LatinX Students in Higher Education

The most recent addition to the "Key Issues on Diverse College Students" series, this important volume bridges theory to practice in order to help higher education professionals support LatinX students in colleges and universities. *LatinX Students in Higher Education* challenges the traditional metrics of student success in higher education for LatinX students, offering a revised definition of student success to re-envision the skills and abilities that these students bring from their communities into institutions of higher education and community-based settings. Garcia's powerful counter-story narratives shed light on the urgent need for systemic reform, and ultimately this book challenges institutions to adopt more inclusive and anti-racist practices that honor cultural identity, community, and resilience. This is a must-read for researchers, educators, student affairs professionals, students, and policymakers committed to creating an equitable higher education system and promoting the success of LatinX populations in higher education.

Nichole Margarita Garcia is Associate Professor of Higher Education at Rutgers University, USA.

KEY ISSUES ON DIVERSE COLLEGE STUDENTS

Series Editors: Marybeth Gasman and Nelson Bowman III

Asian American Students in Higher Education
Samuel D. Museus

Black Men in Higher Education: A Guide to Ensuring Student Success
J. Luke Wood & Robert T. Palmer

Student Veterans and Service Members in Higher Education
Jan Arminio, Tomoko Kudo Grabosky, & Josh Lang

Religious Minority Students in Higher Education
Yoruba T. Mutakabbir, Tariqah A. Nuriddin

Black Women College Students: A Guide to Student Success in Higher
Education
Felecia Commodore, Dominique J. Baker, & Andrew T. Arroyo

Masculinity and Student Success in Higher Education
Jonathan M. Bowman & D. Craig Filar

LatinX Students in Higher Education: Re-Envisioning Student Success
Nichole Margarita Garcia

LatinX Students in Higher Education

Re-Envisioning Student Success

Nichole Margarita Garcia

Routledge
Taylor & Francis Group

NEW YORK AND LONDON

Designed cover image: © Getty Images

First published 2025
by Routledge
605 Third Avenue, New York, NY 10158

and by Routledge
4 Park Square, Milton Park, Abingdon, Oxon, OX14 4RN

Routledge is an imprint of the Taylor & Francis Group, an informa business

Library of Congress Cataloging-in-Publication Data
Names: Garcia, Nichole M., author.
Title: Latinx students in higher education : re-envisioning student success / Nichole Margarita Garcia.
Description: New York, NY : Routledge, 2025. | Series: Key issues on diverse college students | Includes bibliographical references and index.
Identifiers: LCCN 2024046569 (print) | LCCN 2024046570 (ebook) | ISBN 9781032542447 (hardback) | ISBN 9781032534398 (paperback) | ISBN 9781003415909 (ebook)
Subjects: LCSH: Hispanic Americans—Education (Higher). | Education, Higher—Social aspects—United States. | Educational attainment—Social aspects—United States. | Hispanic American college students—Social conditions. | Academic achievement.
Classification: LCC LC2670.6 .G37 2025 (print) | LCC LC2670.6 (ebook) | DDC 378.1/982968073—dc23/eng/20241213
LC record available at https://lccn.loc.gov/2024046569
LC ebook record available at https://lccn.loc.gov/2024046570

ISBN: 978-1-032-54244-7 (hbk)
ISBN: 978-1-032-53439-8 (pbk)
ISBN: 978-1-003-41590-9 (ebk)

DOI: 10.4324/9781003415909

Typeset in Sabon
by Apex CoVantage, LLC

Contents

Series Editors' Introduction   viii

Preface   ix

1   Framing LatinX Demographics and Higher Education Terminology in
    the United States   1

2   Historical Deficit Racial Framing of LatinX Student Academic
    Achievement and Success   42

3   LatinX Academic Achievement and Student Success in the
    Twenty-First Century   73

4   Critical Perspectives on LatinX Student Success: Asset-Based
    Theoretical and Methodological Frameworks from Critical Race
    Theory and Chicana Feminisms   109

5   *LatinX Intergenerational Bendiciones Framework for Student Success*   164

Index   185

Series Editors' Introduction

We are excited to include *LatinX Students in Higher Education: Re-Envisioning Student Success* in our series on Key Issues for Diverse College Students with Routledge Press. LatinX students, one of the fastest-growing demographics in U.S. higher education, continue to face significant challenges within a system still grappling with deeply rooted inequities. While much of the literature often focuses on first-generation students or deficit perspectives, this important volume by Nichole Margarita Garcia turns the lens toward understanding LatinX students through a holistic and asset-based approach.

The book not only addresses the critical need to reframe conversations about student success but also has the potential to have a significant impact on the future of higher education. By grappling with the evolving identities and diverse experiences within the LatinX community, and by centering the familial and community-based strengths of LatinX students, Garcia provides a roadmap for future scholars, practitioners, and institutional leaders on how to create inclusive spaces that foster success.

By exploring the demographic shifts, evolving identities, and the ongoing fight against systemic racism, this work challenges us to rethink how success is defined and measured for LatinX students. In the current landscape of higher education, where diversity, equity, and inclusion are increasingly important despite calls for their elimination, *LatinX Students in Higher Education* is an essential read. We hope that it inspires continued research and action that supports the growing LatinX student population.

Marybeth Gasman and Nelson Bowman III
Series Editors
Key Issues for Diverse College Students

Preface

I wrote this book for my five-year-old Chicana-Boricua self, who dreamed of writing a book that reflected her community and her experiences. My imagination has been intimately formed by LatinX cultural traditions and customs, like the smell of my grandma making fresh tortillas while a pot of beans simmered on the stove—filling the air with the scent of home and the laughter of my cousins filling the room. It might seem rudimentary to begin this book on LatinX student success with such a personal story, but the inspiration for this book has always been based on the stories I heard as a child—especially from my grandmother. As an Associate Professor of Higher Education at Rutgers and a Critical Race Feminista scholar, being a part of the LatinX community has constantly inspired me throughout my academic and professional journey.

The U.S. Census Bureau reports that, as of 2022, the LatinX population comprises 63.7 million of the nation's more than 333 million residents (U.S. Census Bureau, 2022). This makes the LatinX population 19.1 percent of the total population and the largest racial and ethnic group in the United States. LatinX communities are the future of our nation's economic competitiveness and workforce, yet, they have the lowest education attainment level of any group in the United States. Economic progress and education achievement are linked; therefore, educating every LatinX student to not only graduate from high school but also be prepared for college and graduate is a national imperative. By identifying effective and asset-based research that centers the experiences of LatinX students, families, and communities, educational policies and practices can better support their academic achievement and success.

Recent global crises such as COVID-19, racial unrest, racist policies and discourses, and student-debt crises have created unsafe and dangerous conditions for LatinX students in education. As a result, the landscape for postsecondary degree or credential completion and success for LatinX students is more complex than ever before given the heterogeneity that exists within group identities, the states they call home, and where they attend college. There is a shift toward interdisciplinary understandings of how LatinX students not only develop their identities in college environments, but also how they understand the social environments they occupy. Recently, the Biden–Harris administration announced a $50 million investment in Hispanic-Serving Institutions (HSIs) through the U.S. Department of Education. This investment comes at a critical time, as we face an uncertain future in this election year. Historically, efforts to invest in higher education institutions, especially HSIs, that serve LatinX students have been entrenched in white supremacy and racism. And yet, we persevere. The overarching goal of this book is to bridge theory to practice by offering practical and evidence-based recommendations to best serve LatinX students, their families, and communities in college contexts and beyond.

LatinX Students in Higher Education: Re-Envisioning Student Success moves away from standard or conventional notions of "success" to examine how we have persevered. Ahistorical approaches examining the success of LatinX students in higher education have been in juxtaposition to their white counterparts. For too long, LatinX students have had to ascribe to evaluation standards steeped in whiteness and racial inequities. There is much need for a revisionist approach to legitimize the multiple strengths of LatinX students and families. More importantly, there is a need to move away from monolithic definitions of success for LatinX student populations in higher education as they constantly evolve, and change based on the heterogeneity *between and within* group experiences in the United States.

Overall, the main purpose of this book is to provide a revisionist approach to success for LatinX students in higher education, that intends to give students, educators, student affairs practitioners, and scholars a comprehensive examination of contemporary issues and solutions that LatinX students, families, and communities face in navigating and completing a postsecondary degree or credential in U.S. higher education. Using assets-based approaches, this book centers LatinX students as knowledge holders and generators in identifying and naming the skills and abilities they possess and bring with them into institutions of higher education. For LatinX students, success extends beyond standardized assessments. It is also written for those seeking to dismantle the barriers faced by LatinX students and to foster environments where they can thrive academically and personally. The book also serves as a resource for LatinX students, their families, and communities by uplifting their voices based on their unique experiences and strategies for navigating higher education.

DISTINCT FEATURES

One of the most distinctive features of this book is its use of counter-stories. These amplify voices from the margins and serve as rebuttals to majoritarian narratives, which are dominant societal narratives that center on Eurocentric ideologies and dismiss the skills, abilities, and knowledge of LatinX students. The counter-stories throughout this book challenge dominant narratives that often devalue the experiences of LatinX students and provide a more nuanced and accurate understanding of their educational pathways.

Additionally, the book includes reflection questions and discussion prompts at the beginning and end of each chapter. These questions are designed to engage readers in critical thinking and encourage dialogue among educators, students, and community members. By prompting readers to reflect on their own experiences and the experiences of others, the book fosters a deeper understanding of the issues at hand and invites active participation in the work of creating more equitable educational spaces.

OVERVIEW OF CONTENT

The book is structured into five chapters, each of which builds upon the others to develop a comprehensive argument about the re-envisioning of success for LatinX students in higher education.

- **Chapter 1** explores current demographic and postsecondary data trends by deconstructing the assumption that LatinX populations are perpetually identified as one and the same and examines differences and similarities within and between LatinX sub-populations to not commodify their experiences or reinforce a false homogeneity. This chapter also provides terminology often used in institutions of higher education to identify LatinX student populations and current data trends regarding their enrollment and postsecondary degree completion.
- **Chapter 2** takes a historical perspective, providing an analysis of how deficit-oriented racial framing has created the discourse around LatinX student achievement in U.S. educational systems. This chapter explores how white supremacy and racism have systematically undermined the potential of LatinX students. It critiques the historical and contemporary narratives that portray LatinX students as "failing" or "disadvantaged" and emphasizes the resilience that LatinX families cultivate in response to these deficit discourses.
- **Chapter 3** examines foundational scholarship on LatinX academic achievement student success, emphasizing the role of institutional types, such as Hispanic-Serving Institutions (HSIs) and public two-year institutions, in facilitating access to institutions of higher education. The chapter concludes with how social identities such as gender identity, race, and ethnicity impact LatinX students' experiences with a discussion on the need for more specialized research and institutional

strategies that address the array of challenges and strengths that LatinX students bring to their educational pathways.

- **Chapter 4** employs an application of asset-based theoretical and methodological frameworks, particularly within Critical Race Theory (CRT) and Chicana Feminisms in education, to address LatinX academic achievement and student success in institutions of higher education. The chapter outlines the emergence and impact of CRT and Chicana/Latina feminisms in higher education, critiquing the systemic oppression that underlies traditional academic frameworks. Foundational theories are discussed demonstrating how they challenge deficit perspectives and offer transformative approaches to understanding LatinX academic achievement and student success.

- **Chapter 5** introduces the *LatinX Intergenerational Bendiciones Framework for Student Success*, a culturally responsive model for understanding student success. Unlike traditional frameworks that emphasize individual achievement, this model centers on the intergenerational wisdom, cultural affirmation, and community resilience that support LatinX students in their educational pathways. The chapter critiques the dominance of white supremacy culture in framing current definitions of success and proposes the *Bendiciones Framework* as a powerful alternative.

In conclusion, it is my hope that this book will inspire educators, policymakers, and researchers to reconsider how they define and measure success for LatinX students, and that it will serve as a guide for those seeking to create more inclusive and supportive educational environments. Ultimately, this book is a celebration of the resilience, strength, and contributions of LatinX students, their families, and their communities, and a call to action for institutions to honor and uplift these voices in meaningful ways.

REFERENCE

U.S. Census Bureau. (2022). Hispanic Heritage Month: 2023. U.S. Census Bureau. Retrieved from https://www.census.gov/newsroom/facts-for-features/2023/hispanic-heritage-month.html

Chapter 1

Framing LatinX Demographics and Higher Education Terminology in the United States

MARGARITA: THE PHD SHE NEVER KNEW

My first memories revolved around looking at my grandmother's hands. They were calloused, wrinkled, and arthritic. When she would cook, I would ask, "Grandma, do your hands hurt?" She always would reply, "No, princess, they are fine." As she skillfully prepared meals with her hands, despite her limited formal education, she imparted to me a different kind of wisdom. "No one can take away your knowledge. Get your education," she would say, just as she carefully guarded the recipes that had been passed down through generations. For my grandmother, who, like many other Mexican Americans, saw education as the great equalizer, the kitchen was a place of nourishment and a classroom of life lessons. Before she died, I promised her I would attain a PhD and become a faculty member—a "success" story. I never knew how hard it would be to fulfill that promise.

As displayed in Figure 1.1, "The Garcia family educational pipeline," my grandmother, Blandina Tuero Govea, was a Mexican American, World War II veteran,[1] and a single mother of nine children from two marriages. She raised her family in Salt Lake City, Utah. While my grandmother only completed the eigth grade she stressed the importance of education to her children. Of her nine children, all but one graduated from high school; five attended and graduated from four-year institutions of higher education. Three of those five college graduates pursued graduate education and attained master's degrees. My father, Richard Garcia Sr., was one of those three children and holds an M.Ed. and an MSW. My father also pursued a PhD in Education for ten years but did not complete his degree due to being the caretaker of my grandmother. Among the five children who attained bachelor's degrees, they had 14 children. Of all 14, only two have attained a bachelor's degree. On my paternal side, I am the first and

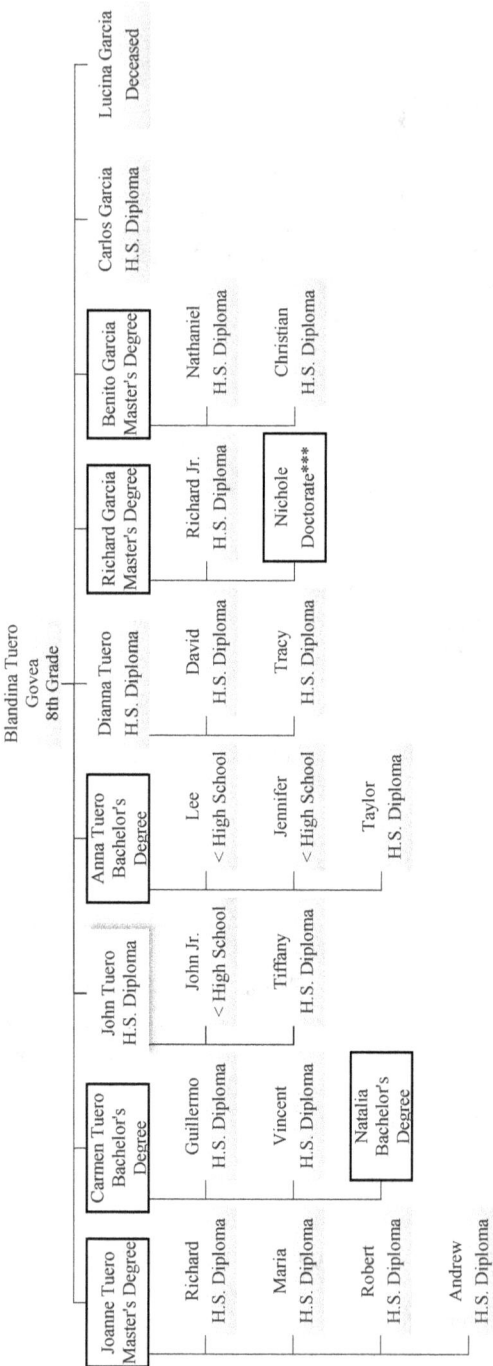

Figure 1.1 The Garcia family educational pipeline. An example of a LatinX familial educational pipeline across generations beginning with grandparents.

only individual to pursue a graduate education, attain a master's, and finish what my father started by earning a doctoral degree. This stark discrepancy is alarming and critical to examine within the LatinX community because education, especially attaining a postsecondary degree,[2] has long been viewed as a vehicle for economic and social mobility (Conteras, 2011). It is increasingly important to examine students considered "high achievers" and "successes" who are *not* the first in their families to attend a four-year institution. I am not considered a first-generation college student because my father pursued higher education and attained a bachelor's and graduate degree. However, let us look at my paternal and maternal familial educational pipelines.[3] One parent with a postsecondary degree may not be enough to transmit the skills and capital necessary to be "successful" in the U.S. higher education system.

On my maternal side, as seen in Figure 1.2, "The Ortiz family educational pipeline," my grandparents, Julio and Guadalupe Ortiz, were, respectively, Puerto Rican and Mexican parents of nine children and raised their family in Salt Lake City, Utah. My grandmother had an eighth-grade education, and my grandfather completed a ninth-grade education. Due to their lack of knowledge and experience about the U.S. educational system, my mother's familial pipeline required a more challenging progression of formal educational attainment. Of my grandparents' nine children, only three graduated from high school. My mother, Julia Ortiz Garcia, was one of them. Among her and her two siblings, all their children graduated with a high school or equivalency diploma. As one of those three, I am the first and only family member on my maternal side to graduate and attain a postsecondary and graduate degree.

In 2018, as I was finishing my post-doctoral fellowship at the University of Pennsylvania, I researched literature for a few projects and found a gem. The project was titled "Saving the Legacy: An Oral History of Utah's World War II Veterans."[4] Within its pages I found an interview with my grandmother. I was unaware she had participated in the project. After taking a moment to cry, I opened the document, and her untold story began. As I read the interview, I could hear my grandmother's voice. I realized the privilege of locating such a rare document. It came at a critical time, as I was in the job market to secure my first tenure-track position. It was unclear whether I had achieved that at the time, but my grandmother left her words as a reminder of why I do what I do. When asked, "How did you feel about your WWII service?" she replied, "I never regretted it. I've always thought that if I could do it over again, I'd do it." I am Nichole Margarita Garcia, the PhD my grandmother never knew. I carry my grandmother's middle name. I publish with my whole name, as my PhD is hers, as well. My legacy is my presence in the ivory tower; if I had to do it again, I would do it! I am reminded that, while LatinX numbers are low in graduate degree completion and pursuing faculty positions as a profession,[5]

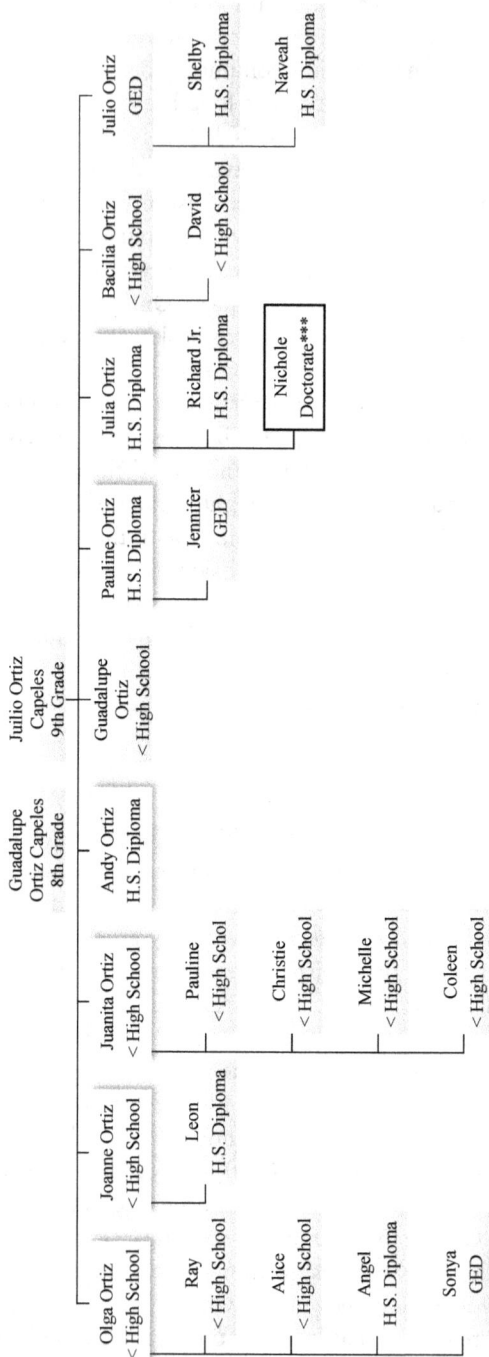

Figure 1.2 The Ortiz family educational pipeline. An example of a LatinX familial educational pipeline across generations beginning with grandparents.

nevertheless, I am here. My grandmother taught me to value and hold pride in my identity as a Chicana and Puerto Rican woman, even when individuals, institutions, or policies may not. We must own our histories, take them into our own hands, and create change by documenting them.

COUNTER-STORY REFLECTION QUESTIONS

- How should LatinX student academic achievement and success be defined or described?
- What specific types of educational processes contribute to or increase the likelihood of LatinX student academic achievement and success?
- How can LatinX student academic achievement and success be measured or assessed throughout the educational pipeline, from early childhood through higher education?

LATINX CHANGING THE LANDSCAPE IN THE UNITED STATES

Milian (2019) introduced the term LatinX and frames the "X" in LatinX as a place of undoing and doing, a dwelling of possibility, and a site of speculative research toward futurity (Wilkie et al., 2017). In doing so, Milian (2019) implies a reconfiguration of the Latino/a lexicon, particularly within the context of the United States, to encompass a broader range of conceptual histories, spaces, and perspectives. The use of LatinX is seen as a way to delve deeper into current and future nomenclature practices, signaling a move toward new understandings and possibilities in LatinX research and discourse. Therefore, throughout this book, I use the term LatinX to create a semiotic shift that locates "X" as a symbol (or sign) that holds different meanings depending on the context (the signifier and the signified).[6] The signifier is the form that the sign takes (in this case, the letter "X") and the signified is the concept it represents (in some cases, this could mean the inclusive and non-binary nature of LatinX identity). As LatinX demographics numerically outpace other racial and ethnic groups, there is a growing need to re-envision how the U.S. landscape will change, particularly within institutions of higher education. Unlike other higher education and college student affairs books on student success, which tend to treat LatinX student experiences as tangential, this book centralizes it as its foci. This book requires that institutions of higher education and institutional actors assume responsibility for meeting the evolving needs of the LatinX student demographic. The overarching framing of this book engages LatinX student experiences within the complex layers of racism, white supremacy, and systemic oppression at the micro (individual), macro (community), and meso (systematic) levels, exploring how social constructs of identity and academic achievement intersect with the concept of student "success" in higher education contexts.

Over the last two decades, much has changed for the LatinX population in the United States. As of 2023, the influence of politically xenophobic leadership during the tenure of the forty-fifth president, ongoing efforts to address climate change, and the management of the global COVID-19 pandemic have significantly altered the present prospects of LatinX communities. Many within this demographic, particularly those designated as "essential workers," endure heightened health risks and face increased financial and medical vulnerabilities. These challenges generated a particularly profound impact on newcomers within the LatinX population. In regions historically unaccustomed to significant immigrant presence, such as the U.S. South, the LatinX population has grown significantly, particularly in Virginia, Georgia, North Carolina, Arkansas, and more recently, Mississippi—now emerging as the Nuevo South (Guerrero, 2017; MacDonald & Carrillo, 2021; Oboler, 2012; Stuesse, 2016). This diasporic shift indicates a changing pattern of where LatinX communities settle, highlighting evolving trends in their distribution and experiences throughout the United States (MacDonald & Carrillo, 2021). While southern states have seen notable growth, the Far West and Midwest regions also began experiencing steady development starting in the 1980s and 1990s, continuing over the last two decades. As of 2022, South Dakota experienced the most rapid growth in its LatinX population, increasing by 6.8 percent or 2,835 residents (U.S. Census Bureau, 2023). The strategic relocation of meatpacking and poultry processing plants to rural areas by major corporations began primarily in the late 1970s and intensified throughout the 1980s and 1990s. During this period, companies like Tyson Foods and others sought to capitalize on various benefits offered by rural towns in states such as Iowa, Kansas, Nebraska, North Dakota, and South Dakota, often employing undocumented workers in hazardous and overcrowded work environments (Zúñiga & Hernández-León, 2006). Indigenous and non-Indigenous migrants from Mexico, Guatemala, and South American countries gravitated toward employment opportunities in these more affordable and rural regions of the United States (Fink, 2003; LeBaron, 2012; Odem & Lacy, 2009).

While LatinX populations are consistently grouped into governmental racial and ethnic categories (Irizarry, 2015; Rodriguez, 2000; López, 2013), the assumption that this is the best way to identify or categorize LatinX people must be challenged, especially in higher education research. For example, Sandoval Girón (2017) found that based on data from the U.S. Census Bureau, Indigenous peoples from Central and South America often choose to identify themselves under the "Hispanic" category rather than opting for specific "tribes" or selecting the race category of "American Indian." These groups perceived both categories as applying to Indigenous peoples in the United States and not reflective of their own racial or ethnic identities. Consequently, Indigenous peoples from Central and South America are likely to be significantly undercounted in the census. Similarly, Afro-Latino was recognized for the first time in the 2020 decennial census (López, 2013). In this case, individuals who indicated Hispanic or Latino identity in the ethnicity question and Black or African American identity in the race question were then automatically tallied as Afro-Latino (U.S. Census Bureau, 2020 Census Special Tabulation). Respondents had various options to express their identification as Hispanic or Latino and Black or African American, including checking multiple boxes and providing specific written identities (López, 2013; U.S. et al., 2020 Census Special Tabulation). While this is progress, much work still remains. Nuñez et al. (2024) emphasize the significance of recognizing the intersectionality of race and ethnicity in data collection processes. They argue that LatinX communities risk misrepresentation in data due to the new Census Bureau question format and analysis methods. Nuñez et al. (2024) advocate for including a "street race" question—reflecting the perceived race based on physical appearance—which could provide a more nuanced understanding of racialization, assisting in the more effective research process that impacts policies and practices.

Far from perfect and significantly complex, LatinX racial and ethnic categorization and socialization contribute to educational inequities and manifest early in childhood and throughout K-20+ education. Understanding future LatinX student populations requires rethinking race, ethnicity, and ethnoracial frameworks, given the evolving migration patterns among LatinX communities across the United States, Mexico, South and Central America, and the Caribbean. Racial and ethnic identities intersect with other social conditions and identities, including immigration and citizenship status, gender, and sexual orientation. In recent times, oppression within LatinX communities has revealed interlocked colonial systems. Specifically, there is critique within Latinidad for historically prioritizing cisheteronormativity in Chicanismo, marginalizing Afro-LatinX and Indigenous LatinX identities, and fostering anti-Black and anti-Indigenous sentiments (Barillas Chón et al., 2024). Busey and Silva (2021) term this phenomenon the "Brown Monolith," describing it as the portrayal of Latinidad as a unified concept under the label of Brown and Browness while simultaneously disregarding its racialized and anti-Black sentiments. These critiques are prompting Chicana/o/x Studies and Latina/o/x Studies toward a crucial phase of self-reflection and transformation (Barillas Chón et al., 2024).

LATINX DEMOGRAPHICS IN THE UNITED STATES

The U.S. Census Bureau reports that, as of 2022, the LatinX population comprises 63.7 million of the nation's more than 333 million residents (U.S.

Census Bureau, 2022). This makes the LatinX population 19.1 percent of the total population and the largest racial and ethnic group in the United States. The Mexican population is the largest LatinX population among 40 states, with seven other states[7] where Puerto Ricans are the largest LatinX group. In the United States, the Mexican population historically grew fastest among LatinX populations but shifted from 2010 to 2020. As of 2010, there has been a decline in the influx of Mexicans entering the United States. This is due to the enforcement of increased and enhanced border security measures between the United States and Mexico, coupled with a rapid escalation in deportations throughout the two administrations of President Barack Obama (Lopez et al., 2011).

Notwithstanding a decrease in the domestic Mexican-born population, every other LatinX sub-ethnic group has experienced an escalated growth rate. For example, data elucidates the impact of international diplomacy, economic stagnation, and climate change-induced catastrophic events on migration patterns from the Caribbean islands of Puerto Rico and Cuba (MacDonald & Carrillo, 2021). Puerto Rico was already grappling with severe economic debt bordering on bankruptcy in the 2000s and experienced the devastating impacts of Category Five Hurricanes Maria and Irma in 2017 (Garcia & Danek, 2023). Enduring prolonged power outages and widespread destruction of homes and essential infrastructure, numerous Puerto Ricans sought refuge in the stateside in the United States, often reuniting with extended family members (Garcia & Danek, 2023; MacDonald & Carrillo, 2021). While Puerto Ricans dispersed across all 50 states, a notable proportion migrated to Orlando, Florida, which has emerged as one of the nation's focal points for the growing Puerto Rican population.

Moreover, the Venezuelan population has grown faster than any other LatinX ethnic group since 2010. Regarding ethnic groups within the broader LatinX population, Colombian and Honduran communities have surpassed a million people for the first time in the United States (Peña et al., 2023). According to the Pew Hispanic Research Center, Central Americans from Guatemala, El Salvador, and Honduras represent the fastest-growing segments of LatinX immigrants in the United States (Cohn et al., 2017). As of 2022, 13 states have 1 million or more LatinX residents: Arizona, California, Colorado, Florida, Georgia, Illinois, New Jersey, New Mexico, New York, North Carolina, Pennsylvania, Texas, and Washington. In terms of states and the LatinX population, California (15,732,180), Texas (12,068,549), and Florida (6,025,030) have the highest concentrations of the LatinX population, with New York (3,867,076) being the only state that has witnessed a recent decline (–0.7%, –27,522) in its LatinX population (U.S. Census Bureau, 2023). California has the highest concentration of Mexicans (12.2 million), followed by Salvadorans (731,697) and Guatemalans (454,917). Florida has the highest concentration of Cubans (1.5 million), Puerto Ricans (1.2 million), and Colombians (403,567). The largest Dominican population (867,304) is in New York, and Texas had the largest Honduran population (168,578) (Peña et al., 2023).

Frey (2018) projects that the United States will attain a "minority white" status by the year 2045, as indicated by current census projections. Frey (2018) contends that this demographic shift will "stimulate growth, counterbalancing an aging, slow-growing, and anticipated declining white population" (p. 1). By the year 2050, the LatinX population will account for 29 percent of the U.S. population (Passel & Cohn, 2008). For the first time in history, the nation will cease to have a majority-white population (Gasman & Conrad, 2015). These demographic shifts will continue contributing to increased diversity within higher education. The U.S. Census Bureau reported that in 2021 the number of LatinX people aged 18 to 24 increased in college enrollments, with the average age of the LatinX population being 30 (Hernandez & McElrath, 2023). Despite demographic growth, LatinX educational attainment across the United States remains inequitable compared with their Asian and white counterparts. LatinX communities continue to grapple with inequitable educational conditions, deficit narratives portraying LatinX parents and students as lacking the capability and motivation to succeed academically, and an educational system that reveals persistently inequitable outcomes for LatinX students.

SOCIAL CONSTRUCTIONS OF LATINX RACE, ETHNICITY, AND ETHNORACIALITY IN THE UNITED STATES

For LatinX communities, the conflation of race and ethnicity is complex, contradictory, and in contention due to varying social constructions based on systematic power, privilege, and/or oppression (Alcoff, 2009; Gracia & Greiff, 2000; Garcia & Mayorga, 2018; Zerquera et al., 2020). Haney López (2006) argues that the U.S. legal system contributed to the construction of whiteness under the law by manipulating and molding specific racial categories through legal decisions to uphold white supremacy and privilege. Haney López (2006) identifies that LatinX communities, in particular Mexican Americans or ChicanX, were classified as being white under the law but socially constructed as inferior. Gracia and Greiff (2000) argue that while the government typically defines Hispanics/Latinos ethnically, the category is frequently used in racial contexts. Alcoff (2009) underscores the challenge of delineating ethnicity and race in practice, particularly among LatinX communities, despite scholarly efforts to distinguish these categories conceptually. More recently, Gómez (2020) has asserted that construction of the LatinX identity in the United States is not a fixed or a natural category but rather a social and political construct invented and reinvented over time to serve specific purposes. Gómez (2020) analyzes how LatinX are racially classified in the U.S. racial system:

> [V]iewing Latinos from an ethnic rather than racial frame . . . pits them against African Americans in a way that supports white supremacy. For example, it encourages Latinos to see themselves as distant from Blacks by adopting the dominant racial narrative that African Americans "deserve" their place at the bottom of the hierarchy, while, in contrast, putting Latinos into the dominant ethnic narrative in which striving "immigrants" overcome the odds to assimilate. In this way, the refusal to see and name anti-Latino racism *qua* racism serves to enlist Latinos in policing the White-over-Black color line.
>
> (pp. 14–15)

By contrasting the operationalization of race and racism, Gómez (2020) delves into the process of racial categorization, both from institutional classification and individuals' self-perceptions of race. Gómez (2020) also sheds light on the complexities and contradictions inherent in LatinX identity and challenges essentialists' understandings of race, ethnicity, and culture in the United States. Furthermore, Busey and Silva (2021) critique the use of Latinidad as a unified proxy for Brown and Browness across U.S., Mexico, South and Central America, and the Caribbean LatinX communities, especially in U.S. educational research. They argue that Latinidad, historically employed as an overarching term, tends to essentialize and homogenize identities, moving away from the concept of mestizaje (mixing of two distinct cultures) and inadvertently neglecting Afro-LatinX and Indigenous LatinX identities. According to Busey and Silva (2021), this approach reflects colonial logics that simplify, standardize, and reproduce the "anti-Black sociopolitical and sociohistorical etymology of Brown" (p. 177). Their analysis challenges the widespread use of Latinidad as a monolithic category, advocating a move toward theorizing race through Afrolatindiades and LatinX Indigeneities in U.S. education research.

Consequently, a racial reckoning regarding anti-Blackness in LatinX communities in the United States must occur. Hernández (2022) refers to this as

> "Latino racial innocence" which acts as a cloak that veils LatinX complicity in U.S. racism. In turn, public ignorance about Latino anti-Blackness undermines the ability to fully address the interwoven complexities of U.S. racism in developing public policies enforcing antidiscrimination law.
>
> (p. 1)

Racial frames in the United States typically function through a lens of a Black/white binary, leaving limited room for discussions involving LatinX individuals and communities who can belong to any race. According to Jiménez Román and Flores (2010), the term "Afro-Latin@" gained prominence in the 1990s as it became evident that race holds significance within the Latin@ community, challenging the notion of Latin@s as a homogenous group (p. 10). Only addressing intergroup ethnic identities falls short, as racial identity carries equal weight, and confronting anti-Blackness is imperative within LatinX communities.

In the next sections, I offer operational definitions of race/racism, ethnicity, and ethnoracial categories to highlight the intricate processes of racial and ethnic socialization that shape LatinX communities in the United States, influencing dynamics within institutions of higher education. Critically analyzing the functions of race/racism, ethnicity, and ethnoracial categories in institutions of higher education reveals complex power dynamics, privilege, and oppression within these constructs, especially as it pertains to academic achievement and student success.

Race and Racism

Race is not a biological phenomenon but rather a social construct encompassing various aspects such as pigmentation, phenotype, and ethnicity (Tatum, 1997). In the United States, the concept of race has significantly influenced law, national policy, and educational institutions through systemic racism, defined as "a system of advantages based on race" (Tatum, 1997, p. 7). This social construction of race, ingrained within institutional policies and practices, perpetuates advantages for certain racial groups and is reflected in the beliefs and actions of individuals or groups. Historically, systemic racism has dictated the social and economic mobility of Black, Indigenous, and People of Color (BIPOC)[8] communities by constraining opportunities for advancement. Additionally, Marable (1992) defines racism as "a system of ignorance, exploitation, and power used to oppress African Americans, Latinos, Asians, Pacific Americans, American Indians, and other people based on ethnicity, culture, mannerisms, and color" (p. 5). According to Solórzano (1997), building on Marable's (1992) and Lorde's (1992) definitions, racism serves three primary functions: (1) promoting belief in one group's superiority; (2) empowering this group to enact racist practices; and (3) results in impacting multiple racial and ethnic groups. Alcoff (2000, 2006) questions whether LatinX identity constitutes a racial identity within LatinX communities. She argues that the complexity of LatinX identity and its relationship to racial categorization remains unresolved, as traditional U.S. racial classifications have historically suggested uniformity and discernible physical traits that do not universally apply to LatinX individuals.

Ethnicity

Race and ethnicity are frequently conflated yet hold distinct meanings (Garcia & Mayorga, 2018; Omi & Winant, 1994, 2014). Omi and Winant (1994, 2014) argue that, in contrast to race paradigms—which are traditionally understood as the biological categorization of groups—ethnicity paradigms are seen as social constructs linked to cultural attributes such as religion, language, customs, nationality, and political affiliations. Ethnicity can be defined as "groups of people who share a common culture; however, like race, ethnicity develops within the context of systems of power" (Anderson & Collins, 2007, p. 82). It is important to note that "the meaning and significance of ethnicity can shift over time and in different social and political contexts" (Anderson & Collins, 2007, p. 82). Unlike race, defined by physical characteristics, ethnicity focuses on shared language, religion, history, and cultural practices and is socially constructed.

Ethnoracial

Goldberg (1993) first refers to ethnorace as a social construction that encompasses a group's identity, which can function interchangeably as either an ethnic group or a racial group.

Hollinger (1995) delves into this concept through his notion of "the ethnoracial pentagon." This framework denotes the United States' five-fold demographic structure commonly used to classify the U.S. population into African American, Asian American, European American, Latino, and Native American categories. For instance, Hitlin et al. (2007) elaborate that among the LatinX community in the United States, perceptions of race and ethnicity often diverge from established social categories, such as those outlined by the U.S. government. Decades of research in the social sciences reveal that LatinX individuals frequently perceive their identities as encompassing race and ethnicity (Hitlin et al., 2007). Specifically, regarding race, LatinX individuals often view themselves as a distinct group that does not neatly fit into categories such as Black, white, Asian, and/or American Indian (Hitlin et al., 2007). Alcoff (2009) argues that LatinX is most accurately characterized as an ethnorace, which she defines as:

> groups who have both ethnic and racialized characteristics, who are historical people with customs and conventions developed out of collective agency, but who are also identified and identifiable by bodily morphology that allows for both group affinity as well as group exclusion and denigration.
>
> (p. 122)

Alcoff (2009) argues that using the term "ethnorace" to describe LatinX communities is more appropriate because it acknowledges the importance of ancestry, history, and culture, and the array of experiences of racialization within these communities. Problematizing ethnorace as a term steeped in colonial logic, white supremacy, and racialization processes, Rosa (2018) states:

> The ethnoracial status of Latinx identity is widely debated in both scholarly and popular discourses, often from the perspective of spectrum-based racial logics that problematically imagine Latinxs as an intermediary "brown" population located between Blackness at one end and Whiteness at the other, or as a phenotypically heterogeneous group that is better understood ethnically (e.g., stereotypically defined culturally or nationally) than racially (i.e., stereotypically defined physically). The former logic is anchored in white supremacist histories of Indigenous erasure and anti-Blackness through which some groups and bodies come to be positioned as desirable for their perceived mixed-race status and proximity to Whiteness; the latter logic is anchored in white supremacist colonial management schemas that homogenize and differentiate populations in varying ways.
>
> (pp. 2–3)

Overall, ethnorace illuminates the nuanced intersection of ethnic and racial identities among LatinX communities while also prompting a reckoning of the historical and contemporary complexities of racial and ethnic categorization and identity formation. Taken together, the social constructions of LatinX race, ethnicity, and ethnoraciality reveal the complexities and contradictions inherent in understanding LatinX identity and underscore the ongoing challenges in addressing anti-Blackness and anti-Indigeneity within LatinX communities. Therefore, this book, where possible, deconstructs and analyzes differences and similarities within and between LatinX sub-populations in higher education student success research to not negate or commodify their experiences but rather avoid reinforcing a false homogeneity.

LATINX AND HIGHER EDUCATION TERMINOLOGY

As demographic characteristics evolve among LatinX students, it is critical to consider how college students are defined and to be cognizant of how social identities are shaped by deeply rooted histories, cultures, and complex social systems. For this book, I provide concise terminology for student populations that institutions of higher education identify as LatinX *and/or* first-generation, low-income, underrepresented, traditional college students, transfer college students, undocumented, and/or adult learners. Identifying how institutions of higher education use nomenclature is essential because LatinX students have multiple nuanced identities, assets, and needs. While these terms identify how to serve different student populations, LatinX students can occupy one or more identities. LatinX students who possess multiple identities may have positive or negative experiences as these identities interact when they navigate institutions of higher education.

In the U.S. higher education research, there is an ongoing transformation regarding the terminology used to refer to LatinX communities across the United States, Mexico, South and Central America, and the Caribbean (Salinas & Lozano, 2019; Salinas, 2020). This evolution spans various labels and identities, including Hispanic, Latin, Latin American, Latino, Latina, Latine, Latina/o, and Latin@ (Salinas & Lozano, 2019). Notably, Latinx has emerged as an inclusive alternative encompassing all genders (Milian, 2019; Salinas & Lozano, 2019), reflecting a concerted effort to recognize the diverse gender and racial identities across the United States, Mexico, South and Central America, and the Caribbean. Additionally, Salinas (2020) has coined the term Latin*, which acts as an umbrella expression accommodating a wide range of identities, including LatinX, Latinx, Latiné, Latini, Latinu, Latino, Latina, Latina/o, Latin@, Latin, or Latin American. Salinas (2020) asserts that Latin* fosters "inclusivity by creating a space that embraces existing gender fluidity and identity labels, as well as those that have yet to gain mainstream recognition" (p. 164). This shift in terminology in higher education contexts acknowledges the need to re-engage possibilities that reflect LatinX students' intersectional experiences. It also underscores the importance of recognizing the dynamic nature of terms and LatinX individual identities, which undoubtedly challenges institutions of higher education and their actors to create knowledge that enhances understanding, advocates for, and amplifies the LatinX student population in higher education (Garcia et al., 2021).

LatinX First-Generation College Students

Traditional college students are generally defined as those attending college immediately following high school. Traditional college students depend financially on their parents and are allocated the resources needed to expense tuition, room, and board. They typically attend college full-time, enroll in college-level courses, and graduate with their bachelor's degree in four to six years. The notion of a traditional college student has shifted as they have become a smaller portion of the nationwide collegiate population (Deli-Amen, 2020). First-generation college students are generally defined as the first person in their family to attend an institution of higher education. Originally defined in 1979 by Fuji Adachi as students who did not have at least one parent with a bachelor's degree, today, higher education researchers have broadened the definition regarding parental level attainment (Nguyen & Nguyen, 2018). The term can be inclusive of students whose parents have a high school diploma or less, or parents who completed some college education, but not a four-year degree. How first-generation college students are defined has policy and empirical implications for how they are counted in terms of enrollment and graduation rates. Being intentionally linked to parental level of education shapes how resources are allocated to this population and ultimately impacts their level of confidence, degree of comfort in college, and possession (or absence) of privileged knowledge of the college-going processes. Approaching first-generation college students as a homogenous student population could deny the complexities and richness of students' lived realities. Based on demographic characteristics, first-generation college students are incredibly heterogeneous. First-generation college students are more likely to be female than male (Nguyen & Nguyen, 2018). In terms of race and ethnic groups, LatinX students are more likely to be first-generation college students in comparison with their Black and Indigenous counterparts, who follow close behind (Nguyen & Nguyen, 2018). According to Excelencia in Education (2024), LatinX people have the highest proportion of first-generation college students among racial and ethnic groups: 51 percent of LatinX individuals were the first in their family to attend college, compared with 38 percent of African Americans, 31 percent of the general student population, 30 percent of Asians, and 22 percent of whites (Excelencia in Education, 2024). These statistics underscore the unique challenges and opportunities faced by LatinX first-generation college students and illuminate the importance of supporting and understanding the specific needs of this demographic within higher education institutions.

LatinX Continuing Generation College Students

Literature on differences in postsecondary degree or credential completion among parents and children is scarce (Garcia, 2016; Garcia & Mireles-Rios, 2019; Garcia, 2019; Garcia & Delgado Bernal, 2021; Kouyoumdjian et al., 2017). Despite limited research, a few studies have explored the experiences of students with parents who graduated from college compared with those whose parents did not (Lohfink & Paulsen, 2005; Pike & Kuh, 2005; Ramos Sánchez & Nichols, 2007; Terenzini et al., 1994). However, higher education researchers need more consensus regarding the terminology used for individuals with parents who have obtained postsecondary degrees in the United States. For instance, terms such as "traditional college student" (Terenzini et al., 1994), "second-generation college student" (Pike & Kuh, 2005), "continuing college student" (Lohfink & Paulsen, 2005), and "non-first-generation college student" (Ramos Sánchez & Nichols, 2007) are often used interchangeably. Lohfink and Paulsen (2005) identify a research gap in higher education studies that compares first-generation college students with continuing-generation students. They define first-generation college students as those whose parents have not attended a four-year institution, while continuing-generation students have at least one parent who has done so. Using data from the Beginning Postsecondary Students Longitudinal Study, Lohfink and Paulsen (2005) specifically investigated persistence and completion rates in postsecondary education and the broader impacts of postsecondary education on individuals. They discovered significant disparities in persistence between first-generation and continuing-generation college students. Notably, they found that "being Hispanic and first-generation is an example of how race and ethnicity intersect with parental education to negatively impact persistence" (Lohfink & Paulsen, 2005, p. 418).

In my scholarship, I conducted a comparative study of ChicanX and Puerto Rican nuclear families considered continuing-generation students (Garcia, 2016). By advancing intergenerational academic achievement and success narratives, I challenged deficit views held by institutions of higher education that attribute low enrollment and postsecondary degree or credential competition among LatinX communities to non-nuclear family structures. I found that ChicanX and Puerto Rican families whose parents received a postsecondary degree or higher in the United States positively influenced their children's postsecondary degree competition. However, outside factors such as race, racism, and white supremacy tended to stunt linear trajectories of postsecondary degree completion among these families (Garcia, 2016).

LatinX Adult Learners and Nontraditional LatinX College Students

Adult learner and nontraditional college student are often interchangeable terms used in institutions of higher education (Kasworm, 2012; Kennedy, 2023). Both have generally been defined based on age (i.e., 25 years of age or older) (National Center of Educational Statistics, 2015). Like the term first-generation college student, the definition of adult learners or nontraditional college students must capture the heterogeneity of a huge population of adult students in a diverse nation (Wyatt, 2011). Notably, higher education researchers have now differentiated nontraditional students from adult learners based on meeting at least one of the following criteria: are 25 years of age or older, delay postsecondary enrollment by one year or more after high school, enroll on a part-time status, are employed full time, are not financially dependent on their parents, have dependents other than a spouse, are single parents, or do not have a high school diploma (Choy, 2002). Nearly three-quarters (73 percent) of all undergraduates are nontraditional in some way, making them the majority in today's college campuses (National Center for Education Statistics, 2019a).

While these terms are used interchangeably, not all nontraditional students are adult learners. Adult learners generally are defined as being 25 years of age or older but have been identified by varying characteristics as compared with nontraditional students such as, but not limited to, the following: are more likely to pursue a program that leads to a vocational certificate or degree; are more likely to enroll in two-year community colleges; are more likely to enroll in distance education; self-identify as workers rather than students; have educational goals advancing their work skillsets; and are more likely to leave postsecondary education without finishing their degrees or credentials (Compton et al., 2006). Person et al. (2019) found that fewer than half of the 170 million U.S. residents between the ages of 25 and 64 had completed a post-secondary degree or credential, and 15 percent had completed some college but still needed a degree. Adult learners often are from BIPOC communities who historically have been excluded from institutions of higher education and, when they do enroll, are less likely to complete a postsecondary degree or credential (Ross-Gordon, 2005; Rosser-Mims et al., 2014; Community College Research Center, 2021). From 2000 to 2020, the LatinX adult population in the United States almost doubled (Santiago et al., 2024). During this period, LatinX adults advanced in higher education while balancing full-time jobs and family commitments. The decade of 2012 to 2022 saw more LatinX adults earning postsecondary degrees, though attainment gaps remained low (Santiago et al., 2024). Nearly 31 percent of LatinX undergraduates were adult learners aged 25 and older in the 2019–20 academic year (Santiago et al., 2024). This proportion is close to that of white undergraduates at 33 percent, lower than the 41 percent of Black undergraduates, and higher than the 25 percent of Asian undergraduates (National Center for Education Statistics, 2021). More than half of Latina female adult learners aged 25 and older are caring for dependent children (Santiago et al., 2024). During the 2019–20 academic year, 56 percent of Latina female undergraduates had dependent children, in contrast to 31 percent of their Latino male counterparts (Cruse et al., 2019; Santiago et al., 2024).

LatinX College Students from Low-income Backgrounds or Economic Disadvantage

The U.S. federal government generally defines low-income students as those whose family income is at or below 150 percent of the federal poverty threshold. Taylor and Turk (2019) found that, more commonly, students who are female, People of Color, from immigrant backgrounds, and speak languages other than English at home represent a larger share of those living below the poverty line. Regarding race and ethnicity, more LatinX students from low-income backgrounds are enrolled across all types of institutions of higher education, especially in public two-year community colleges and for-profit institutions (Fry & Cilluffo, 2019; Taylor & Turk, 2019). As equity and inclusion progress, moving toward asset-based terminology is critical for the well-being of LatinX students. A shift centering LatinX from low-income to economically disadvantaged backgrounds will be used throughout this book.

LatinX Transfer Students

Transfer students are typically assumed to be students who start at a two-year institution and then transfer to a four-year university to attain their postsecondary degree. However, definitions vary when "transfer" is associated with a student as they are not a monolithic group (Jain et al., 2020; Kirk-Kuwaye & Kirk-Kuwaye, 2007). A vertical transfer or upward transfer is a student who attends a two-year institution and then transfers to a four-year university (Kirk-Kuwaye & Kirk-Kuwaye, 2007). A lateral transfer is a student who transfers between two-year institutions and four-year institutions. Reverse transfer students can be defined as undergraduate students who begin their education at a four-year institution and then transfer credits to a two-year institution (Townsend, 1999). Research shows that various transfer patterns are increasing, and it is estimated that two out of five postsecondary students attend two or more institutions within four years of initial enrollment (Bahr, 2009). Santiago et al. (2024) found that more than one-third (36 percent) of LatinX college students in the fall of 2020 were enrolled at a public two-year college, compared with 47 percent at a public four-year institution. The predominant transfer pathway for LatinX students involves transferring within the same institutional type, known as lateral transfer (Santiago et al., 2024). In fall 2022, nearly half (49 percent) of LatinX transfer students opted for lateral transfer, whether from a two-year to another two-year institution or from a four-year to another four-year institution (Santiago et al., 2024).

LatinX Undocumented Students

Despite the diverse national and cultural origins of undocumented students, LatinX communities are often racially profiled in immigration discourse and have become the face of immigration rhetoric (Huber et al., 2008). LatinX students make up 46 percent of the undocumented student population in U.S. higher education (American Immigration Council, 2023). Since the landmark

Plyler v. Doe case in 1982, the Supreme Court of the United States (SCOTUS) has afforded undocumented children access to public K-12 education. This decision invalidated Texas' authority to allow school districts to deny free public education to undocumented children (Olivas, 2020). This constitutional guarantee, however, only extends to K-12 education and not institutions of higher education, resulting in state-level policies and practices that unfairly impact the college admission and success of undocumented students (Nienhusser, 2018). As a result, federal and state laws vary in their treatment of undocumented students in higher education, often resulting in limited access to financial aid and in-state tuition or outright bans in some states. LatinX undocumented students constitute a vulnerable demographic due to the intersectionality of their social identities. Undocumented LatinX students are frequently first-generation college students from economically disadvantaged backgrounds (Abrego, 2011; Bjorklund, 2018; Golash-Boza & Valdez, 2018; Teranishi et al., 2015). Negotiating their multiple identities poses challenges in pursuing postsecondary degrees or credentials, as having an "undocumented status" can exacerbate these difficulties (Aguilar, 2021). Research has shown that undocumented students face unique challenges in higher education, including discrimination, microaggressions, and institutional barriers that complicate their educational journey (Nienhusser et al., 2016). These challenges are often intensified by their undocumented status, which can limit their opportunities and heighten the difficulties of navigating multiple identities in a college setting.

LATINX HIGHER EDUCATIONAL ATTAINMENT AND DEGREE OR CREDENTIAL TYPE

In fall 2021, approximately 15.4 million undergraduate students enrolled at degree-granting postsecondary institutions in the United States (National Center for Education Statistics, 2021). The educational landscape holds significant importance for the LatinX community in the United States, especially considering its relatively youthful median age of 30.5 years in 2021. In fact, as of 2021, most LatinX adults fell within the age range of 25 to 34. Within this demographic, the LatinX population exhibited the highest college attainment rate (bachelor's degree or beyond) and the lowest high school non-completion rate. In 2021, the U.S. Census Bureau reported the Mexican population had the most substantial increase in college enrollment at a 12-percentage-point rise from 21 percent in 2005 to 33 percent in 2021. Additionally, Puerto Rican, Dominican, Central American, and other sub-ethnic LatinX populations witnessed enrollment increases of 7.5 percentage points or more (Hernandez & McElrath, 2023). While there has been notable growth in educational enrollment among LatinX over the past two decades, they remain less likely to hold a postsecondary degree or credential, and they are disproportionately represented among adults with a high school diploma or less.

In 2021, The National Student Clearinghouse Research Center revealed a concerning trend: LatinX enrollment in higher education dropped by 5.4 percentage points in 2020 amidst the COVID-19 global pandemic. When examining differences across institutions of higher education types, these declines appear even more distressing. While all enrollment at public four-year colleges decreased by nearly two percentage points, community colleges experienced a significant decline of 10.6 percentage points overall, with Latino males facing an even steeper drop of nearly 17 percentage points, compared with a 6.2 percentage point decline for Latina females. These declines are particularly worrisome given that over 52 percent of LatinX college students attend community colleges. Still, LatinX students continue to be underrepresented in both two- and four-year institutions compared with their demographic proportions and their white counterparts.

Also in 2021, the U.S. Census Bureau reported that over the span of 16 years, South American (46 percent) and Cuban (35.9 percent) demographics exhibited bachelor's degree completion rates compared with other LatinX sub-ethnic groups. The South American cohort experienced the most significant surge, a 12 percent increase. Mexican and Central American demographics showed approximately a 10-percentage-point rise in bachelor's degree attainment. Puerto Rican, Dominican, and other LatinX communities demonstrated comparable growth patterns in bachelor's degree completion, commencing 2021 at rates between 15 percent and 20 percent and advancing to levels between 27 percent and 28 percent (Hernandez & McElrath, 2023).

As one of the largest and fastest-growing segments of the U.S. population, LatinX stands to benefit greatly from college attendance, which is strongly linked to improved health, employment, and economic outcomes. Without concerted efforts to address these declines, the educational opportunity gaps in the United States will only widen, leaving LatinX students at a disadvantage. Academic achievement and student success in higher education are a complex concept influenced by various demographic factors such as gender, race, ethnicity, socioeconomic status, and age. Certain barriers disproportionately affect LatinX groups, hindering their access to and completion of postsecondary degrees or credentials in higher education. To enhance academic achievement and student success rates, it's crucial to identify and address these barriers that impede progress for LatinX communities.

Extensive research in higher education over the years indicates that attaining a postsecondary degree or credential increases significant economic advantages to students (Yannelis & Tracey, 2022). Colleges and universities play pivotal roles as conduits for employment opportunities, enhancing the socioeconomic well-being of individuals, facilitating enhancement of vocational skills, serving as focal points for cultural enrichment within broader societal contexts, and serving as catalysts for attracting employers who value the elevated quality of life often associated with proximal higher education institutions (Hearn & Holdsworth, 2002). Interestingly, in 2008, the Lumina Foundation committed to ensuring that 60 percent of U.S. adults aged 25 to 65 attain a postsecondary degree or credential by 2025. To date, the Foundation reported that in the United States, 48 out of 50 states have implemented state policies to increase the higher education attainment to at least 60 percent among adults aged 25 to 65 to assist in the nation's economic growth. It is essential to distinguish between the different types of postsecondary degrees or credentials, the quality of the degrees or credentials, how they are awarded, and what type of degrees or credentials LatinX students are pursuing, as there may be inequities in who is pursuing various degrees or credentials, given the immense diversity among LatinX students.

For LatinX students, the educational opportunity gap has increased with the changing landscape of higher education, especially COVID-19, college affordability, and student debt. Now, the repeal of affirmative action could drastically impact equity moving forward. As seen in the previous section, it is critical to note that specifically for LatinX students, despite being the largest racial and ethnic student population, enrolling in a postsecondary pathway only *sometimes* equates to completing a postsecondary degree or credential. While the changing landscape of higher education poses challenges, illuminating successful processes and pathways for LatinX populations to attain postsecondary degrees or credentials is critical to understanding where institutions of higher education and institutional actors should focus their efforts moving forward to 2025 and beyond.

In 2014, the U.S. Department of Labor signed the Workforce Innovation and Opportunity Act (WIOA) into law, which was implemented to strengthen and increase the nation's workforce and assist individuals in gaining access to employment, education, training, and support services. The Workforce Innovation and Opportunity Act defines and recognizes a postsecondary degree or credential as "an industry-recognized certificate or certification, a certificate of completion of an apprenticeship, a license recognized by the State involved or Federal Government, or an associate or baccalaureate degree" (U.S. Department of Labor, n.d.). Postsecondary degrees or credentials are commonly identified as associate or bachelor's degrees but can include diplomas, certificates, or degrees. Non-degree credentials signify sufficient knowledge or mastery of a wide range of knowledge, skills, and abilities, evidenced by credit and noncredit certificates, industry certifications, occupation licensure, apprenticeships, and micro-credentials (Van Noy, 2020). There is vast variation in non-degree credentials and their requirements, so it can be challenging for students and employers to determine the quality of programs that grant them. In fact, there is little consensus among students, employers, and institutional actors about measuring the quality of non-degree credentials. In 2019, the National Skills Coalition asserted that not all non-degree credentials are created equitably; as such, this remains a continuing issue that institutions of higher education, their actors, and respective states will face in meeting and measuring its attainment goal of 65 percent by 2025 (National Skills Coalition, 2019).

The U.S. Department of Education defines a baccalaureate degree as one that typically requires at least four years, but not more than five, of full-time equivalent college-level courses. Completing a bachelor's degree comes with a range of individual and economic growth opportunities. For example, in 2020, the U.S. Bureau of Labor Statistics reported the median earnings of individuals with a bachelor's degree (but no higher degree) working full time was $36,000 or 84 percent higher than those of high school graduates. Additionally, the unemployment rate for individuals with a bachelor's degree is about half the unemployment rate for individuals with a high school diploma. Santiago et al. (2024) identified that during 2019–2020, the top 25 institutions where LatinX students earned baccalaureate degrees were primarily public institutions (24 out of 25), with 21 classified as Hispanic-Serving Institutions (HSIs) and 17 recognized with the Seal of Excelencia.[9] California boasted the highest number of these institutions (12), followed by Texas (8). Despite these advancements, the Pew Research Center (2022) reports that 62 percent of U.S. adults aged 25 and older lack a bachelor's degree, including approximately 79 percent of LatinX individuals.

The U.S. Department of Education defines an associate degree as an award that requires completion of an organized program of study of at least two years, but less than four, of full-time academic study or more than 60 but less than 120 semester credit hours, usually equating to two years of full-time study. An associate degree is a recognized higher education degree, with many students being granted Associate of Arts (AA) or Associate of Science (AS) degrees. At times, professional, technical, and terminal programs can offer an associate degree, called an Associate of Applied Science (AAS). An associate degree is usually earned at a community or junior college. It is considered a pathway of growth for individuals who otherwise may not have been able to earn a full degree, whether due to financial reasons or other circumstances. Associate degrees offer a level of flexibility and affordability. The number of individuals working to earn an associate degree has risen to almost half of the general college students (Gittell et al., 2017). In many ways, associate degrees benefit both the individual and the overall economy. Recent studies have shown that associate degrees are associated with individual income growth by over 30 percent (Gittell et al., 2017). This is due to an associate degree facilitating students' abilities to qualify for "good jobs" that provide more benefits and increased earnings. During the 2019–20 academic year, every one of the top 25 institutions where LatinXs earned associate degrees was a public institution and held the status of Hispanic-Serving Institution (Santiago et al., 2024).

The Adult Training and Education Survey (ATES) conducted by the National Center for Education Statistics defines certificates as an award granted upon successful completion of a postsecondary program that awards credentials below a bachelor's degree and sometimes below an associate degree (National Center for Education Statistics, 2019a). As the National Center for Education Statistics (2019a) stipulates, a certificate can be categorized by the time spent attaining it. For example, a certificate may take less than one year of study, at least one year but less than two years, and/or at least two years but less than four. Certificates are typically awarded in career technical education or vocational education and potentially offer coursework similar to an associate degree, but without general educational requirements (National Center for Education Statistics, 2019a). Certificates are not bound by time and do not have to be renewed. In addition, the National Skills Coalition defined apprenticeship certificates as licensures either earned through work-based programs or postsecondary earn-and-learn models applicable to industry trades and professions (National Skills Coalition, 2020). Unlike certificates that are tied to specific educational programs, the National Skills Coalition differentiates certificates from certifications, mainly as it applies to industry certifications, which qualify as credentials that are awarded by a certification body (i.e., not an educational institution or government agency) in which individuals demonstrate their knowledge, skills, and abilities through an examination process exemplifying mastery of a specific occupation or skill. Certifications are bound by time and renewable through re-certification (National Skills Coalition, 2020). While limited, the Adult Training and Education Survey is among the most nationally comprehensive data sources available on work-related credentials held by adults in the United States. In 2016, ATES found that overall, 21 percent of adults have a license or certification, with licenses being more prevalent than certifications (National Center for Education Statistics, 2017). Certifications were more prevalent among adults with a college degree versus those with less educational attainment. Most adults with a certification reported that it helped them gain and maintain employment, sustain marketability, and increase their work skills (National Center for Education Statistics, 2017). Santiago et al. (2024) reported that in 2019–20, the majority of the top 25 institutions where LatinXs earned certificates were public (23 out of 25) and the vast majority were HSIs (23 out of 25), with three institutions receiving the Seal of Excelencia. California housed the highest number of these institutions (13), followed by Florida (4), and Texas (3). LatinX representation at these institutions varied widely, ranging from 33 percent to 100 percent, with an overall representation of 54 percent. Furthermore, these top 25 institutions were responsible for conferring one-fifth of all certificates earned by LatinXs during that academic year (Santiago et al., 2024).

The National Student Clearinghouse Research Center has one of the most comprehensive data sources (segmented by state) on the students who have completed "some college, no credential." As previously discussed, using precise nomenclature is of utmost importance when discussing different LatinX student populations, as they are not monolithic. This is especially true for LatinX students with "some college, no degree" versus those with "non-degree credentials." The National Student Clearinghouse Research Center (NSCRC) and the Lumina Foundation have moved toward the term "some college, no credential" (SCNC), which may or may not have benefits associated with aggregating both these student groups into the same population. In 2023, the NSCRC reported that the population who has completed "some college, no credential" has reached 40.4 million, up 1.4 million from 39 million the previous year. The National Student Clearinghouse Research Center produced a four-part report series addressing the "some college, no credential" student population. They found that 23.6 percent of LatinX students who stop out[10] tend to encounter various circumstances that influence their family, work, and education priorities. At times, personal circumstances (e.g., financial, caregiving, parenthood), policies (e.g., institutional, state, or federal level), basic needs (e.g., transportation, food, technology, health care access), or a combination of all can result in LatinX students being stunted in their progress toward a postsecondary degree or credential.

ACADEMIC ACHIEVEMENT AND STUDENT SUCCESS

A key focus in the literature on LatinX student success in higher education is the definition of academic achievement. According to Kuh et al. (2006), academic achievement is understood as measurable outcomes that include a range of indicators such as "GPA [grade point average], standardized test scores for college entry, attainment of knowledge and skills, persistence, educational attainment post-college, and subsequent performance" (p. 10). This definition emphasizes the extent to which individuals meet specific, measurable goals within educational contexts. Academic achievement is often viewed narrowly in terms of academic outputs—how well a student meets the academic requirements and expectations of their program. In contrast, student success is a broader term that encompasses academic achievement and other factors like college readiness, student satisfaction or engagement, and/or career readiness (Steinmayr et al., 2014). However, in higher education research and literature, the definition of student success is widely debated, especially when referring to LatinX students, which is the focus of Chapters 2, 3, and 5 of this book.

Notwithstanding, LatinX students' pathways to academic achievement and success[11] are often non-linear, influenced by factors such as familial support, the value placed on education, and personal achievement (Zalaquett, 2006). Still, existing scholarship on the assets LatinX students bring to higher education institutions and the strategies that support their success remains limited (Hurtado et al., 2020; Rendón et al., 2014). Efforts are needed to highlight effective strategies and move away from deficit-oriented approaches that overshadow LatinX students' strengths and contributions (Valencia, 2010). LatinX students often face institutional biases and stereotypes that question their commitment to learning and pursuit of a postsecondary degree or credential despite their determination to succeed amidst challenges (Zalaquett, 2006). Moreover, systemic issues affecting student progression are sometimes overlooked, with student departures often viewed as personal failures rather than systemic shortcomings (Rendón et al., 2014). Current academic achievement and student success research predominantly relies on quantitative methodologies emphasizing measurable variables such as graduation and retention rates (Bensimon, 2007). This approach may overlook the unique contexts of marginalized students' lives and perpetuate disparities in educational outcomes (Bensimon, 2007). Graduation rates, often used to measure institutional success, provide a narrow view of academic achievement and student success, while retention rates may only partially account for diverse student experiences (Stohs & Schutte, 2019). Recent efforts in student success research are diversifying methodologies to include qualitative approaches that center students' perspectives (Cejda, 2010; Wirth & Padilla, 2008). These approaches aim to understand "successful students" strategies despite barriers rather than solely identifying signs of potential pushout (Wirth & Padilla, 2008). Recent studies also consider institutional factors, such as whether students attend Minority Serving Institutions (MSIs) or Predominantly White Institutions (PWIs), in understanding LatinX academic achievement and student success (Cuellar, 2012; Chang et al., 2019; McKeown-Moak et al., 2013).

THE ORGANIZATION OF THIS BOOK: RE-ENVISIONING SUCCESS FOR LATINX STUDENTS AND FAMILIES

Institutions of higher education face unprecedented challenges, prompting a critical reassessment and re-envisioning of how institutional actors define and research LatinX student success. As previously discussed, traditionally, success for LatinX students has been narrowly defined by metrics such as standardized assessments and GPA, which offer only partial insights. Ewell and Wellman (2007) conceptualize student success as "encompassing various dimensions, including educational progression (high school graduation, college enrollment, retention, and degree completion), learning outcomes, and positive educational experiences like engagement and satisfaction" (p. 2). The question arises: How can we quantify, if at all, the intangible aspects of success, especially among LatinX communities?

In the United States, unlearning conventional notions of student success is crucial to re-envision a brighter future for LatinX students. Pérez Huber et al. (2018) assert that higher education degrees symbolize more than mere documents for LatinX students—they represent a communal struggle and triumph that extends beyond the individual. Often, attaining a postsecondary degree or credential is a collective accomplishment shared with parents, mainly as many LatinX students are the first in their families to complete a postsecondary degree or credential. It embodies a collective endeavor and is a labor of love shaped by the guidance and sacrifices of ancestors, kin, and parents, marking a shared moment of profound joy that transcends institutional metrics. Honoring the LatinX community begins with acknowledging the profound influence of family and friends on educational journeys.

Institutions of higher education and institutional actors must hold themselves accountable by recognizing and centering on the skills, abilities, and knowledge LatinX communities consistently bring to these environments. As documented in this chapter, there is a need to move away from monolithic definitions of LatinX student success as this population in higher education is constantly evolving and changing based on the heterogeneity *between and within* group experiences in the United States. It is crucial not to homogenize the sources of support or challenges faced by different LatinX sub-ethnic and racial groups. Each group is unique and deserves to be embraced rather than subjected to a one-size-fits-all approach. As seen in this chapter, nomenclature is of utmost importance when approaching understanding and working with LatinX students, their families, and communities.

As a newly tenured Associate Professor of Higher Education at Rutgers and a Critical Race Feminista scholar, my research ensures that academic literature reflects and values LatinX students and their families' experiences. LatinX families are pivotal in nurturing their children's and relatives' educational aspirations, resilience, and perseverance in higher education. As underrepresented students, we often ponder our place and worth in academia regarding economic advancement and stability for ourselves and our families. I have learned to self-define my worth and determine what is meaningful to me and the narrative I wish to create. What story do you want to tell now, during your college years, and beyond graduation? My connection to the LatinX community has constantly inspired me throughout my academic and professional journey. I dedicate much of my time to mentoring students, guiding them through their academic pursuits, graduation, and transition into the next phase of their lives. Witnessing the brilliance of future generations reaffirms the significance of my work. I cherish my role because of the affirmations I received and because I can share these accomplishments with my family. That is what I define as LatinX student success—intergenerational nurturing, care, love, and joy!

I began this book and chapter on re-envisioning LatinX student success by examining my familial educational pipelines with my counter-story. Emerging in the early 2000s, the ChicanX educational pipeline illustrates these dynamics (Solórzano & Yosso, 2000). The impetus for this book stems from a desire to fulfill the promise made to my grandmother, due to her hard work and sacrifices, though she never got to witness or benefit from my fulfilled promise. Storytelling is foundational to survival, resistance, and knowledge within ChicanX and Puerto Rican families. Although institutions of higher education may not recognize the power of storytelling, it is intertwined with normalcy within ChicanX and Puerto Rican communities. Storytelling and counter-stories, in particular, are used as pedagogical tools that save our own lives when encountering racism, white supremacy, and other forms of systemic oppression.

Unique to this book, each chapter provides a counter-story that frames the chapter's content. Solórzano and Yosso (2002) apply Critical Race Theory to develop counter-storytelling methodology in educational research. This approach integrates "race and racism throughout the research process" (Solórzano & Yosso, 2002, p. 24). While their methodology centers on race and racism in education research, they also acknowledge the intersecting influences of class, gender, sexuality, and other social identities on the experiences of LatinX students in institutions of higher education settings. Historically, researchers have overlooked these intersections and often depicted these experiences in deficit terms. A critical race methodology challenges and disrupts conventional research paradigms by highlighting the racialized, gendered, and class-based experiences of students of color, considering these experiences as sources of strength (Solórzano & Yosso, 2002). Counter-storytelling emerges as one method within this approach.

Yosso (2005) argues that dominant societal narratives, or majoritarian stories, center on Eurocentric ideologies and dismiss the community cultural wealth of LatinX students, their families, and communities. These majoritarian stories, naturalized and unchallenged in mainstream discourse, often portray LatinX students, their families, and communities through a deficit lens. In response, counter-stories amplify voices from the margins and serve as rebuttals to majoritarian narratives. They draw from interdisciplinary sources such as academic research, social sciences/humanities literature, legal precedents, and quantitative data to "document the persistence of racism from the perspective of those affected and victimized by its enduring legacy" (Yosso, 2005, p. 10). Counter-stories can take various forms, including autobiographical,

biographical, or composite narratives, all aimed at documenting the impacts of race, racism, and white supremacy. In Chapters 2 through 5, a composite counter-story is utilized, integrating diverse data sets, personal and professional experiences, and scholarly research to challenge systems of oppression. Employing the critical race methodology of counter-storytelling, this book relies on engaging with intersectional analysis of individual and collective experiences. It challenges ahistorical approaches to examining LatinX student success in institutions of higher education, which has traditionally been viewed in juxtaposition to the success of their white counterparts. For far too long, LatinX students have had to ascribe to evaluation standards steeped in racism, white supremacy, and colonial logic (Garcia et al., 2021). There is a need for a revisionist approach to legitimize the multiple strengths of LatinX students, their families, and communities.

To do this, in Chapter 2, I provide a historical analysis of the deficit racial framing that has shaped academic achievement and success discourse of LatinX students in U.S. educational systems. It explores how white supremacy and racism have influenced deficit discourses, portraying LatinX students as "failing" or "disadvantaged," thus marginalizing their academic potential. Through the counter-story of Mari, a Salvadorian/Chicana student navigating learning disabilities and cultural misconceptions, the chapter emphasizes the ongoing struggle of LatinX families to advocate for their children in an educational system that often undermines their potential. The chapter also critically examines how ethnic, racial, and cultural socialization practices within LatinX families cultivate resilience and academic success, challenging these deficit narratives. Finally, it reviews "traditional" definitions and measures of student success and emphasizes the need for more inclusive, equitable frameworks that recognize the distinct experiences of LatinX students. The chapter calls for a re-envisioning of traditional definitions and measures of student success in institutions of higher education, advocating for strategies that empower LatinX students to thrive academically despite white supremacy, racism, and other forms of systematic oppression.

In Chapter 3, I investigate the complexities of LatinX academic achievement and student success in institutions of higher education, focusing on the experiences of marginalized identities within this community. Through the counter-story of Ariel, an Afro-LatinX non-binary student, the chapter illustrates the intersection of personal, cultural, and academic struggles that inform the educational pathways of LatinX students. The chapter explores foundational scholarship on LatinX academic achievement student success, emphasizing the role of institutional types, such as Hispanic-Serving Institutions (HSIs) and public two-year institutions, in facilitating access to institutions of higher education. Foundational research is analyzed to define LatinX student success and assess indicators of academic achievement and postsecondary degree or credential completion among LatinX students. The chapter concludes with how social identities such as gender identity, race, and ethnicity impact LatinX students' experiences with a discussion on the need for more specialized research and institutional strategies that address the array of challenges and strengths that LatinX students bring to their educational pathways.

In Chapter 4, I explore the application of asset-based theoretical and methodological frameworks, particularly within Critical Race Theory (CRT) and Chicana Feminisms, to address LatinX academic achievement and student success in institutions of higher education. The chapter begins with the counter-story of Yamaris, a Dominican undergraduate, who navigates the challenges of disaster preparedness amid familial and academic responsibilities. Her story exemplifies how familial support, community resilience, and aspirations serve as sources of support against socioeconomic and academic challenges. The chapter outlines the emergence and impact of CRT and Chicana/ Latina feminisms in higher education, critiquing the systemic oppression that underlies traditional academic frameworks. Foundational theories are discussed, demonstrating how they challenge deficit perspectives and offer transformative approaches to understanding LatinX academic achievement and student success. By bridging theory and methodology, the chapter emphasizes the importance of Critical Race Feminista methodologies and Quantitative Ethnographic practices, offering innovative ways to integrate qualitative and quantitative approaches to better represent LatinX student experiences in higher education.

Finally, in Chapter 5, I conceptualize and introduce the LatinX Intergenerational Bendiciones Framework for Student Success, a culturally responsive framework that re-envisions how academic achievement and student success are defined for LatinX students in institutions of higher education. Drawing from a counter-story on Felix, an undocumented Bolivian student, the chapter examines the impacts of anti-Diversity, Equity, and Inclusion (DEI) legislation, white supremacy, and racism on LatinX students' educational pathways. It demonstrates how white supremacy, racism, and other forms of systematic oppression continue to shape their experiences, while offering resistance strategies these students employ to challenge oppression. The chapter critiques traditional definitions of success, which are grounded in the characteristics of white supremacy culture and introduces the concept of *bendiciones* (blessings)—the intergenerational wisdom, cultural affirmation, and community resilience that support LatinX students in their educational pathways. In centering intergenerational collective milestones rather than individual achievement, the framework shifts the focus to the shared cultural and familial bonds that sustain LatinX students. The chapter concludes by urging institutions of higher education and their actors to adopt anti-racist practices and recognize the value of family and community in cultivating LatinX student academic achievement and success.

CONCLUSION

This book seeks to advance a deeper understanding of LatinX academic achievement and student success by challenging "traditional" and/or deficit frameworks and embracing a more inclusive, dynamic, and culturally appropriate approach—a LatinX attentive approach (Flores et al., 2021). The term "LatinX," as introduced by Milian (2019), serves as a crucial tool for rethinking and expanding the lexicon used to describe the experiences of LatinX individuals, particularly within the context of U.S. higher education. By employing critical race methodology of counter-storytelling and engaging with intersectional analyses, this book aims to reframe the discourse around the academic achievement and success of LatinX students, centering their experiences within the broader contexts of racism, white supremacy, and other forms of systemic oppression. This book contributes to the ongoing conversation about how to best support and empower LatinX students in higher education, ensuring their success is not measured by white academic standards but rather by their abilities to thrive in a complex and changing world.

DISCUSSION QUESTIONS

Using the content within this chapter, consider the following questions for reflection and discussion:

- How can institutions of higher education develop more holistic metrics that better capture the diverse and intangible aspects of success for LatinX students beyond standardized assessments and GPA?
- What strategies can institutions of higher education adopt to better support and engage with the families and communities of LatinX students, acknowledging their significant influence on educational aspirations and resilience?
- How can counter-storytelling be integrated into higher education curricula to address systemic racism and white supremacy, and what impact might this have on the educational experiences of LatinX students?

NOTES

1. For more information on Mexican American women who served in World War II see: Escobedo, E. R. (2013). *From coveralls to zoot suits: The lives*

of Mexican American women on the World War II home front. UNC Press Books.

2. Postsecondary degrees or credentials are commonly identified as associate or bachelor's degrees, but they can include diplomas, certificates, or degrees. Non-degree credentials include a wide range of knowledge, skills, and abilities, such as credit and non-credit certificates, industry certifications, occupation licensure, apprenticeships, and micro-credentials (Van Noy, 2020). For the purposes of this book, I use postsecondary degree or credential as umbrella terms to denote both.

3. I was inspired and draw from the Chicana and Chicano educational pipelines, which refer to the educational trajectories of ChicanX or Mexican American communities as they progress through the educational system in the United States. These pipelines often highlight the systemic barriers, inequities, and challenges that ChicanX students face, as well as the factors that contribute to their "success" or "failure" in their academic achievement. The visual pipelines are frequently used in Critical Race Theory (CRT) to examine how race, class, gender, and citizenship intersect and impact the educational outcomes of this population. Please see: Solórzano, D., & Yosso, T. (2000). Toward a critical race theory of Chicana and Chicano education. In C. Tejeda, C. Martinez, & Z. Leonardo (Eds.), *Charting new terrains of Chicana(o)/Latina(o) education* (pp. 35–65). Hampton Press.

4. Saving the Legacy: An Oral History of Utah's Veterans. The University of Utah. American West Center. For more information on this oral history project, see: https://awc.utah.edu/oral-histories/veterans.php

5. For educational pipelines that document these phenomena, see: Pérez Huber, L., Malagón, M. C., Ramirez, B. R., Gonzalez, L. C., Jimenez, A., & Vélez, V. N. (2015). Still falling through the cracks: Revisiting the Latina/o education pipeline. *CSRC Research Report.* Number 19. UCLA Chicano Studies Research Center.

6. Please refer to semiotics; see Saussure, F. de (2011). *Course in general linguistics* (P. Meisel, H. Saussy, & W. Baskin, Trans.). Columbia University Press (original work published 1916) and Barthes, R. (1977). *Image, music, text* (S. Heath, Trans.). Hill and Wang.

7. Connecticut, Hawaii, Massachusetts, New Jersey, Pennsylvania, New Hampshire, and New York.

8. I use BIPOC as critiques among scholars and grassroots activists advocating against Black murder at the hands of police and the ongoing Indigenous genocide prefer using BIPOC (Black, Indigenous, and People of Color). This term underscores solidarity among marginalized groups while respecting the distinct experiences within each community, avoiding the erasure of voices from the most institutionally marginalized individuals.

9. Excelencia in Education grants a certificate or what is referred to as the Seal of Excelencia to institutions of higher education that serve and support LatinX students effectively on their pathways to postsecondary degree or credential completion.

10. Stop-out often refers to students who temporarily leave their respective institutions of higher education with the intention of returning. I use this term rather than drop-out to shift deficit discourse to asset-based discourse.

11. Due to the conflation of terms throughout this book, I use academic achievement and success as umbrella terms.

31

REFERENCES

Abrego, L. J. (2011). Legal consciousness of undocumented Latinos: Fear and stigma as barriers to claims-making for first- and 1.5-generation immigrants. *Law & Society Review*, 45(2), 337–370. https://doi.org/10.1111/j.1540-5893.2011.00435.x

Aguilar, C. (2021). Undocumented critical theory in education. In N. M. Garcia, C. Salinas Jr., & J. Cisneros (Eds.), *Studying Latinx/a/o students in higher education* (pp. 149–163). Routledge.

Alcoff, L. M. (2000). Is Latina/o identity a racial identity? In J. J. E. Gracia & P. M. de Greiff (Eds.), *Hispanics/Latinos in the United States* (1st ed., pp. 23–44). Routledge. https://doi.org/10.4324/9780203613566

Alcoff, L. M. (2006). *Visible identities: Race, gender, and the self*. Oxford University Press. https://doi.org/10.1093/0195137345.001.0001

Alcoff, L. M. (2009). Latinos beyond the binary. *Southern Journal of Philosophy*, 47(S1), 112–128.

American Immigration Council. (2023). *Undocumented students in U.S. higher education*. Retrieved from https://www.americanimmigrationcouncil.org/research/undocumented-college-students-2023

Anderson, M. L., & Collins, P. H. (2007). *Race, class, and gender: An anthology* (6th ed.). Wadsworth.

Bahr, P. R. (2009). College hopping: Exploring the occurrence, frequency, and consequences of lateral transfer. *Community College Review*, 36(4), 271–298.

Barillas Chón, D. W., Landeros, J., & Urrieta, L. (2024). Critical Latinx Indigeneities: Love letters to Chicanx and Latinx studies. *Journal of Latinos and Education*, 1–13.

Barthes, R. (1977). *Image, music, text* (S. Heath, Trans.). Hill and Wang.

Bensimon, E. M. (2007). The underestimated significance of practitioner knowledge in the scholarship on student success. *The Review of Higher Education*, 30(4), 441–469. https://doi.org/10.1353/rhe.2007.0032

Bjorklund Jr, P. (2018). Undocumented students in higher education: A review of the literature, 2001 to 2016. *Review of Educational Research*, 88(5), 631–670.

Busey, C. L., & Silva, C. (2021). Troubling the essentialist discourse of Brown in education: The anti-Black sociopolitical and sociohistorical etymology of Latinxs as a Brown monolith. *Educational Researcher*, 50(3), 176–186.

Cejda, B. D. (2010, October). In their own words: Latina success in higher education. *Journal of Women in Educational Leadership*, 8(4).

Chang, E., London, R. A., & Foster, S. S. (2019). Reimagining student success: Equity-oriented responses to traditional notions of success. *Innovative Higher Education*, 44(6), 481–496.

Choy, S. P. (2002). Nontraditional undergraduates: Findings from *The Condition of Education 2002*. National Center for Education Statistics. Retrieved from https://nces.ed.gov/pubs2002/2002012.pdf

Cohn, D., Passel, J. S., & Gonzalez-Barrera, A. (2017). Rise in U.S. immigrants from El Salvador, Guatemala, and Honduras outpaces growth from elsewhere. Pew Research Center. Retrieved from http://www.pewhispanic.org/2017/12/07/rise-in-u-s-immigrants-from-el-salvador-guatemala-and-honduras-outpaces-growth-from-elsewhere/

Community College Research Center. (2021). *Strategies for improving postsecondary credential attainment among Black, Hispanic, and Native American adults.* https://ccrc.tc.columbia.edu/media/k2/attachments/credential-attainment-black-hispanic-native-american-adults.pdf

Compton, J. I., Cox, E., & Laanan, F. S. (2006). Adult learners in transition. *New Directions for Student Services, 2006*(114), 73–80.

Conteras, F. E. (2011). *Achieving equity for Latino students: Expanding the pathway to higher education through public policy*. Teachers College Press.

Cruse, L. R., Holtzman, T., Gault, B., Croom, D., & Polk, P. (2019). *Parents in college: By the numbers*. Institute for Women's Policy Research.

Cuellar, M. (2012). *Latina/o student success in higher education: Models of empowerment at Hispanic-serving institutions (HSIs), emerging HSIs, and non-HSIs* (Order No. 3497388). ProQuest Dissertations & Theses A&I. https://www.proquest.com/dissertations-theses/latina-o-student-success-higher-education-models/docview/925618798/se-2

Deli-Amen, R. (2020). The "traditional" college student: A smaller and smaller minority and its implications for diversity and access institutions. In E. P. St. John, & M. Wilkerson (Eds.), *Remaking college* (pp. 134–166). Stanford University Press. https://doi.org/10.1515/978080479

Escobedo, E. R. (2013). *From coveralls to zoot suits: The lives of Mexican American women on the World War II home front*. UNC Press Books.

Ewell, P., & Wellman, J. (2007). *Enhancing student success in education: Summary report of the NPEC initiative and national symposium on postsecondary student success*. National Postsecondary Education Cooperative. Retrieved from https://nces.ed.gov/npec/pdf/Ewell_Report.pdf

Excelencia in Education. (2024). *Latinx first-generation college students*. Retrieved from https://www.edexcelencia.org/media/2520

Fink, L. (2003). *The Maya of Morganton: Work and community in the nuevo new south*. The University of North Carolina Press.

Flores, S. M., Carroll, T., & Lyons, S. M. (2021). Beyond the tipping point: Searching for a new vision for Latino college success in the United States. *The ANNALS of the American Academy of Political and Social Science, 696*(1), 128–155.

Frey, W. H. (2018, March 14). The US will become "minority White" in 2045, census projects. *Brookings: The Avenue.* https://www.brookings.edu/blog/the-avenue/2018/03/14/the-us-will-become-minority-white-in-2045-census-projects/

Fry, R., & Cilluffo, A. (2019, May 22). A rising share of undergraduates are from poor families, especially at less selective colleges. *Pew Research Center.* https://www.pewresearch.org/social-trends/2019/05/22/a-rising-share-of-undergraduates-are-from-poor-families-especially-at-less-selective-colleges/

Garcia, N. M. (2016). Adelante y Pa'lante: College-educated Chicana/o and Puerto Rican family educational oral histories [doctoral dissertation, University of California]. eScholarship, California Digital Library. https://escholarship.org/uc/item/9rr1h330

Garcia, N. M. (2019). Pa'lante, siempre pa'lante: Pedagogies of the home among Puerto Rican college educated families. *International Journal of Qualitative Studies in Education, 32*(6), 576–590. https://doi.org/10.1080/09518398.2019.1609116

Garcia, N. M., & Danek, V. (2023). Shelter from the storm: Disaster capitalism and Puerto Rican undergraduates in post-Hurricane María stateside higher education. *Teachers College Record, 125*(4), 182–211.

Garcia, N. M., & Delgado Bernal, D. (2021). Remembering and revisiting pedagogies of the home. *American Educational Research Journal, 58*(3), 567–601.

Garcia, N. M., & Mayorga, O. J. (2018). The threat of unexamined secondary data: A critical race transformative convergent mixed methods. *Race Ethnicity and Education, 21*(2), 231–252.

Garcia, N. M., & Mireles-Rios, R. (2019). "You were going to go to college": The role of Chicano fathers' involvement in Chicana daughters' college choice. *American Educational Research Journal, 57*(5). https://doi.org/10.3102/0002831219892004

Garcia, N. M., Cisneros, J., & Salinas Jr, C. (2021). *Studying Latinx/a/o students in higher education.* Routledge.

Gittell, R., Samuels, J. D., & Tebaldi, E. (2017). The contribution of associate's degree holders to US earnings, labor quality, productivity, and overall economic growth. *Southern Economic Journal, 84*(2), 600–636.

Golash-Boza, T., & Valdez, Z. (2018). Nested contexts of reception: Undocumented students at the University of California, Central. *Sociological Perspectives, 61*(4), 535–552.

Goldberg, D. T. (1993). *Racist culture: Philosophy and the politics of meaning.* Basil Blackwell.

Gómez, L. E. (2020). *Inventing Latinos: A new story of American racism.* The New Press.

Gracia, J. J. E., & De Greiff, P. (Eds.). (2000). *Hispanic/Latino ethnicity, race, and rights: An introduction.* Routledge.

Guerrero, E. (2017). *Nuevo south: Latina/o immigration, race, and community in the changing south.* University Press of Mississippi.

Haney López, I. (2006). *White by law: The legal construction of race* (10th Anniversary ed.). New York University Press.

Hearn, J. C., & Holdsworth, J. M. (2002). The societally responsive university: Public ideals, organizational realities, and the possibility of engagement. *Tertiary Education and Management*, 8(2), 127–144.

Hernández, T. K. (2022). *Racial innocence: Unmasking Latino anti-Black bias and the struggle for equality*. Beacon Press.

Hernandez, E. L., & McElrath, K. (2023, May 10). Significant educational strides by young Hispanic population. Gains in educational attainment, enrollment in all Hispanic groups, largest among south American population. U.S. Census Bureau. Retrieved from https://www.census.gov/library/stories/2023/05/significant-educational-strides-young-hispanic-population.html#:~:text=The%20number%20of%20Hispanic%20people,age%20(30.5%20in%202021).

Hitlin, S., Brown, J. S., & Elder, G. H. (2007). Measuring Latinos: Racial vs. ethnic classification and self-understandings. *Social Forces*, 86(2), 587–611.

Hollinger, D. A. (1995). *Postethnic America: Beyond multiculturalism*. Basic Books.

Hurtado, S. S., Gonyea, R. M., Graham, P. A., & Fosnacht, K. (2020). The relationship between residential learning communities and student engagement. *Learning Communities: Research & Practice*, 8(1), article 5.

Huber, L. P., Lopez, C. B., Malagon, M. C., Velez, V., & Solorzano, D. G. (2008). Getting beyond the "symptom," acknowledging the "disease": Theorizing racist nativism. *Contemporary Justice Review*, 11(1), 39–51.

Irizarry, Y. (2015). Utilizing multidimensional measures of race in education research: The case of teacher perceptions. *Sociology of Race and Ethnicity*, 1(4), 564–583. https://doi.org/10.1177/2332649215580350

Jain, D., Bernal Melendez, S. N., & Herrera, A. R. (2020). *Power to the transfer: Critical race theory and a transfer receptive culture*. Michigan State University Press.

Jiménez Román, M. & Flores, J. (2010). *The Afro-Latin@ reader: History and culture in the United States*. Duke University Press.

Kasworm, C. E. (2012). Adult learners in a research university: Negotiating undergraduate student identity. *Adult Education Quarterly*, 62(3), 279–296. https://doi.org/10.1177/0741713611402044

Kennedy, A. (2023). Nontraditional students: The way to improving enrollment and completion. *Journal of Applied Research in the Community College*, 30(2), 141–149. https://login.proxy.libraries.rutgers.edu/login?qurl=https%3A%2F%2Fwww.proquest.com%2Fscholarly-journals%2Fnontraditional-students-way-improving-enrollment%2Fdocview%2F2934226819%2Fse-2%3Faccountid%3D13626

Kirk-Kuwaye, C., & Kirk-Kuwaye, M. (2007). A study of engagement patterns of lateral and vertical transfer students during their first semester at a public research university. *Journal of the First-Year Experience & Students in Transition*, 19(2), 9–27.

Kouyoumdjian, C., Guzman, B. L., Garcia, N. M., & Talavera-Bustillos, V. (2017). A community cultural wealth examination of sources of support and challenges among Latino first-and second-generation college students at a Hispanic serving institution. *Journal of Hispanic Higher Education, 16*(1), 61–76. https://doi.org/10.1177/1538192715619995

Kuh, G. D., Kinzie, J., Buckley, J. A., Bridges, B. K., & Hayek, J. C. (2006). *What matters to student success: A review of the literature* (Vol. 8). National Postsecondary Education Cooperative.

LeBaron, G. (2012). Migrant workers in the United States. In E. Goldsmith & D. Hall (Eds.), *Handbook of international migration* (pp. 122–138). Oxford University Press.

Lohfink, M. M., & Paulsen, M. B. (2005). Comparing the determinants of persistence for first-generation and continuing-generation students. *Journal of College Student Development, 46*(4), 409–428.

Lopez, M. H., Gonzalez-Barrera, A., & Motel, S. (2011). As deportations rise to record levels, most Latinos oppose Obama's policy. *Pew Hispanic Center.* Retrieved from http://www.pewhispanic.org/2011/12/28/as-deportations-rise-torecord-levels-most-latinos-oppose-obamas-policy

López, N. (2013). Killing two birds with one stone? Why we need two separate questions on race and ethnicity in the 2020 census and beyond. *Latino Studies, 11*(4), 428–438.

Lorde, A. (1992). Age, race, class, and sex: Women redefining difference. In M. Andersen & P. Hill Collins (Eds.), *Race, class, and gender: An anthology* (pp. 495–502). Wadsworth.

MacDonald, V.-M., & Carrillo, J. F. (2021). The United Status of Latinx: 2010–2020 remix. In *Handbook of Latinos and education.* Taylor & Francis.

Marable, M. (1992). *Black America.* Open Media.

McKeown-Moak, M. P., Zaken, O., Olson, J., Vesely, R. S., Jimenez-Castellanos, O., & Okhremtchouk, I. (2013). The "new" performance funding in higher education. *Educational Considerations, 40*(2), 3–12.

Milian, C. (2019). *LatinX.* University of Minnesota Press.

National Center for Education Statistics. (2015). *The condition of education 2015* (NCES 2015–144). U.S. Department of Education. Retrieved from https://nces.ed.gov/pubs2015/2015144.pdf

National Center for Education Statistics. (2017). *Adult training and education: Results from the National Household Education Surveys Program of 2016 (NCES 2017–103).* U.S. Department of Education. https://nces.ed.gov/pubs2017/2017103.pdf

National Center for Education Statistics. (2019a). *Classification of Instructional Programs (CIP 2010).* U.S. Department of Education. Retrieved from https://nces.ed.gov/ipeds/cipcode/Default.aspx?y=55

National Center for Education Statistics. (2019b). *The condition of education 2019*. Retrieved from https://nces.ed.gov/programs/coe/

National Center for Education Statistics. (2021). *Undergraduate enrollment*. U.S. Department of Education. Retrieved from https://nces.ed.gov/programs/coe/indicator_cha.asp

National Skills Coalition. (2019). *Expanding opportunities: Defining quality non-degree credentials for states*. Retrieved from https://nationalskillscoalition.org/resource/publications/expanding-opportunities-defining-quality-non-degree-credentials-for-states/

National Skills Coalition. (2020). *Measuring non-degree credential attainment*. Retrieved from https://www.nationalskillscoalition.org/resources/publications/file/Measuring-Non-Degree-Credential-Attainment.pdf

National Student Clearinghouse Research Center. (NSCRC). (2021). *Undergraduate enrollment declines show no signs of recovery from 2020*. Retrieved from https://www.studentclearinghouse.org/news/undergraduate-enrollment-declines-show-no-signs-of-recovery-from-2020/

National Student Clearinghouse Research Center. (NSCRC). (2023). *Some college, no credential population increased by 1.4 million*. Retrieved from https://www.studentclearinghouse.org/news/college-student-stop-out-population-increased-3-6-from-previous-year/

Nguyen, T. H., & Nguyen, B. M. D. (2018). Is the "first-generation student" term useful for understanding inequality? The role of intersectionality in illuminating the implications of an accepted—yet unchallenged—term. *Review of Research in Education, 42*(1), 146–176.

Nienhusser, H. K. (2018). Higher education institutional agents as policy implementers: The case of policies that affect undocumented and DACAmented students. *The Review of Higher Education, 41*(3), 423–453. https://doi.org/10.1353/rhe.2018.0014

Nienhusser, H. K., Vega, B. E., & Carquin, M. C. S. (2016). Undocumented students' experiences with microaggressions during their college choice process. *Teachers College Record, 118*(2), 1–33.

Nuñez, C., Silver, J., Galdámez, M., & López, N. (2024, August 7). *Latino is not a race: Understanding lived experiences through street race*. Latino Policy & Politics Institute. https://latino.ucla.edu/research/latino-is-not-a-race/

Oboler, S. (2012). *Latino immigrants in the United States*. Routledge.

Odem, M. E., & Lacy, E. R. (2009). *Latino immigrants and the transformation of the U.S. South*. University of Georgia Press.

Olivas, M. A. (2020). *Perchance to DREAM: A legal and political history of the DREAM Act and DACA*. New York University Press.

Omi, M., & Winant, H. (1994). *Racial formation in the United States: From the 1960s to the 1990s*. Routledge.

Omi, M., & Winant, H. (2014). *Racial formation in the United States*. Routledge.

Passel, J. S., & Cohn, D. (2008). *U.S. population projections, 2005–2050* (p. 20). Pew Research Center. https://www.pewresearch.org/hispanic/2008/02/11/us-population-projections-2005-2050/

Peña, J. E., Lowe Jr., R. H., & Rios-Vargas, M. (2023, September 26). Eight Hispanic groups each had a million or more population in 2020. Colombian and Honduran populations surpassed a million for first time; Venezuelan population grew the fastest of all Hispanic groups since 2010. U.S. Census Bureau. Retrieved from https://www.census.gov/library/stories/2023/09/2020-census-dhc-a-hispanic-population.html

Pérez Huber, L., Vélez, V. N., & Solórzano, D. (2018). More than "papelitos": A QuantCrit counterstory to critique Latina/o degree value and occupational prestige. *Race, Ethnicity and Education, 21*(2), 208–230.

Pérez Huber, L., Malagón, M. C., Ramirez, B. R., Gonzalez, L. C., Jimenez, A., & Vélez, V. N. (2015). Still falling through the cracks: Revisiting the Latina/o education pipeline. *CSRC Research Report*. Number 19. UCLA Chicano Studies Research Center.

Person, A. E., Bruch, J., & Goble, L. (2019). Why equity matters for adult college completion. *Education Issue Brief*. Mathematica. https://www.mathematica.org/publications/why-equity-matters-for-adult-college-completion

Pew Research Center. (2022). *Hispanic enrollment reaches new high at four-year colleges in the U.S., but affordability remains an obstacle*. Retrieved from https://www.pewresearch.org/short-reads/2022/10/07/hispanic-enrollment-reaches-new-high-at-four-year-colleges-in-the-u-s-but-affordability-remains-an-obstacle/

Pike, G. R., & Kuh, G. D. (2005). First- and second-generation college students: A comparison of their engagement and intellectual development. *The Journal of Higher Education, 76*(3), 276–300.

Plyler v. Doe 457 U.S. 202 (1982).

Ramos-Sánchez, L., & Nichols, L. (2007). Self-efficacy of first-generation and non-first-generation college students: The relationship with academic performance and college adjustment. *Journal of College Counseling, 10*(1), 6–18.

Rendón, L. I., Nora, A., & Kanagala, V. (2014). *Ventajas/assets y conocimientos/knowledge: Leveraging Latin@ strengths to foster student success*. Center for Research and Policy in Education, The University of Texas at San Antonio.

Rodriguez, C. E. (2000). *Changing race: Latinos, the census, and the history of ethnicity in the United States* (Vol. 41). NYU Press.

Rosa, J. (2018). *Looking like a language, sounding like a race: Raciolinguistic ideologies and the learning of Latinidad*. Oxford University Press. https://doi.org/10.1093/oso/9780190634728.001.0001

Ross-Gordon, J. M. (2005). The adult learner of color: An overlooked college student population. *The Journal of Continuing Higher Education, 53*(2), 2–11. https://doi.org/10.1080/07377366.2005.10400064

Rosser-Mims, D., Palmer, G. A., & Harroff, P. (2014). The reentry adult college student: An exploration of the Black male experience. *New Directions for Adult and Continuing Education, 2014*(144), 59–68. https://doi.org/10.1002/ace.20114

Salinas Jr, C. (2020). The complexity of the "x" in Latinx: How Latinx/a/o students relate to, identify with, and understand the term Latinx. *Journal of Hispanic Higher Education, 19*(2), 149–168.

Salinas, C., & Lozano, A. (2019). Mapping and recontextualizing the evolution of the term Latinx: An environmental scanning in higher education. In E. G. Murillo Jr. (Ed.), *Critical readings on Latinos and education* (pp. 216–235). Routledge.

Sandoval Girón, A. B. (2017). Central and South American Indigenous, American Indian or Hispanic/Latino respondents? Navigating racial identity categories in U.S. census forms. *Center for Survey Measurement, U.S. Census Bureau.*

Santiago, D., Arroyo, C., & Cuellarsola, L. (2024, April). *Latinos in higher education: 2024 compilation of fast facts.* Excelencia in Education.

Saussure, F. de (2011). *Course in general linguistics* (P. Meisel, H. Saussy, & W. Baskin, Trans.). Columbia University Press (original work published 1916).

Solórzano, D. G. (1997). Images and words that wound: Critical race theory, racial stereotyping, and teacher education. *Teacher Education Quarterly, 24*(3), 5–19. https://www.jstor.org/stable/23478088

Solórzano, D., & Yosso, T. (2000). Toward a critical race theory of Chicana and Chicano education. In C. Tejeda, C. Martinez, & Z. Leonardo (Eds.), *Charting new terrains of Chicana(o)/Latina(o) education* (pp. 35–65). Hampton Press.

Solórzano, D. G., & Yosso, T. J. (2002). Critical race methodology: Counter-storytelling as an analytical framework for education research. *Qualitative Inquiry, 8*(1), 23–44.

Steinmayr, R., Meiñer, A., Weideinger, A. F., & Wirthwein, L. (2014). *Academic achievement.* Oxford University Press. https://doi.org/10.1093/obo/9780199756810-0108

Stohs, M. H., & Schutte, J. G. (2019). The graduation rate myth and the equity gap. *Journal of Applied Social Science, 13*(2), 94–114.

Stuesse, A. (2016). *Scratching out a living: Latinos, race, and work in the deep south.* University of California Press.

Tatum, B. D. (1997). *Why are all the Black kids sitting together in the cafeteria? And other conversations about race.* Basic Books.

Taylor, M., & Turk, J. M. (2019). *Race and ethnicity in higher education: A look at low-income undergraduates.* American Council on Education.

Teranishi, R. T., Suárez-Orozco, C., & Suárez-Orozco, M. (2015). *In the shadows of the ivory tower: Undocumented undergraduates and the liminal state of immigration reform.* The UndocuScholars Project at the Institute for Immigration, Globalization, and Education, University of California, Los Angeles. https://www.undocuscholars.org/2015-report

Terenzini, P. T. (1994). The transition to college: Diverse students, diverse stories. *Research in Higher Education, 35,* 57–73.

Townsend, B. K. (1999). Understanding the impact of reverse transfer students on community colleges. In *New Directions for Community Colleges, Number 106.* Jossey-Bass.

U.S. Bureau of Labor Statistics. (2020). Retrieved from https://www.bls.gov/

U.S. Census Bureau. (2020). 2020 census special tabulation. U.S. Government Printing Office.

U.S. Census Bureau. (2022). Hispanic Heritage Month: 2023. U.S. Census Bureau. Retrieved from https://www.census.gov/newsroom/facts-for-features/2023/hispanic-heritage-month.html

U.S. Census Bureau. (2023, June 22). America is getting older. New population estimates highlight increase in national median age. U.S. Census Bureau. Retrieved from https://www.census.gov/newsroom/press-releases/2023/population-estimates-characteristics.html

U.S. Department of Labor. (n.d.). Workforce Innovation and Opportunity Act. Attachment 1. Credential resources. Retrieved from https://www.dol.gov/sites/dolgov/files/ETA/advisories/TEN/2020/TEN_25-19_Attachment_1.pdf

Valencia, R. R. (2010). *Dismantling contemporary deficit thinking: Educational thought and practice.* Routledge.

Van Noy, M. (2020). *Identifying high quality industry certifications.* Rutgers Education and Employment Research Center.

Wilkie, A., Savransky, M., & Rosengarten, M. (Eds.). (2017). *Speculative research: The lure of possible futures.* Routledge. https://doi.org/10.4324/9781315655317

Wirth, R. M., & Padilla, R. V. (2008). College student success: A qualitative modeling approach. *Community College Journal of Research and Practice, 32*(9), 688–711. https://doi.org/10.1080/10668920701380942

Wyatt, L. G. (2011). Nontraditional student engagement: Increasing adult student success and retention. *The Journal of Continuing Higher Education, 59*(1), 10–20. https://doi.org/10.1080/07377363.2011.544977

Yannelis, C., & Tracey, G. (2022). Student loans and borrower outcomes. *Annual Review of Financial Economics, 14,* 167–186.

Yosso, T. J. (2005). Whose culture has capital? A critical race theory discussion of community cultural wealth. *Race Ethnicity and Education, 8*(1), 69–91.

Zalaquett, C. P. (2006). Study of successful Latina/o students. *Journal of Hispanic Higher Education*, *5*(1), 35–47. https://doi.org/10.1177/1538192705282568

Zerquera, D. D., Haywood, J., & De Mucha Flores, M. (2020). More than nuance. In R. T. Teranishi, B. M. D. Nguyen, C. M. Alcantar, & E. R. Curammeng (Eds.), *Measuring race: Why disaggregating data matters for addressing educational inequality* (pp. 154–172). Multicultural Education.

Zúñiga, V., & Hernández-León, R. (2006). *New destinations: Mexican immigration in the United States*. Russell Sage Foundation.

Chapter 2

Historical Deficit Racial Framing of LatinX Student Academic Achievement and Success

MARI: OVERCOMING LEARNING DISABILITIES AND DEFICIT CULTURAL MISCONCEPTIONS

The teacher's voice rang through the frost-covered windows, announcing, "It is time for math and reading. Those of you who need to leave, please line up at the back. The teacher from the learning resource trailer will come get you." Outside, the sky loomed in shades of gray, with the promise of a looming snowstorm. Eight students rushing reached for their coats, ready to brave the harsh wind and rain, while 22 others chuckled quietly, immersed in their textbooks. As the door swung open against the gusts, a knock signaled the arrival of the learning resource teacher, prompting the eight to step outside into the onslaught of angry winds and water droplets.

These students were bound for the learning center, a Title 1 program[1] for "delayed learners." Among them was Mari, a Latina native of California,[2] raised by her Salvadorian mother and Chicano[3] father. Her mother, a high school graduate who worked in insurance, and her father, who began his college education at a community college by working as a janitor at the college to pay for tuition while she was growing up, had chosen private Catholic schooling for Mari and her brother, believing it offered the best education. Mari's potential shone brightly in first grade—she was hard-working, loved books, and possessed a vivid imagination, often filling her diaries with drawings and writings. Her passion for storytelling and the written word developed early. However, by second grade, challenges emerged in math and reading. Numbers escaped her grasp, and word problems proved overwhelming. The mixture of letters and numbers became a perplexing puzzle, often causing confusion where little to none should exist.

A pivotal moment came during a reading quiz when Mari, unsure of what to write, resorted to copying answers from her peers. Caught in the act, she endured public humiliation as her teacher scolded her, the sting of criticism

 DOI: 10.4324/9781003415909-2

slicing through her like a thousand paper cuts. Her failing grade branded her "at risk,"[4] unfairly correlating her struggles with her "Hispanic" culture.[5] Sent home with a red "0" and a demand for a parental signature, Mari's shame was heightened.

Returning home, she handed the test to her mother, who sensed her daughter's distress. Mari struggled to articulate her confusion, feeling overwhelmed by a sense of inadequacy. It was then that Mari's mother recognized a familiar struggle—her own battles with learning disabilities that had plagued her educational journey. Together with Mari's father, they advocated for their daughter, demanding she be tested for learning disabilities. Their suspicions were confirmed, and Mari attended a specialized learning center from second to sixth grade.

Despite their sacrifices—working overtime to afford tutoring and dedicating summers to one-on-one learning—Mari's confidence remained fragile. Despite her parents' advocacy, the school failed[6] to support her. Now, navigating through college, Mari carries the scars of past struggles, her determination to succeed fueled by the unwavering support of her family amidst educational challenges and systemic barriers.

COUNTER-STORY REFLECTION QUESTIONS

- Based on your professional, personal, or community-based experiences, what happened to Mari?
- What role do LatinX parents or kin have in assisting their children's academic achievement and student success?
- What roles do elementary, secondary, and postsecondary institutions have in assisting the academic achievement of LatinX students, families, and communities?

To date, much of the educational research on LatinX students has focused on Mexican American and ChicanX populations, often generalizing implications for other subgroups without acknowledging their distinct characteristics (Montero-Sieburth & Batt, 2000, p. 294). Moreover, quantitative and qualitative research conducted by social scientists and policymakers on LatinX students has typically examined between-group and within-group relationships, and comparisons of academic achievement and student success between immigrant and U.S.-born LatinX students (Soto, 2006). Between-group studies explore the longitudinal educational experiences of LatinX students compared with their high-achieving white peers, highlighting disparities in academic outcomes among African Americans and Asians (Soto, 2006). Within-group research focuses on the educational outcomes among subgroups such as Mexicans, Cubans, Puerto Ricans, and, more recently, Central Americans (Soto, 2006).

Examining shifts in academic paradigms that analyze academic achievement and student success processes among LatinX students is crucial for accurately portraying their experiences in secondary and postsecondary contexts. A significant aspect of the literature on LatinX student success in higher education involves defining what constitutes academic achievement. Drawing on a comprehensive review of student success literature, Kuh et al. (2006) define academic achievement as measurable outcomes "such as GPA, standardized test scores for college entry, attainment of knowledge and skills, persistence, educational attainment post-college, and subsequent performance" (p. 10). As such, academic achievement signifies how students achieve specific goals set within educational environments that are measured and qualified as outcomes. Student success is an umbrella term encompassing academic achievement and other factors such as college readiness, student engagement and satisfaction, and/or a sense of belonging (Nuñez et al., 2013; Steinmayr et al., 2014). Due to the conflation of terms throughout this chapter and the entire book, I use LatinX student academic achievement and success to refer to measurable academic outcomes and broader factors, including personal development and identity formation.

As discussed in Chapter 1, the depiction of LatinX communities in the U.S. elementary, secondary, and postsecondary systems is multifaceted and often fails to recognize their ethnic and racial diversity (Gomez, 2008). This chapter aims to provide a critical historical overview of LatinX academic achievement and student success, emphasizing the intersection of these with issues of white supremacy and racism. Aligned with Crisp et al. (2015), before exploring factors influencing LatinX student academic achievement and success in higher education, it is essential to acknowledge the broader structural and cultural contexts that shape their experiences.

Therefore, I first extend Montero-Sieburth and Batt's (2000) framework of paradigm shifts across secondary and postsecondary research to explore the racial narratives that underlie LatinX academic achievement and student success in institutions of higher education, which are deeply embedded in systems of white supremacy and racism. I provide a historical perspective on how deficit discourses subtly reinforce notions of LatinX students as "failing," "disadvantaged," or "the problem." I intend to assist institutions of higher education and their actors in recognizing and countering deficit discourses that have become normalized within U.S. educational systems. Next, to challenge these assumptions, this chapter explores ethnic, racial, and cultural socialization practices within LatinX families that relate to academic achievement and parental involvement. This exploration does not aim to place the burden on LatinX students, their families, or communities but rather to document their responses to and resistance against white supremacy and racism.

Lastly, I conclude the chapter with an examination of research in the field of higher education to examine how to define and what constitutes student success in institutions of higher education. The concept of student success remains challenging to define and measure, with ongoing debates and research discrepancies (Ramos & Sifuentez, 2021). In 2006, the National Postsecondary Cooperative (NPEC) convened a symposium, bringing together leading researchers to investigate this complex issue. The commissioned papers offered various perspectives, revealing multiple dimensions of student success, from academic achievement to personal development and post-graduation outcomes. I conclude this chapter with insights from the NPEC symposium, examining the evolving definitions and metrics of student success in the twenty-first century.

SEGREGATIONIST EDUCATIONAL EXPLANATIONS 1800S–1950S

Segregationist educational explanations are rooted in overt racist notions justified by "scientific evidence." Hofstadter (1992) argues that proponents of Social Darwinism and Eugenics constructed a hierarchy based on a typology of biology and race. Social Darwinist ideology contends for the "survival of the fittest," meaning that individuals, groups, and cultures collectively determined as weak will ultimately be eliminated in any given human society. At the same time, those who are understood as vital will rise to power and maintain cultural influence over the disenfranchised (Hofstadter, 1992). Following suit, Eugenics is the science of intentionally improving a human population by controlled breeding to increase the occurrence of desirable heritable characteristics (Galton, 1869). Within this Western, pseudo-scientific movement, a convenient racialized typology cultivated the biological superiority and purity of Anglo-Saxons, resulting in a spectrum of phenotype and inferiority of BIPOC communities. Racial histories of the 1800s tend to focus on the strict racial categorization of Black individuals concerning the one-drop rule of hypodescent (Galton, 1869). In actuality, LatinX (specifically Mexican Americans) were not defined by their ethnicity or race distinctively (Gomez, 2008).

The systemic categorization of LatinX in the United States originated within the institution of law that rendered LatinX as racially ambiguous (Gomez, 2008). The ambiguous nature of LatinX racialization greatly influenced their status and subsequent treatment within U.S. educational institutions. Legal scholars (Gomez, 2008; Haney López, 2006) have documented how the law has been utilized to construct and deploy "race" as a vehicle for determining the social experiences of LatinX communities. For example, Haney López (2006) contends that the "law constructs race at every [societal] level: changing the physical features borne by people in this country, shaping the social meanings that define races, and rendering concrete the privileges and disadvantages justified by racial ideology" (p. 104). Commenting on the materialization of these processes amongst LatinX, Gomez (2008) asserts that the involuntary descendants of Spanish and Portuguese slaves and colonizers have been depicted as a monolithic "ethnic" group that will eventually benefit from "straight-line" integration into the U.S. "melting pot." Instead, Gomez (2008) argues that LatinX has been (and will continue to be) regarded, analyzed, understood, and rigidly treated as a distinct marginalized racial group. In comparison with Native and African Americans, the racialization process for LatinX has varied widely due to the disparate manifestations of colonization among these groups. Further complicating these differences, European-American settler-colonists diabolically and effectively leveraged the law to legitimize artificial racial formations, construct inequitable resource allocations by race, and ferment conflict amongst BIPOC communities (Omi & Winant, 1994). This conflict pitted BIPOC communities against one another, helping sustain white supremacy and racism (Omi & Winant, 1994).

The signing of the Treaty of Guadalupe Hidalgo in 1848 ended the Mexican-American War. It marked a historical moment for Mexican Americans and LatinX in general because it granted the United States ownership of the Southwest and, of particular importance, facilitated the racial ambiguity of Mexican Americans (Haney López, 2006). After the signing of the treaty, Mexican nationals in the Southwest automatically became citizens, whereas the 14th Amendment legalized African Americans as citizens two decades later in 1868. Gomez (2008) states, "groups [came] to be identified and to identify themselves in racial terms and learn their place as deserving or underserving in the racial hierarchy" (p. 2). Unfortunately, many early nineteenth-century Mexican Americans engaged in racial bargains that disenfranchised and distanced them from Native Americans and African Americans while simultaneously elevating LatinX in the racial hierarchy, ostensibly out of second-class citizenship status (Gomez, 2008).

Similarly, the Spanish-Cuban-American War in 1898 dictated the fate of Puerto Rico and its relationship with the United States. On December 10, 1898, the Treaty of Paris was signed, ensuring the Spanish Empire's end. As a result, Spain relinquished Cuba, Puerto Rico, and Guam. The U.S. government undertook the notions of manifest destiny coupled with racial superiority to drive U.S. expansion and colonial rule into Puerto Rico (Nieto, 2000). Subsequently, the United States enforced a military occupation from 1898 to 1900. It issued the Foraker Act (first Organic Act of 1900–1917), which granted Puerto Ricans civilian rule while strategically displacing their participation in their government (Nieto, 2000). Under the Foraker Act, political representation shifted political power directly to U.S. government officials.

The U.S. President, the U.S.-appointed Governor, and the U.S. Congress all had the power to veto local legislation.

Nieto (2000) further articulates colonial rule as she states, "Given its status as a colony of larger world powers for almost 500 years, Puerto Rico has always been at the mercy of policies and practices over which it has had little control" (p. 7). In 1917, U.S. Congress passed the Jones Act, declaring all Puerto Ricans as citizens of the United States and English as the island's official language. Between World War I and World War II, Puerto Rico encountered drastic economic change, and the United States restricted emigration among Europeans. Whalen and Vazquez-Hernandez (2005) emphasize that "displaced by economic change at home, recruited as a source of cheap labor, and seeking work to improve their lives, Puerto Ricans boarded steamships and came to the States in large numbers" (p. 13). Consequently, Puerto Ricans, as newly designated U.S. citizens, became a preferred source of low-wage workers for jobs in the stateside United States (Nieto, 2000).

Therefore, for many LatinX in the 1800s, seeking and/or embracing the legal designation "white," had to do with their acknowledgment of the importance of a white racial positionality in a society that determined citizenship and granted related rights through a rigid, racially hierarchical lens. Thus, LatinX (namely Mexican Americans) utilized jurisprudence to be legally understood as white to obtain citizenship and hopefully gain access to institutions, like education, to which they had previously been denied entry (Valencia, 2008). For example, *Mendez v. Westminster* (1946) is an influential case that demonstrates the utilization of white racial positionality within the context of law (Valencia, 2008). Gonzalo and Felicitas Mendez resided in Westminster, California and wanted their three children to attend Westminster Elementary School with their cousins during the 1944 to 1945 school year. However, when Soledad Vidaurri, the aunt of the three children, went to enroll them, they were denied admission. Soledad later discovered that her children could only attend because of their French last name and light complexion. This discrimination by phenotype and surname became crucial in the Mendez case (Valencia, 2008). The winning argument in the trial strategically avoided addressing race directly. Instead, the argument asserted that the "segregation of Mexican students deprived them of their federal right to equal treatment by the state" (p. 61). The argument would ensure that California state law recognized Mexican Americans as white, and as a result, Mexican children gained access to schools (Valencia, 2008; Strum, 2010).

Ironically, LatinX were legally defined as white, yet socially constructed as decidedly non-white. The U.S. law defined African Americans as non-white through the rule of hypodescent (Galton, 1869). The one-drop rule served LatinX rather differently: "One drop of Spanish blood allowed them to claim whiteness under certain circumstances" (Gomez, 2008, p. 5). The racial ideologies that were constructed for LatinX and African Americans during this time period expose the complexities and inconsistencies of white supremacy and racism (Gomez, 2008). Ultimately,

> both ideologies reproduced the racial subordination of blacks and Mexicans, but they did so in very different ways. Without understanding how they worked—and how they worked in tandem—we cannot fully understand American racial dynamics in the twentieth century and beyond.
>
> (Gomez, 2008, p. 6)

Illuminating the multilayered racial history of LatinX during the 1800s to 1950s reveals their complex social positions within the law and education institutions. By law, some LatinX benefited and gained access to specific arenas but were still deemed inferior to their white counterparts and were not socially accepted. As a result, the inferiority of LatinX would be transmitted into the educational system, and the LatinX family, culture, and values were cited as the cause of their "underachievement."

CULTURAL EXPLANATIONS: 1960S–1970S

LatinX racial discourse underwent a significant shift at the turn of the twentieth century and centered on cultural explanations of LatinX academic underachievement. The concepts of cultural deficit, cultural deprivation, and cultural differences suggest that disappointing learning outcomes among LatinX students are often attributed to perceived shortcomings in LatinX families and under-resourced homes, including inadequate preparation or lack of motivation (Soto, 2006). During the 1960s and 1970s, dominant groups in the United States viewed LatinX families as deficient compared with white middle-class families. LatinX individuals were seen as "failing [due to] not having access to reading, writing, computing, and ways of speaking that mainstream white students had" (Soto, 2006, p. 12). Lewis (1966) coined the term "culture of poverty" after conducting an ethnographic study of Mexican communities. Lewis (1966) suggested that due to poverty, Mexicans were prone to violence, lacked a sense of history, and neglected to plan. Lewis's (1966) findings were based on stereotypes and, unfortunately, still endure as systematic explanations of why LatinX families lag behind their white counterparts and other racial and ethnic groups. Lewis's study influenced how educational researchers focus on culture in reproducing societal structure. Educational institutions, while appearing impartial, tend to legitimize certain forms of knowledge, speaking, and relating to the world (i.e., cultural capital) that privilege the dominant class. Conversely, educational institutions marginalize and devalue the knowledge, ways of speaking, and perspectives of marginalized communities.

Gonzalez (1997a) provides a prominent historical example of the cultural deficit approach through the Americanization programs that Mexican Americans were subjected to during the early twentieth century. Gonzalez (1997a) argues that early Americanization programs enforced segregation and the dismantling of the Mexican culture, language, and customs. The United States government was convinced that "traditional ethnic culture rejected external governmental methods to achieve social relations characteristics of modern societies" (Gonzalez, 1997a, p. 32). Americanization programs were one path the U.S. government took within the educational system to target LatinX immigrants. The educational system served as the fastest means to achieve Americanization since children spent the majority of their day in school. The fundamental goal was to eliminate the use of the Spanish language because the "lack of a common language makes social cohesion impossible" (Gonzalez, 1997a, p. 33). The U.S. government concluded that language and identity were inseparable; one could not exist without the other. As a result, the Mexican American home was viewed as "a source of Mexican culture and consequently a reinforcer of the 'Mexican educational problem'" (Gonzalez, 1997a, p. 47). Consequently, government officials targeted mothers and daughters within the household as focal points for assimilation. Mexican daughters and mothers could enforce the Americanization of homemaking, and the likelihood of creating an American-like home could be achieved. Gonzalez (1997a) states,

> Americanization proponents identified the Mexican girls as potential carriers of American culture, the social gene who upon her marriage and subsequent motherhood could create a type of home in which the next generation could be raised in an American cultural atmosphere.
>
> (p. 48)

Villenas (2009) argues that deficit perspectives have "historically served to label Latina/os parents as backward, incompetent people who do not care about their children's education" (p. 129). Furthermore, Soto (2006) explains:

> The cultural deficit and cultural deprivation theories fell into misuse because they tended to place the blame on the families and students and presented a passive picture of the agency of these parents and students to act on their behalf. Latina/os parents are engaged in the education of their children, yet accessing that education requires understanding the infrastructure of educational policies as well as practices. In this regard, identifying the culture of the home as static and non-adaptive is in itself problematic.
>
> (p. 13)

Historically, a substantial amount of the literature that examines the experience of LatinX students in higher education takes on a cultural-deficit model; that is, a model which contends that minority students are ill-equipped to attaining educational mobility due to their inability to adapt and assimilate into mainstream society (Kretovics & Nussel, 1994; Solórzano, 1997; Valencia, 1997). This literature suggests that LatinX students have lower levels of college readiness and a higher number of stressors and familial obligations that deter them from obtaining a postsecondary degree or credential as compared with their white counterparts (Longerbeam et al., 2004; Torres et al., 2003). Moreover, LatinX students encounter numerous financial challenges, as they are less likely to receive financial aid, have lower incomes, and are more likely to be employed while attending college (Santiago, 2011). Educational institutions, from K-12 through higher education, have reproduced class inequities by privileging the dominant class's culture and marginalizing the culture of LatinX communities.

SOCIOLOGICAL EXPLANATIONS: 1970S–PRESENT

Sociological explanations from the 1970s to the present focus on the upward or downward assimilation of LatinX individuals in the United States. Assimilation theories (Alba & Nee, 2003; Jiménez, 2010; Lacy, 2007; Wilson, 1980), while undergoing important revisions over the past 70 years, remain shaped by a preoccupation with culture as a measure of social inclusion and boundary maintenance. Because assimilation is closely linked to factors such as language, values, and customs, it often presupposes that cultural reasons alone explain why assimilation does or does not. Traditional assimilation theory assumes that social inclusion follows a predictable process, with immigrant groups expected to integrate into the mainstream culture within two or three generations of arrival (Perlmann, 2005). If integration does not happen, it raises the question of whether the immigrant group lacks certain forms of cultural capital.

Gordon (1964) examined how the social structure in the United States encourages ethnic groups to create their own enclaves because institutions outside of these established enclaves are often shut off to those not assimilated or part of the dominant group(s). This lack of assimilation, in turn, leads to cultural pluralism, where ethnic groups live alongside the dominant group but do not assimilate. Assimilation, however, was viewed as a solution for incorporating white ethnic groups into the United States during the World War II era as biological determinism began to lose its legitimacy. Although Gordon (1964) warned that ethnic groups failing to assimilate into the dominant group would promote racial prejudice, he argued that the systematic formation of the United States hinders the assimilation of ethnic groups and, in turn, promotes the conservation of their separate ethnic identities and enclaves. Interestingly, although Gordon emphasized the inevitable creation of ethnic communities, he also stated that social class is more important than ethnicity and that ethnic groups will begin to identify with others according to their social class and not their ethnicity. This directly contradicts his earlier statement, and this conflicted argument has reemerged into contemporary assimilation arguments for LatinX communities (Alba & Nee, 2003; Jiménez, 2010; Lacy, 2007; Wilson, 1980). Gordon (1964) is limited in his argument because he was solely concerned with white-ethnic communities who, during that time, were able to assimilate into White Anglo-Saxon Protestant (WASP) society. Consequently, Gordan (1964) essentially conflates ethnicity with race.

Omi and Winant (1994) critique particular ideas of traditional assimilation and ultimately disagree with Gordon's (1964) structural assimilation argument. Omi and Winant (1994) argue that race has been classified into three common paradigms within the United States: ethnicity, class, and nation. Omi and Winant (1994) categorize the ethnicity paradigm into three major stages: 1) pre-1930s—ethnic groups were able to assimilate into U.S. society, challenging the Social Darwinism and Eugenics; 2) 1930s to 1965—progressive/liberal "common sense" approach to race with the themes of assimilation and cultural pluralism come to the forefront; and 3) post-1965—the ethnicity paradigm was used to defend and sustain white supremacy (pp. 14–16). Omi and Winant (1994) challenge the notion of structural assimilation as functioning in a straight-line convergence. They state, "yet this assumption is quite unwarranted with respect to racial minorities, whose distinctiveness from the white majority is often not appreciably altered by the adoption of the norms and values of the white majority" (p. 21). In other words, despite the ability that BIPOC communities have to adopt the white dominant group norms, the capability to assimilate is not a straight-line integration as it is for white immigrants due to *race* and not ethnicity.

Moreover, while Gordon (1964) provides one of the first conceptualizations of classic assimilation and Omi and Winant (1994) critique his scholarship that incorporates race and racism, the construction of these theories is deeply rooted in the context of a white/Black paradigm, which places LatinX in a complex space as discussed in Chapter 1. Telles and Ortiz (2008) move beyond these limited notions to examine how groups such as Mexican Americans fall outside conventional explanations of immigrant or ethnic integration in the United States. In particular, assimilation and ethnic integration might be processes with no clear end, riddled with bumps, contours, and unforeseen outcomes that previous theories do not take into account. In other words, there are multiple dimensions to measure the extent of assimilation, which may not always be cohesive. Telles and Ortiz (2008) argue that assimilation involves not only adopting the values of a new place but also participating in its institutions. When assimilation fails, the explanation often given is that the group does not share the mainstream belief system. However, social inclusion is not just about values but about integrating into institutions such as the educational system. Simply valuing education is not enough; attending and navigating these institutions play a crucial role in advancement, a trajectory heavily influenced by social structures and the distributions of privilege and status. Therefore, studies of the assimilation of LatinX students in education need to complicate how ethnicity and race are understood to reveal systematic oppression that could be stunting pathways into institutions of higher education and processes of postsecondary degree or credential completion (Alcoff, 2009).

Using Montero-Sieburth and Batt's (2000) framework of paradigm shifts to examine the historical racial discourse of LatinX students in education, it becomes evident that LatinX students have historically been positioned and socially constructed as inferior and incapable of academic achievement due to their race and/or ethnicity. These paradigm shifts operate at organizational and individual levels, historically influencing how LatinX college student success is characterized (Murphy & Murphy, 2018). Deficit discourses remain embedded in the very fabric of educational institutions, often framing academic underachievement as a cultural, traditional, or family issue within LatinX communities. In the following section, I explore ethnic, racial, and cultural socialization practices among LatinX families and their relationship to academic achievement. By examining LatinX family dynamics, I demonstrate how these households foster ethnic, racial, and cultural identities, support academic achievement, and prepare their children to navigate encounters with racism, white supremacy, and colonial ideologies through K-12 and higher education educational institutions.

ETHNIC, RACIAL, AND CULTURAL SOCIALIZATION PRACTICES AMONG LATINX FAMILIES AND ACADEMIC ACHIEVEMENT

Parent–Child Socialization and Children's Academic Achievement

Within Child Development and Family Studies, parent–child relationships are examined in the context of socialization. Parent–child socialization refers to "the manner by which a child, through education, training, observation, and experience, acquire[s] skills, motives, attitudes, and behaviors that is [sic] required for successful adaptation to a family and a culture" (Spera, 2005, p. 126). The socialization process is reciprocal between parent and child, as parents transmit messages to their children, their children can vary in their "level of acceptance, receptivity, and internalization of these messages" (Spera,

2005, p. 126). Scholars have become increasingly interested in parent–child socialization and the relationship between the child's home environment (i.e., family), school environment, and educational attainment (Brown & Iyengar, 2008; Davis-Kean, 2005; Spera, 2005). For instance, research has consistently shown that parents' education and income are significant in predictors of children's academic achievement, but how parents practice socialization in the household concerning their children's academic achievement warrants further exploration (Brown & Iyengar, 2008; Davis-Kean, 2005; Duncan et al., 1994; Haveman & Wolfe, 1994; Spera, 2005). Parenting practices and parenting styles are two distinct mechanisms categorized as parent–child socialization.

Spera (2005) conducted an integrated literature review to examine parent–child socialization by analyzing the relationship among parenting practices, parenting styles, and adolescent school achievement. In describing the research, Spera (2005) argues that researchers have often used the labels of parenting styles and practices interchangeably. However, Darling and Steinberg (1993) and Spera (2005) suggest that to understand socialization processes better, it is essential to distinguish between parenting practices and styles. Parenting practices are defined as particular actions that parents utilize to socialize their children (Darling & Steinberg, 1993; Spera, 2005). For example, activities such as doing homework with their children, reading aloud to their children, and/or attending school functions can be activities. Such actions model performance that parents wish for their children to adopt to be successful in the world, whereas parenting styles refer to the emotional climate or strategies parents utilize to raise their children. Baumrind (1966) established three parenting styles: permissive, authoritarian, and authoritative. A permissive parenting style refers to parents who behave in a non-punitive, accepting, and affirmative way in response to a child's impulses, desires, and actions. An authoritarian parenting style refers to parents who act to shape, control, and evaluate the child's behavior and attitudes following a set standard of conduct. An authoritative parenting style refers to parents directing the child's activities rationally and in an issue-oriented manner. The relationship between parenting practices and parenting styles on children's academic achievement varies (Davis-Kean & Sexton, 2009; Dubow et al., 2009; Pettit et al., 2009; Spera, 2005).

Spera (2005) identifies three areas of parenting practices that affect children's educational outcomes: 1) parental involvement, 2) parental monitoring, and 3) parental goals, values, and aspirations. For these parenting practices, the research suggests that when parents are involved in their children's education and monitor their children's after-school activities, they facilitate academic achievement and educational attainment. The research indicates that authoritative parenting styles are associated with higher levels of adolescent academic achievement. Spera (2005) concludes that these findings about parenting practices, parenting styles, and adolescent school achievement are not consistent across ethnicity, culture, or socioeconomic status. Further, Hauser-Cram (2009) argues that more attention is needed for moderation or group analysis among parents and their children. Hauser-Cram (2009) suggests that tests of moderation "can lead to conclusions about whether findings from some groups are stronger than others, and from a policy and practice perspective, the findings related to subgroups that are more at risk for low educational attainment deserve careful scrutiny" (p. 355). At this critical juncture, I shift direction to analyze this inconsistency in the literature to examine how BIPOC families use racial and ethnic parenting practices concerning their children's academic achievement.

Parent Practices of Racial and Ethnic Socialization and Children's Academic Achievement

In the previous section, I identified considerable research on parenting practices, parenting styles, and adolescent academic achievement centered on white families and the processes critical for success in those families (Davis-Kean & Sexton, 2009). Less research has examined different race and/or ethnicity groups to determine whether similar processes are important for success in these groups. Therefore, there is little understanding of the complex roles that socioeconomic status, race and/or ethnicity, and parenting practices may play in the development of children (Conger & Donnellan, 2007; Davis-Kean & Sexton, 2009). As previously mentioned, families and parents play a critical role in socializing children to enter a world where they may encounter stigmatization due to their race or ethnicity. Therefore, it is important to ask how LatinX parents communicate with their children about issues of racial discrimination, prejudice, and negative stereotypes. How do racial or ethnic socialization messages impact LatinX children's educational persistence or their understanding of their social positions in the educational system?

Scholars (Pessar, 1995; Rodríguez & Sánchez Korrol, 1996; Suárez-Orozco & Suárez-Orozco, 1995; Urciuoli, 1996; Waters, 1990, 1994) have become more interested in these relationships as the percentage of BIPOC communities in the United States advances to surpass their white counterparts. According to the 2022 U.S. Census, BIPOC children will constitute a numerical majority in public elementary and secondary school enrollment. Therefore, understanding how parents' levels of education and practices of ethnic and racial socialization among families of color influence their children's academic achievement is necessary, as these children are indeed our future. The following section comprises: 1) definitions of ethnic, racial, and cultural socialization and how BIPOC families utilize these strategies to prepare their children for a world where race and racism exist; 2) how parent practices of racial and ethnic socialization affect their children's academic achievement; and 3) how LatinX families' ethnic or racial socialization practices influence their children's academic achievement.

Literature pertaining to ethnic, racial, and cultural socialization practices among families of color is complex, limited, and in contention. Child Development scholars often conflate race, ethnicity, and culture as if they were synonymous (Chao & Otsuki-Clutter, 2011; Quintana et al., 2006). Quintana et al. (2006) state, "Development research has been attempting to disentangle the various components associated with ethnic and racial minority children by examining the individual contribution of each sociocultural characteristic (e.g., race, culture, social class) as well as the interactions of multiple sociocultural features" (p. 1131). Racial socialization and ethnic socialization are broadly defined as the transmission of messages from parents to children about their ethnicity or race (Hughes et al., 2006). Hughes et al. (2006) found a lack of consensus among scholars as they use different terminology when explaining similar processes for BIPOC families. In fact, researchers (Boykin & Toms, 1985; Hughes & Chen, 1997; Hughes et al., 2006; Peters, 1985; Phinney & Chavira, 1995; Spencer & Markstrom-Adams, 1990) consistently refer to *racial socialization* when discussing African American families, whereas, research on *ethnic socialization* analyzes the experiences of LatinX, Asian, and Native American families (Hughes et al., 2006; Knight et al., 1993; Ou & McAdoo, 1993; Phinney & Chavira, 1995; Quintana & Vera, 1999).

Hughes et al. (2006), due to the conflation in defining ethnic and racial socialization, opt to combine ethnic-racialization and operationalize the two as "a class of adaptive practices that ethnic minority parents use to promote children's functions in a world that is stratified by ethnicity and race" (p. 16). Ethnic-racial socialization within the family assists children to prepare for racial bias and discrimination and helps them to cope with these experiences. Quintana et al. (2006) further complicate the definition of terms, as their research identified that racial and cultural socialization were often separated when studying African American families. Cultural socialization refers to teaching children about their heritage and/or history while promoting cultural customs and traditions and instilling a sense of pride associated with a child's race, ethnicity, or culture (Hughes et al., 2006; Quintana et al., 2006). Quintana et al. (2006) found that racial socialization was more strongly related to adverse outcomes (e.g., external locus of control) and less strongly related to positive outcomes (e.g., cognitive development) than cultural socialization. Quintana et al. (2006) urge scholars to make a clear distinction between racial and cultural socialization among BIPOC families, as race and culture are not one and the same.

Furthermore, in addressing the discrepancies in the literature, Burton et al. (2010) provide an integrated literature review in the field of Family Studies entitled "Critical Race Theories, Colorism, and the Decade's Research on Families of Color," where they discuss the racial socialization of children in the United States. They are concerned with two issues: 1) the role of demographic changes that will contribute to Black, Indigenous, and other People of Color becoming the majority of the population, resulting in literature and research pertaining to the racial socialization of children; and 2) how critical race and colorism can inform new conceptualizations about the racialization of children. They put forth their definition of racial socialization as "a set of overt and covert behaviors parents use, over and above those responsibilities shared by all parents, to prepare children psychologically for success in a racially stratified American society" (Burton et al., 2010, p. 452). After presenting this definition, Burton et al. (2010) respectfully challenge the fields of Child Development and Family Studies to integrate Critical Race Theory and make several advances. First, they identify that researchers lack attention concerning how colorism shapes group racial or ethnic socialization practices of families. Second, studies of racial socialization assume that BIPOC communities will encounter racism, but studies do not examine the socialization process that leads white people to discriminate against them. They argue that by only focusing on BIPOC families, the representation of whites as a non-racial group sustains color-evasive ideologies that privilege white children in comparison with BIPOC children. These perspectives are essential in examining the racial socialization practices across diverse groups as the conflation of terms limits our understanding of how parenting practices and beliefs of different ethnic groups have different impacts on and relationships to child academic achievement.

LatinX Families' Ethnic or Racial Socialization Practices Influence Their Children's Academic Achievement

In general, children with a strong sense of ethnic identity and high self-esteem are more likely to be academically successful than those without (Chavous et al., 2003; Hughes et al., 2006; Wigfield & Eccles, 2002). Hughes et al. (2006) found that only a few studies address ethnic-racial socialization practices among children concerning academic achievement. These studies frequently focus on the parenting practices within African American families. Marshall (1995) studied the relationship between ethnic socialization and academic achievement among middle-class African American mothers and their 9- and 10-year-old children who attended predominantly white schools. Marshall (1995) found that African American children whose parents addressed race in their parenting practices appeared to be further along in their identity development but performed poorly in schools. Marshall (1995) concludes that ethnic socialization may predict lower grades. Further, he explains "that the data are cross-sectional and one cannot determine whether socialization leads to lower grades or lower grades brought about more ethnic socialization" (p. 395).

Contrary to Marshall (1995), Caughy et al. (2002) examined parent-racial socialization and child competence among a socioeconomically diverse group of African American parents and their preschool-aged children. Caughy et al.'s (2002) findings suggest that African American parents who provide homes that stress the importance of African American culture had children who demonstrated more instances of factual knowledge and problem-solving skills. Similar to Caughy et al., Smith et al. (2003) examined family, school, and community factors in relation to racial-ethnic attitudes and academic achievement among 98 African American fourth-grade children. Smith et al. (2003) found that having more educated parents was related to higher levels of children's racial and ethnic pride. Community context also influenced children's racial-ethnic attitudes. Increased educational attainment and mobility in their communities were related to children feeling more confident of their possibilities for academic achievement.

Much of the literature concerning LatinX families predominantly uses the term "family ethnic socialization" instead of ethnic-racial socialization (Hughes et al., 2006; Kulish et al., 2019). Empirical research on ethnic-racial socialization among LatinX children and academic achievement has primarily emphasized ethnic identity. Studies consistently demonstrate that developing a strong ethnic identity can produce positive emotional, social, and academic outcomes (Else-Quest & Morse, 2015). Ayón et al. (2018a) and Else-Quest and Morse (2015) have shown a strong link between parents' cultural socialization practices and the ethnic identity development of LatinX parents and their children's academic achievement. Cultural socialization practices have enduring positive effects in LatinX families, where parents play a pivotal role in their children's microsystems. These practices include daily activities such as cooking traditional meals together, conversing in Spanish, attending family gatherings, sharing experiences through stories and pictures, engaging in religious practices, and, for some, traveling to visit hometowns outside of the United States—sometimes sending their children alone if parents are undocumented and unable to travel across borders (Ayón et al., 2018a). Studies on LatinX families have also indicated that parents' cultural socialization enhances parent–child communication, fostering stronger bonds between parents and their children and contributing to their academic achievement (Ayón et al., 2018a, 2018b).

LatinX culture strongly emphasizes interpersonal relationships and family-oriented values such as familism, where the family unit takes precedence. LatinX children become culturally socialized to practice positive social behaviors within their families by caring for their siblings and the elderly or assisting with household chores. Research suggests that LatinX children who engage in positive social behaviors or actions to benefit others are more socially adjusted and less likely to engage in negative social behaviors (Calderón-Tena et al.,

2011). The literature has shown that parents and cultural values play a significant role in developing positive social behaviors and academic achievement (Calderón-Tena et al., 2011).

Villenas and Deyhle (1999) apply Critical Race Theory to examine LatinX schooling and family education as portrayed in seven ethnographic studies among LatinX adolescents and their parents. The findings revealed that despite the school rhetoric of parent involvement and deficit framing of LatinX parents, these mothers and fathers are actually kept out of schools by the negative ways they are treated through insensitive administrative requirements. Administrative views of parent involvement resulted in disregarding LatinX knowledge and culture bases. Relatedly, Dumka et al. (2013) reviewed theory and evidence regarding family influences on Mexican American adolescents' academic success. They concluded that research results on the impact of parents' ethnic socialization of their children to date have been equivocal (Hughes et al., 2006). Dumka et al. (2013) found that Mexican American parents' ethnic socialization "predicted adolescents' later ethnic pride, which, in turn, was related to higher levels of traditional Mexican American values, which mediated the effects of discrimination on adolescents' academic efficacy" (p. 169). Lastly, Ceballo (2004) examined the role of parents and home characteristics on the academic success of LatinX first-generation college students from low-income immigrant families who attended Yale University. Ceballo (2004) concluded that four factors contributed to their academic success: a strong parental commitment to the importance of education, parental facilitation of their child's autonomy, an array of non-verbal parental expressions of support for educational goals and tasks, and the presence of supportive faculty mentors and roles models in their lives.

Therefore, historically, it seems that the findings within these studies (Caughy et al., 2002; Marshall, 1995; Smith et al., 2003) are mixed with respect to ethnic, racial, and cultural socialization practices and academic achievement among LatinX families. Umaña-Taylor and Hill (2020) recently conducted a comprehensive literature review on the evolving role of family ethnic-racial socialization over the past decade. Analyzing 259 empirical articles across various ethnic-racial groups, their findings consistently underscore the positive association between ethnic-racial socialization and academic achievement. Their integrated review reaffirms and builds upon earlier findings from Hughes et al. (2006), highlighting the ongoing significance of this emerging area of research. Despite these inconclusive findings, LatinX families discussed in this literature consistently demonstrate that they are active participants in their children's academic trajectories, which counteracts the deficit framing of LatinX in education. In the following section, I analyze student success in the twenty-first century, exploring fundamental research that documents the changing definitions and measures of student success.

STUDENT SUCCESS IN THE TWENTY-FIRST CENTURY

In the field of higher education, student success remains a challenging concept to define and measure, with ongoing debate and research discrepancies (Ramos & Sifuentez, 2021). In November 2006, The National Postsecondary Cooperative (NPEC) hosted a symposium and commissioned a series of five papers by higher education researchers to address and explore the question "What is student success?" from various perspectives, creating one of the most comprehensive research resources on student success in higher education. The commissioned papers presented different perspectives, uncovering multiple dimensions of student success in higher education, ranging from academic achievement to personal development and post-graduation outcomes. Hearn (2006), a highly influential higher education scholar, was tasked with summarizing the papers, discussing similarities and differences, and offering directions for future research. Ewell and Wellman (2007), well-known higher education policy researchers and practitioners, were also commissioned to summarize and synthesize the papers and discussions after attending the NPEC symposium. Table 2.1, National Postsecondary Cooperative Commissioned Papers on Student Success, displays each commissioned paper's title, author and affiliation, and published year.

Defining and Measuring Student Success

According to the 2024 *Merriam-Webster Dictionary*, "success" is a favorable or desired outcome. In the context of higher education, student success may refer to students achieving their desired educational goals. However, such a broad definition may pose challenges in measuring student success. Hearn's (2006) synthesis of the five commissioned papers emphasizes this as an important debate: whether to narrow or broaden the definition of student success and how to measure it. Hearn (2006) states:

> Perhaps most fundamental of all the topics meriting continuing emphasis and attention is the question of effectively defining and measuring student success. Graduating with a desired degree is unquestionably an appropriate indicator of a student's success, and aggregated institutional and system rates of graduation can be a significant indicator of an institution's or system's performance. Simple and straightforward, graduation rates are very much on the minds of policymakers, educational leaders, the public, and students themselves. But institutions differ in the capabilities of their students to do college work. A focus on raw graduation rates runs the risk of embellishing the reputations of selective schools while tarnishing the perceptions of those serving a wider range of students.
>
> (p. iv)

Table 2.1 National Postsecondary Cooperative Commissioned Papers on Student Success

Commissioned Paper Title	Author & Affiliation	Year
Faculty Professional Choices in Teaching That Foster Student Success	John M. Braxton *Vanderbilt University*	June 2006
What Matters to Student Success: A Review of the Literature	George D. Kuh, Jillian Kinzie, and Jennifer A. Buckley, *Indiana University Bloomington* Brian K. Bridges, *American Council on Education* John C. Hayek, *Kentucky Council on Postsecondary Education*	July 2006
A Framework for Reducing the College Success Gap and Promoting Success for All	Laura W. Perna, *University of Pennsylvania* Scott L. Thomas, *University of Georgia*	July 2006
Holland's Theory and Patterns of College Student Success	John C. Smart, PhD, *The University of Memphis* Kenneth A. Feldman, PhD, *SUNY at Stony Brook* Corinna A. Ethington, PhD, *The University of Memphis*	July 2006
Moving From Theory to Action: Building a Model of Institutional Action for Student Success	Vincent Tinto, *Syracuse University* Brian Pusser, *University of Virginia*	June 2006
Summary and Synthesis of Papers and Symposium		
Student Success: What Research Suggests for Policy and Practice	James C. Hearn, *University of Georgia*	October 2006
Enhancing Student Success in Education: Summary Report of the NPEC Initiative and National Symposium on Postsecondary Student Success	Peter Ewell *National Center for Higher Education Management Systems (NCHEMS)* Jane Wellman Delta *Project on Postsecondary Costs, Productivity, and Accountability*	May 2007

As Hearn (2006) suggests, defining and measuring student success remains an ongoing challenge for higher education scholars, practitioners, and institutions of higher education and their actors. Therefore, it is crucial to fully assess the strengths and limitations of the five working definitions provided by the commissioned authors.

In defining student success, Braxton (2006), drawing from higher education literature,[7] identifies eight categories as markers of student success: academic attainment, acquisition of general education, development of academic competence, development of cognitive skills and intellectual dispositions, occupational attainment, preparation for adulthood and citizenship, personal accomplishments, and personal development (p. 2). For Braxton, each category provides multiple indicators for measuring student success. For example, an indicator for measuring academic achievement includes persistence in college, whether a student continues their education through to senior year, or earning a postsecondary degree on time. Regardless of the category, Braxton (2006) underscores the significant role of faculty and institutional leaders (i.e., presidents and chief academic officers) in promoting student success, mainly through effective teaching. Faculty should make informed pedagogical choices, conduct meaningful course assessments, and implement practices contributing to student learning and success. Braxton (2006) argues that institutional leaders influence a culture of teaching that promotes student success by recognizing faculty and student achievements and providing necessary resources for success. Lastly, Braxton (2006) provides recommendations for faculty hiring that prioritize pedagogy, educational philosophies, and reward systems aimed at promoting success in institutions of higher education. While Braxton (2006) focuses on specific categories and indicators of student success, Kuh et al. (2006) take a broader approach, examining student success through multiple theoretical perspectives and the importance of student engagement, institutional support, and assessment.

According to Kuh et al. (2006), traditionally, student success has been discussed from five theoretical perspectives/disciplines: sociological, psychological, economic, organizational, and cultural. Kuh et al. (2006) argue that there is no single definition for student success in higher education, though many indicators can be used to measure it. Kuh et al. (2006) state that there are indicators to measure student success that are commonly used, such as "academic achievement; engagement in educationally purposeful activities; satisfaction; acquisition of desired knowledge, skill, and competencies; persistence; and attainment of educational objectives" (p. 10). Kuh et al. (2006) emphasize that student success encompasses a broad range of factors across four major areas: students' backgrounds and pre-college experiences, engagement in educational activities during postsecondary education, institutional conditions within postsecondary institutions that promote student success, and students' intended achievements during and after college. According to Kuh et al. (2006), students' ability to integrate and engage in their campus environments is a significant component of student success. Finally, effective assessment and accountability practices are necessary to ensure that institutions of higher education continuously improve teaching and student outcomes.

Similar to Braxton (2006) and Kuh et al. (2006), Perna and Thomas (2006) review theoretical and empirical literature to address persistent racial/ethnic,[8] socioeconomic, and other social identities in defining student success. Perna and Thomas (2006) distinguish that scholarship on student success varies theoretically and methodologically within various disciplines, and viewing this research through a conceptual model provides a comprehensive way to approach it. They propose a longitudinal conceptual model of student success, identifying four instrumental "transitions for the success process": college readiness, college enrollment, college achievement, and post-college attainment (p. 3). Perna and Thomas (2006), like Braxton (2006), identify ten indicators that contribute to student success across these four transitions. They define student success as the fulfillment or optimization of these indicators. The first transition involves students' preparation for college, which can be assessed by their educational aspirations and college readiness. The second, college enrollment, depends on students' access to relevant information and their choice of institution. The third transition, college achievement, is reflected in academic performance, institutional transfers, and persistence toward degree completion. Finally, post-college attainment is assessed by "enrollment in graduate or professional programs, income levels, and educational attainment" (p. 4). Similar to Kuh et al. (2006), Perna and Thomas (2006) situate student success within various disciplines, including education, psychology, sociology, and economics, to comprehensively approach success as a multi-faceted process that spans from pre-college to post-baccalaureate studies. While Perna and Thomas (2006) use a multidisciplinary approach to student success, examining it through various theoretical and methodological lenses, Smart et al. (2006) focus specifically on Holland's person-environment fit theory to discuss how the congruence between students' personalities and academic environments impacts their educational outcomes.

Smart et al. (2006) employed Holland's person-environment fit theory (1966) to define and examine student success. Holland's person-environment fit theory (1966) suggests that individuals can be classified into six personality types: Realistic, Investigative, Artistic, Social, Enterprising, and Conventional, and that the congruence between students' personality types and their academic environments leads to greater educational success. Smart et al. (2006) identify that Holland's (1966) theory has two assumptions, congruence, and socialization, which can lead to different profiles in student success. The congruence assumption suggests that students' success is tied to growth in characteristics congruent with personality type. In contrast, the socialization assumption implies that students develop characteristics reinforced by their academic environments regardless of congruence. Smart et al. (2006) argue that academic environments significantly influence student success irrespective of the congruence assumption; students learn and grow based on the competencies and values reinforced by their academic majors. For Smart et al. (2006), academic environments should be central in assessing student success, with criteria based on the cognitive and affective outcome specific to their field of study.

Tinto and Pusser (2006) emphasize the need for a practical model of institutional action to improve student success by analyzing research on student persistence and success. Tinto and Pusser (2006) argue that, often, student success research tends to be too abstract and lacks actionable strategies that institutions can implement. They focus on institutional factors, such as climate, faculty support, performance feedback, and student engagement, which institutions can influence to enhance student outcomes. Tinto and Pusser (2006) identify state and national policies that are most effective for student success, such as bridging elementary, secondary, and postsecondary education, building longitudinal databases to track students through their educational pathways, providing resources for the educational development of less prepared students, creating programming as a form of outreach for underrepresented students, enhancing course alignment between two- and four-year colleges, implementing ongoing assessment of student readiness for postsecondary education, and introducing progressive financial policies to boost overall financial assistance and provide direct aid to students with the most significant financial need. Tinto and Pusser (2006) provide a comprehensive framework for improving student success through practical, actionable strategies at the institutional and policy levels.

Based on the symposium and synthesis of the commissioned papers, Hearn (2006) emphasizes that graduating with the degree a student intends to pursue is one of the most fundamental, if not the most crucial, indicators of student success. Similarly, Ewell and Wellman (2007) argue that student success "can be understood in its simplest form as getting students into and through college to a degree or certificate" (p. 2). While Hearn (2006) and Ewell and Wellman (2007) agree on how to define student success, they, along with their colleagues, acknowledge that there are various indicators of student success. Ewell and Wellman (2007) persuasively state:

"Student success" is thus a generic label for a topic with many dimensions, ranging from *student flow* across the entire educational pipeline (high school graduation, college enrollment, retention, and degree completion), to the *quality and content* of learning and skills achieved as a result of going to college, to positive *educational experiences* (such as student engagement or satisfaction).

(p. 2)

Success is measured differently depending on whether it is evaluated for individual students, groups defined by diverse characteristics, or institutions, with each level potentially aggregated at state and national levels (Ewell & Wellman, 2007). Ewell and Wellman (2007) make it evident that while there has been a steady increase in student success in the United States, the future appears bleak due to a growing divide between the nation's demand for post-secondary degree completion and the system's ability to meet these demands. Ewell and Wellman (2007) identify the following disparities contributing to the growing divide. First, quantitatively, postsecondary access and degree completion lag behind population growth and global economic competitiveness. Qualitatively, the skills, abilities, and knowledge that students gain upon postsecondary degree completion fall short of the nation's academic and workforce needs. Second, the United States faces a shortage of skilled workers to meet occupational demands. Third, racial, socioeconomic, and educational opportunity gaps continue to widen for marginalized communities, especially in postsecondary degree completion. Finally, increasing college affordability issues and widening funding disparities between institutions and states exacerbate the problem. Overall, the NPEC symposium and commissioned papers show that student success is not a one-size-fits-all matter. Instead, student success is a multi-faceted process that includes various dimensions before college enrollment or selection, including how well students' college experiences unfold during their higher education trajectories and how and what students learn after college.

Building on the understanding that student success is a multi-faceted process, it is particularly important to focus on LatinX students, who are more vulnerable to white supremacy and racism, contributing to disparities in postsecondary degree or credential completion. LatinX students are often misunderstood, overlooked, or forgotten. Therefore, LatinX students' success must be examined to assess what is currently known and what is needed to assist them in meeting their full potential regardless of the persistent inequities they face. Like the NPEC symposium and commissioned papers, it is critical to ask, "What is LatinX student success?"

CONCLUSION

In conclusion, this chapter has provided a historical analysis of LatinX student academic achievement and success, emphasizing the role of deficit racial framing in shaping their educational experience. By examining the role of white supremacy and racism and how they contribute to disparities in postsecondary degree or credential completion, institutions of higher education and their actors can better understand the systemic barriers that LatinX students encounter, and develop more inclusive and equitable strategies to support their educational pathways. Despite persistent inequities, LatinX families demonstrate resilience through ethnic, racial, and cultural socialization practices that foster their children's academic success. Existing research on student success demonstrates that traditional models of student success often overlook the unique experiences of

LatinX students, particularly in how they navigate educational systems that have historically marginalized them. As institutions of higher education continue to evolve, institutional actors must critically reassess and adapt their definitions and measures of success to reflect the realities faced by LatinX students, ensuring they are included and empowered to thrive academically.

DISCUSSION QUESTIONS

Using the content within this chapter, consider the following questions for reflection and discussion:

- How has deficit racial framing historically impacted the academic achievement and success of LatinX students and their families? What are some specific examples of this framing, and how can institutions of higher education and their actors work to dismantle it?
- How do white supremacy and racism contribute to the disparities in postsecondary degree or credential completion for LatinX students? How can institutions of higher education and their actors address these issues?
- LatinX families demonstrate resilience through ethnic and racial socialization practices. How do these practices contribute to LatinX students' academic achievement and success, and what can elementary, secondary, and postsecondary institutions learn from them?

NOTES

1. In 1965, under President Johnson's administration, the Elementary and Secondary Education Act (ESEA) was implemented, which included Title I programs. It was later revised to Every Student Succeeds Act (ESSA). These programs were established to provide financial assistance to schools nationwide and to improve academic achievement, particularly in reading, language, arts, and mathematics. ESEA would set a precedent for Title VII, known as the Bilingual Education Act, which has a complex and long history.
2. Historically, California has had high proportions of LatinX elementary and secondary school students who are overrepresented within Title I programs throughout the state.
3. California has one of highest concentrations of Mexican and Salvadoran populations in the United States. Please see: https://www.census.gov/quickfacts/CA
4. For research on "at risk" to "at promise," please see: Mireles-Rios, R., Rios, V. M., Auldridge-Reveles, T., Monroy, M., & Castro, I. (2020). "I was pushed out of school": Social and emotional approaches to a youth promotion program. *Journal of Leadership, Equity, and Research*, 6(1), n1.
5. For research debunking Oscar Lewis's notion of a "culture of poverty," please see: Valencia, R. R. (2010). *Dismantling contemporary deficit thinking: Educational thought and practice*. Routledge.

6. See Valencia (2010).
7. Braxton (2006) draws from the following scholars' research: Astin and Panos (1969), Astin (1977, 1993), Banta (1985), Baird (1976), Becker (1964), Bowen (1977, 1996), Feldman and Newcomb (1969), Lenning, Munday, Johnson, Vander Weil, and Brue (1974), Pace (1979), Pascarella and Terenzini (1991, 2005), and Willingham (1985).
8. Perna and Thomas (2006) use the term "racial/ethnic" when referring to race and ethnicity. In this section, I will adopt their terminology when discussing their research findings.

REFERENCES

Alba, R., & Nee, V. (2003). *Remaking the American mainstream: Assimilation and contemporary immigration.* Harvard University Press.

Alcoff, L. M. (2009). Latinos beyond the binary. *Southern Journal of Philosophy, 47*(S1), 112–128.

Astin, A. W. (1977). *Four critical years. Effects of college on beliefs, attitudes, and knowledge.* U.S. Department of Education.

Astin, A. W. (1993). *What matters in college? Four critical years revisited.* Jossey-Bass.

Astin, A. W., & Panos, R. J. (1969). *The educational and vocational development of college students.* American Council on Education.

Ayón, C., Marsiglia, F. F., & Bermudez-Parsai, M. (2018a). Latino family cultural values and the effects on children's development. *Journal of Family Studies, 20*(4), 212–229. https://doi.org/10.1002/jcop.20392

Ayón, C., Ojeda, I., & Ruano, E. (2018b). Cultural socialization practices among Latino immigrant families within a restrictive immigration socio-political context. *Children and Youth Services Review, 88,* 57–65. https://doi.org/10.1016/j.childyouth.2018.02.042

Baird, L. L. (1976). *Using self-reports to predict student performance.* College Entrance Examination Board.

Banta, T. W. (1985). *Performance funding in higher education: A critical analysis of Tennessee's experience.* National Center for Higher Education Management Systems.

Baumrind, D. (1966). Effects of authoritative parental control on child behavior. *Child Development, 37*(4), 887–907.

Becker, G. S. (1964). *Human capital: A theoretical and empirical analysis, with special reference to education.* National Bureau of Economic Research.

Bowen, H. R. (1977). *Investment in learning: The individual and social value of American higher education.* Jossey-Bass.

Bowen, H. R. (1996). *The economics of higher education.* Princeton University Press.

Boykin, A. W., & Toms, F. D. (1985). Black child socialization: A conceptual framework. In H. P. McAdoo & J. L. McAdoo (Eds.), *Black children: Social, educational, and parental environments* (pp. 33–51). Sage.

Braxton, J. M. (2006). Student success in higher education. In *Five Dimensions of Student Success* (pp. 2–3). National Postsecondary Education Cooperative.

Brown, E. D., & Iyengar, S. (2008). The effects of family income and maternal education on child's academic achievement. *Developmental Psychology, 44*(4), 857–866.

Burton, L. M., Bonilla-Silva, E., Ray, V., Buckelew, R., & Freeman, E. H. (2010). Critical race theories, colorism, and the decade's research on families of color. *Journal of Marriage and Family, 72*(3), 440–459.

Calderón-Tena, C. O., Knight, G. P., & Carlo, G. (2011). The socialization of pro-social behavioral tendencies among Mexican American adolescents: The role of familism values. *Cultural Diversity and Ethnic Minority Psychology, 17*(1), 98–106. https://doi.org/10.1037/a0021825

Caughy, M. O., Randolph, S. M., & O'Campo, P. J. (2002). The influence of racial socialization practices on the cognitive and behavioral competence of African American preschoolers. *Child Development, 73*(5), 1611–1625.

Ceballo, R. (2004). From barrios to Yale: The role of parenting strategies in Latino families. *Hispanic Journal of Behavioral Sciences, 26*(2), 171–186.

Chao, R. K., & Otsuki-Clutter, M. (2011). Racial and ethnic differences: Sociocultural and contextual explanations. In N. S. Landale (Ed.), *Handbook of child psychology* (pp. 582–652). Wiley.

Chavous, T. M., Bernat, D. H., Schmeelk-Cone, K., Caldwell, C. H., Kohn-Wood, L., & Zimmerman, M. A. (2003). Racial identity and academic attainment among African American adolescents. *Child Development, 74*(4), 1076–1090.

Conger, R. D., & Donnellan, M. B. (2007). An interactionist perspective on the socioeconomic context of human development. *Annual Review of Psychology, 58*, 175–199.

Crisp, G., Taggart, A., & Nora, A. (2015). Student characteristics, pre-college, and environmental factors predicting Latino/a academic success in higher education: A moderated mediation analysis. *Research in Higher Education, 56*(6), 595–645.

Darling, N., & Steinberg, L. (1993). Parenting style as context: An integrative model. *Psychological Bulletin, 113*(3), 487–496.

Davis-Kean, P. E. (2005). The influence of parent education and family income on child achievement: The indirect role of parental expectations and the home environment. *Journal of Family Psychology, 19*(2), 294–304.

Davis-Kean, P. E., & Sexton, H. R. (2009). Race differences in parental influences on child achievement: Multiple pathways to success. *Merrill-Palmer Quarterly, 55*(3), 285–318.

67

Dubow, E. F., Boxer, P., & Huesmann, L. R. (2009). Long-term effects of parents' education on children's educational and occupational success: Mediation by family interactions, child aggression, and teenage aspirations. *Merrill-Palmer Quarterly, 55*(3), 224–249.

Dumka, L. E., Roosa, M. W., & Jackson, K. M. (2013). Protective factors for resilience in Mexican American youth: The role of cultural and family influences. *Journal of Applied Developmental Psychology, 22*(4), 469–482.

Duncan, G. J., Brooks-Gunn, J., & Klebanov, P. K. (1994). Economic deprivation and early childhood development. *Child Development, 65*(2), 296–318.

Else-Quest, N. M., & Morse, M. C. (2015). Ethnic variations in parental involvement in children's schooling: Perceptions and practices. *Cultural Diversity and Ethnic Minority Psychology, 21*(4), 438–450.

Ewell, P., & Wellman, J. (2007). *Enhancing student success in education: Summary report of the NPEC initiative and national symposium on postsecondary student success.* National Postsecondary Education Cooperative [NPEC].

Feldman, K. A., & Newcomb, T. M. (1969). *The impact of college on students.* Jossey-Bass.

Galton, F. (1869). *Hereditary genius: An inquiry into its laws and consequences.* Macmillan.

Gomez, L. E. (2008). *Manifest destinies: The making of the Mexican American race.* New York University Press.

Gonzalez, G. G. (1997a). *Culture of empire: American writers, Mexico, and Mexican immigrants, 1880–1930.* University of Texas Press.

Gonzalez, G. G. (1997b). Culture, language, and the Americanization of Mexican children. In *Latinos and education: A critical reader* (pp. 158–173).

Gordon, M. M. (1964). *Assimilation in American life: The role of race, religion, and national origins.* Oxford University Press.

Haney López, I. (2006). *White by law: The legal construction of race* (10th Anniversary ed.). New York University Press.

Hauser-Cram, P. (2009). Family influences on the achievement of children with disabilities. *Educational Psychology Review, 21*(3), 355–369.

Haveman, R., & Wolfe, B. (1994). *Succeeding generations: On the effects of investments in children.* Russell Sage Foundation.

Hearn, J. C. (2006). Theories of student success: Reflections and future directions. *National Postsecondary Education Cooperative.*

Hofstadter, R. (1992). *Social Darwinism in American thought.* Beacon Press.

Holland, J. L. (1966). *The psychology of vocational choice: A theory of personality types and model environments.* Blaisdell Publishing Company.

Hughes, D., & Chen, L. (1997). When and what parents tell children about race: An examination of race-related socialization among African American families. *Applied Developmental Science, 1*(4), 200–214.

Hughes, D., Rodriguez, J., Smith, E. P., Johnson, D. J., Stevenson, H. C., & Spicer, P. (2006). Parents' ethnic-racial socialization practices: a review of research and directions for future study. *Developmental Psychology, 42*(5), 747.

Jiménez, T. R. (2010). *Replenished ethnicity: Mexican Americans, immigration, and identity.* University of California Press.

Knight, G. P., Bernal, M. E., Garza, C. A., Cota, M. K., & Ocampo, K. A. (1993). Family socialization and the ethnic identity of Mexican-American children. *Journal of Cross-Cultural Psychology, 24*(1), 99–114.

Kretovics, J., & Nussel, E. J. (1994). *Transforming higher education curriculum for student success.* Allyn and Bacon.

Kuh, G. D., Kinzie, J., Buckley, J. A., Bridges, B. K., & Hayek, J. C. (2006). *What matters to student success: A review of the literature* (Vol. 8). National Postsecondary Education Cooperative.

Kulish, A. L., Cavanaugh, A. M., Stein, G. L., Kiang, L., Gonzalez, L. M., Supple, A., & Mejia, Y. (2019). Ethnic–racial socialization in Latino families: The influence of mothers' socialization practices on adolescent private regard, familism, and perceived ethnic–racial discrimination. *Cultural Diversity and Ethnic Minority Psychology, 25*(2), 199.

Lacy, K. R. (2007). *Blue-chip black: Race, class, and status in the new black middle class.* University of California Press.

Lenning, O. T., Munday, L. A., Johnson, R. W., Vander Weil, D. R., & Brue, E. J. (1974). *The outcomes structure: A guide for systematic planning, evaluating, and reporting of institutional outcomes.* National Center for Higher Education Management Systems.

Lewis, O. (1966). The culture of poverty. *Scientific American, 215*(4), 19–25. https://www.jstor.org/stable/24931078

Longerbeam, S. D., Sedlacek, W. E., & Alatorre, H. M. (2004). In their own voices: Latino student retention. *NASPA Journal, 41*(3), 538–550. https://doi.org/10.2202/1949-6605.1360

Marshall, S. (1995). Ethnic socialization of African American children: Implications for parenting, identity development, and academic achievement. *Journal of Youth and Adolescence, 24*(4), 377–396.

Mendez v. Westminster School District, et al., 64 F. Supp. 544 (C.D. Cal. 1946).

Mireles-Rios, R., Rios, V. M., Auldridge-Reveles, T., Monroy, M., & Castro, I. (2020). "I was pushed out of school": Social and emotional approaches to a youth promotion program. *Journal of Leadership, Equity, and Research, 6*(1), n1.

Montero-Sieburth, M., & Batt, M. C. (2000). An overview of the educational models used to explain the academic achievement of Latino students: Implications for research and policies into the new millennium. In R. E. Slavin and M. Calderón (eds), *Effective programs for Latino students* (pp. 331–368). Routledge.

Murphy, J. P., & Murphy, S. A. (2018). Get ready, get in, get through: Factors that influence Latino college student success. *Journal of Latinos and Education, 17*(1), 3–17.

Nieto, S. (2000). Puerto Rican students in US schools: A brief history. *Puerto Rican Students in US Schools* (pp. 5–38). https://doi.org/10.4324/9781410606082

Nuñez, A.-M., Crisp, G., & Elizondo, D. (2013). Hispanic-serving institutions: Advancing research and transformative practice. *Journal of Latinos and Education, 12*(3), 150–165.

Omi, M., & Winant, H. (1994). *Racial formation in the United States: From the 1960s to the 1990s*. Routledge.

Ou, Y.-s., & McAdoo, H. P. (1993). Socialization of Chinese American children. In H. P. McAdoo (Ed.), *Family ethnicity: Strength in diversity* (pp. 245–270). Sage Publications.

Pace, C. R. (1979). *Measuring outcomes of college: Fifty years of findings and recommendations for the future.* Jossey-Bass.

Pascarella, E. T., & Terenzini, P. T. (1991). *How college affects students: Findings and insights from twenty years of research.* Jossey-Bass.

Pascarella, E. T., & Terenzini, P. T. (2005). *How college affects students: A third decade of research* (Vol. 2). Jossey-Bass.

Perlmann, J. (2005). *Italians then, Mexicans now: Immigrant origins and the second-generation progress, 1890–2000.* Russell Sage Foundation.

Perna, L. W., & Thomas, S. L. (2006). A framework for reducing the college success gap and promoting success for all. *National Postsecondary Education Cooperative.*

Pessar, P. R. (1995). *A visa for a dream: Dominicans in the United States.* Allyn & Bacon.

Peters, M. F. (1985). Racial socialization of young Black children. In H. P. McAdoo & J. L. McAdoo (Eds.), *Black children: Social, educational, and parental environments* (pp. 159–173). Sage Publications.

Pettit, G. S., Yu, T., Dodge, K. A., & Bates, J. E. (2009). A developmental process analysis of cross-generational continuity in educational attainment. *Merrill-Palmer Quarterly, 55*(3), 250–284.

Phinney, J. S., & Chavira, V. (1995). Parental ethnic socialization and adolescent coping with problems related to ethnicity. *Journal of Research on Adolescence, 5*(1), 31–53. https://doi.org/10.1207/s15327795jra0501_2

Quintana, S. M., & Vera, E. M. (1999). Mexican American children's ethnic identity, understanding of ethnic prejudice, and parental ethnic socialization. *Hispanic Journal of Behavioral Sciences, 21*(4), 387–404.

Quintana, S. M., Chao, R. K., Cross, W. E., Jr., Hughes, D., Nelson-Le Gall, S., Aboud, F. E., Contreras-Grau, J., Hudley, C., Liben, L. S., & Vietze, D. L. (2006). Race, ethnicity, and culture in child development: Contemporary research and future directions. *Child Development, 77*(5), 1129–1141.

Ramos, A., & Sifuentez, M. (2021). *Equity and inclusion: A Latino perspective on higher education*. Harvard Education Press.

Rodríguez, C. E., & Sánchez Korrol, V. (1996). *Historical Perspectives on Puerto Rican Survival in the United States*. Markus Wiener Publishers.

Santiago, D. A. (2011). *Ensuring America's future by increasing Latino college completion*. Excelencia in Education. Retrieved from http://www.edexcelencia.org/research/roadmap-ensuring-americas-future

Smart, J. C., Feldman, K. A., & Ethington, C. A. (2006, July). Holland's theory and patterns of college student success. In *Commissioned report for the national symposium on postsecondary student success: Spearheading a dialog on student success* (p. 50). National Postsecondary Education Cooperative.

Smith, P. J., & Yosso, T. J. (2003). Latino/a identity and educational attainment: Racialized and classed practices. *Harvard Educational Review, 73*(3), 355–391.

Solórzano, D. G. (1997). Images and words that wound: Critical race theory, racial stereotyping, and teacher education. *Teacher Education Quarterly, 24*(3), 5–19. https://www.jstor.org/stable/23478088

Soto, L. D. (2006). *The politics of early childhood education*. Peter Lang.

Spencer, M. B., & Markstrom-Adams, C. (1990). Identity processes among racial and ethnic minority children in America. *Child Development, 61*(2), 290–310. https://doi.org/10.2307/1131095

Spera, C. (2005). A review of the relationship among parenting practices, parenting styles, and adolescent school achievement. *Educational Psychology Review, 17*(2), 125–146.

Strum, P. (2010). *Mendez v. Westminster: School desegregation and Mexican-American rights*. University Press of Kansas.

Suárez-Orozco, C., & Suárez-Orozco, M. M. (1995). *Transformations: Immigration, family life, and achievement motivation among Latino adolescents*. Stanford University Press.

Telles, E., & Ortiz, V. (2008). *Generations of exclusion: Mexican Americans, assimilation, and race*. Russell Sage Foundation.

Tinto, V., & Pusser, B. (2006). Moving from theory to action: Building a model of institutional action for student success. National Postsecondary Education Cooperative.

Torres, V., Winston Jr, R. B., & Cooper, D. L. (2003). Hispanic American students' cultural orientation: Does geographic location, institutional type, or level of stress have an effect. *NASPA Journal, 40*(2), 153–172.

Umaña-Taylor, A. J., & Hill, N. E. (2020). Ethnic–racial socialization in the family: A decade's advance on precursors and outcomes. *Journal of Marriage and Family, 82*(1), 244–271. https://doi.org/10.1111/jomf.12622

Urciuoli, B. (1996). *Exposing prejudice: Puerto Rican experiences of language, race, and class.* Westview Press.

Valencia, R. R. (1997). *The evolution of deficit thinking: Educational thought and practice.* RoutledgeFalmer.

Valencia, R. R. (2008). *Chicano students and the courts: The Mexican American legal struggle for educational equality.* New York University Press.

Valencia, R. R. (2010). *Dismantling contemporary deficit thinking: Educational thought and practice.* Routledge.

Villenas, S. A. (2009). Knowing and unknowing transnational Latino lives in teacher education: At the intersection of educational research and the Latino humanities. *The High School Journal, 92*(4), 129–136.

Villenas, S., & Deyhle, D. (1999). Critical race theory and ethnographies challenging the stereotypes: Latino families, schooling, resilience and resistance. *Curriculum Inquiry, 29*(4), 413–445. https://doi.org/10.1111/0362-6784.00140

Waters, M. C. (1990). *Ethnic options: Choosing identities in America.* University of California Press.

Waters, M. C. (1994). *Black identities: West Indian immigrant dreams and American realities.* Harvard University Press.

Whalen, C. T., & Vazquez-Hernandez, R. (2005). *The Puerto Rican diaspora: Historical perspectives.* Temple University Press.

Wigfield, A., & Eccles, J. S. (2002). The development of competence beliefs, expectancies for success, and achievement values from childhood through adolescence. In A. Wigfield & J. S. Eccles (Eds.), *Development of achievement motivation* (pp. 91–120). Academic Press.

Willingham, W. W. (1985). Success in college: The role of personal qualities and academic ability. College Board Publications, New York.

Wilson, W. J. (1980). *The declining significance of race.* University of Chicago Press.

Chapter 3

LatinX Academic Achievement and Student Success in the Twenty-First Century

ARIEL: AN ASPIRING AFRO-LATINX POET

Ariel slammed their[1] book on their desk before exiting their summer class at Brooklyn College.[2] Their air pods, snug within their ears, became conduits for the soul-stirring rhythms of "Pa'lante" by Hurray for the Riff Raff.[3] Each bass note thrummed through Ariel like a heartbeat, propelling them toward the subway station to catch the 5 to Hunter College.[4] Ariel's steps matched the tempo of the song, their spirit lifting with Alynda Mariposa Segarra's piercing lyrics. They took a deep breath and inhaled the must that permeated the train stop's air. Ariel stood with eyes closed, a silent recitation of Pedro Pietri's "Puerto Rican Obituary"[5] syncing with the music's crescendo. The powerful words meshed with the melody, wrapping Ariel in a cloak of cultural reverence that soothed and energized them. As the train roared in, Ariel murmured a burring "¡Pa'lante!" feeling the phrase's ancestral weight and promise.

Ariel was born and raised in Brooklyn, New York, in a predominately Puerto Rican neighborhood. Their grandparents were Young Lords[6] and activists in the community for the empowerment of the people and the self-determination of Puerto Rico. As a child, they remembered them telling them stories of Pedro Pietri reciting Puerto Rican Obituary at a rally[7] supporting the Young Lords Party. These narratives were the foundation of Ariel's identity as a non-binary Afro-Nuyorican[8]—a legacy of struggle and strength that pulsed in their blood.

Their parents, researchers in Centro[9] (The Center for Puerto Rican Studies), participated in ASPIRA[10]—a college preparation program that promotes the empowerment of the Puerto Rican and LatinX community by developing and nurturing the leadership, intellectual potential, and cultural potential of its youth to build and contribute their skills and dedication to the fullest development of the Puerto Rican and LatinX community everywhere.

DOI: 10.4324/9781003415909-3

Ariel's parents expected them to attend college and pursue a career in Science, Technology, Engineering, and Mathematics (STEM). Now, as a sophomore grappling with the weight of familial expectations and their budding voice, Ariel was journeying to Centro not for science but to revisit the handwritten manuscripts of Pedro Pietri.[11] In the quiet sanctuary of the archive, surrounded by the penned thoughts of their literary hero, Ariel felt a profound connection to their roots and path. Ariel's soul was tied to the rhythm of words. Recently, after declaring their non-binary identity, Ariel found solace and expression through poetry, channeling their experiences into verses that echoed the giants of Afro-LatinX literature.

Inspired by contemporary LatinX authors like Elizabeth Acevedo and Gabby Rivera,[12] Ariel was determined to carve out space for their voice within the literary world. Their writings, raw and introspective, explored the complexities of non-binary identity against the backdrop of societal upheaval— particularly the rise of anti-Blackness in the LatinX community and the global racial reckoning stemming from the murder of George Floyd during COVID-19. In every word they wrote, Ariel sought to tell a story and ignite conversation, challenge norms, and affirm identities.

COUNTER-STORY REFLECTION QUESTIONS

- How can LatinX student success be defined, and what unique challenges might Ariel face in achieving this success due to their non-binary identity?
- How can different institutional types of higher education and institutional actors promote LatinX student success, and how can these institutions better support students like Ariel who navigate multiple marginalized identities?
- How can LatinX student success be measured or assessed, and what role do parents play in influencing the academic pathways and majors of students like Ariel, particularly those with non-binary identities?

LatinX student academic achievement and success in higher education are a multi-layered issue that demands a nuanced understanding of students' experiences, identities, and the institutional and societal environments they navigate. Recent searches in academic databases show a growing body of research on LatinX student academic achievement and success in the field of higher education. However, I argue that inconsistencies in search results demonstrate the challenges of defining and understanding LatinX academic achievement and student success in higher education. As discussed in Chapter 1, while terms like "Hispanic" and "Latino" are well established in academic research, relatively newer terms such as "Latinx," "LatinX," and "Latine" yield fewer

results, reflecting ongoing discussions and variations in how the LatinX population is identified and studied in higher education research. These variations raise the critical question: "What is LatinX student success?" Despite
emerging terminology, I argue that three critical bodies of scholarship are
foundational in higher education research on LatinX academic achievement
and student success. First, Nuñez et al. (2013b) provide an empirical analysis
of LatinX academic achievement and student success, emphasizing the crucial
role of institutional types, such as Hispanic-Serving Institutions (HSIs), and
the support offered by institutional actors such as faculty and student affairs
professionals. Second, Crisp et al. (2015) systematically review the factors
influencing LatinX student academic achievement and success, examining the
importance of persistence, academic performance, and degree completion.
Finally, Valverde (2002, 2012) presents a practical guide aimed at assisting
LatinX students with navigating the educational pipeline from elementary to
graduate education.

Therefore, in this chapter, I examine these three foundational bodies of
work and explore the complexities of LatinX student academic achievement
and success by analyzing the various definitions and indicators of success
proposed in the research (Crisp et al., 2015; Nuñez et al., 2013b; Valverde
2002, 2012). Further, scholars (Crisp et al., 2015; Garcia, 2017; Marin &
Pereschica, 2017; Nuñez et al., 2013a, 2013b) have identified that the type of
institution of higher education LatinX students attend, such as public two-year
colleges or Hispanic-Serving Institutions (HSIs), significantly influences their
pathways to postsecondary degree or credential completion. Additionally,
institutional actors—including faculty, administrators, and staff—are essential
in determining campus culture, providing support services, and preparing
students academically to cultivate LatinX student success. Taken together,
I examine public two-year institutions and HSIs, exploring why LatinX students pursue these pathways and the institutional factors and actors that
influence their success in completing a postsecondary degree or credential in
these contexts. I conclude the chapter by discussing the social identities LatinX
students bring with them into institutions of higher education, emphasizing
the gaps in current research and the need for more inclusive, direct strategies
to support the success of all LatinX students.

LATINX STUDENT SUCCESS

A search on ProQuest for "Hispanic college student success" within the
past 12 months across scholarly journals returned 1,270 results, including
1,772 dissertations and theses. A similar search for "Latino college student
success" yielded 1,190 dissertations and theses and 731 academic journal
articles. However, searching for the more recent term "Latinx college student

success" resulted in 605 dissertations and theses and 515 scholarly journals, with a prompt asking, "Did you mean *Latin* college student success?" These varied search outcomes demonstrate how academic search engines generate different results based on terminology. More importantly, the inconsistencies in these results raise questions about the soundness of LatinX academic achievement and student success literature and how the field of higher education research considers or defines LatinX student success. To date, and to my knowledge, three comprehensive bodies of work examine LatinX student success in higher education research—two are empirical (Nuñez et al., 2013b; Crisp et al., 2015) and the third addresses the implementation of practice (Valverde, 2002, 2012). First, Nuñez et al. (2013b) examine LatinX student postsecondary degree or credential completion and institutional types and contexts, specifically in attunement to HSIs and their institutional actors, such as faculty and student affairs professionals. Second, Crisp et al. (2015) conducted a systematic review of research on factors contributing to LatinX undergraduate student academic success and outcomes. Lastly, Valverde (2002, 2012), in an edited volume first published in the early 2000s and in its second edition, provides a step-by-step roadmap for LatinX student pathways toward success from completing and transitioning from elementary to graduate education.

Nuñez et al.'s (2013b) book, *Latinos in Higher Education and Hispanic-Serving Institutions: Creating Conditions for Success*, provides a comprehensive review of the state of Latino[13] students in U.S. higher education, attuned to the challenges they encounter and the role of HSIs. Nuñez et al.'s (2013b) monograph is structured into six chapters, covering a diverse set of approaches to examining LatinX student success. These methods range from traditional methods of approaching student success in higher education scholarship through mainstream notions of human capital (Bourdieu, 1986) to culturally responsive approaches (Gay, 2018) that center LatinX students' experiences that are not necessarily validated by institutions of higher education (Solórzano & Delgado Bernal, 2001). Nuñez et al. (2013b) emphasize that while the demographic growth of the Latino population is the largest among all racial and ethnic groups in the United States, persistent educational inequities remain, especially in postsecondary degree completion, where Latino students have the lowest rates as compared with their white counterparts. Nuñez et al. (2013b) explore how Latino students' demographic, social, and cultural characteristics impact academic success, focusing on variation among the three largest ethnic subgroups in the United States (Mexican, Puerto Rican, and Cuban). Namely, they examine how family dynamics, language, religious values, neighborhood compositions, immigration experiences, and citizenship status affect Latino educational experiences. Applying Latino Critical Race Theory (LatCrit), Nuñez et al. (2013b) analyze the role of student identity development regarding Latino student success. They then use a "multiple capitals" approach to describe the various forms of capital—academic, financial, cultural, and social—that Latino students need to successfully navigate higher education while also foregrounding the significance of asset-based approaches to view Latino families as sources of strength rather than barriers to success.

Furthermore, shifting the responsibility away from Latino students and urging institutions of higher education to take greater accountability in offering tailored support, Nuñez et al. (2013b) thoroughly examine institutional supports and best practices that can enhance Latino student success, emphasizing the role of faculty, staff, and administrators in creating inclusive and culturally responsive campus environments. Most notably, they discuss the critical role of HSIs, which, despite often being underfunded, provide vital access to Latino students and contribute significantly to the production of postsecondary degrees and credential completers, particularly in STEM fields. Additionally, Nuñez et al. (2013b) examine the importance of community colleges in Latino students' educational pathways, noting that these institutions are often under-researched as central sites of Latino student success and how community colleges are often where they attend. Overall, their scholarship defines LatinX students as "success [that] can encompass initial enrollment characteristics, academic performance, social sense of belonging, persistence, and degree completion" (Nuñez et al., 2013b, p. 2). As discussed in Chapter 2, Nuñez et al.'s (2013b) broad definition reflects discussions at the National Postsecondary Cooperative (NPEC) symposium and its commissioned papers, highlighting the central importance of postsecondary degree or credential completion in the definition of LatinX student achievement and success.

Crisp et al. (2015) conducted a systematic review of Latino student success in higher education research based on empirical studies centered on traditional academic success outcomes, which they defined as "behaviors necessary to accomplish students' academic goals, including course completion, course grades or grade point average, persistence in higher education, transfer to another postsecondary institution, and certificate or degree completion" (p. 251). Focusing on indicators of LatinX student success, Crisp et al. (2015) identified 190 empirical studies to analyze using those studies' inclusion and exclusion criteria; 63 met the requirements and were included in their study. Among the studies analyzed, the majority (62 percent) examined students from four-year institutions, while 27 percent concentrated solely on two-year institutions. The institution of higher education type was often unspecified, though some studied HSIs (17 percent), predominantly white institutions (PWIs) (5 percent), or institutions with selective admissions criteria (6 percent). Crisp et al. (2015) found that the predominant indicators of LatinX student success were course grades or grade point average (GPA), persistence, and postsecondary degree or credential completion. Their findings suggest nine indicators for LatinX student success (Crisp et al., 2015):

1. LatinX students' sociocultural attributes, such as gender, parent education, and income level, influence persistence, grades, and the likelihood of postsecondary degree or credential completion.
2. LatinX students' self-confidence regarding academic tasks contributes to their persistence, grades, and completion of postsecondary degrees or credentials.
3. LatinX students' awareness of their ethnic and racial identities, belief systems regarding justice-oriented equity, responsiveness to stereotypes, and engagement in adaptative coping might contribute to their persistence in postsecondary degree or credential completion.
4. LatinX students' precollege characteristics, such as how well they perform in high school, can dictate how well they will perform in college, especially regarding their grades and persistence to a postsecondary degree or credential completion, regardless of institutional type.
5. LatinX students' college experiences, such as college affordability, financial aid packages, student and employment status (e.g., full-time or part-time), and academic performance, influence their postsecondary degree or credential completion.
6. LatinX students' internal motivation and commitment profoundly impact their drive to succeed and their academic performance.
7. LatinX students need supportive relationships from peers, parents, mentors, or others who contribute to their grades and persistence in pursuing postsecondary degrees or credentials.
8. LatinX students who have negative experiences due to hostile campus climate may deter their persistence and postsecondary degree or credential completion.
9. For LatinX students, the institutional type they attend may impact their persistence in obtaining a postsecondary degree or credential completion.

Crisp et al.'s (2015) and Nuñez et al.'s (2013b) definitions of LatinX student success share similarities and differences. Both their definitions of LatinX student success emphasize the significance of academic performance. For example, Crisp et al. (2015) identify course grades, GPA, and persistence, while Nuñez et al. (2013b) include academic performance explicitly. Each of their definitions is explicit in that completing a postsecondary degree or certificate is a critical element of success while emphasizing the importance of persistence in higher education, which involves continuing through graduation or transferring without interruption. Additionally, both definitions view success as multidimensional, incorporating factors such as performance, persistence, and a postsecondary degree or credential completion rather than focusing solely on academic achievement. Despite the similarities in their definitions of LatinX student success, there are significant differences. Crisp et al. (2015) focus on specific behaviors necessary to achieve academic success, such as course completion and GPA, while Nuñez et al.'s (2013b) definition includes broader social factors like a "social sense of belonging," which relates to emotional and community engagement. Moreover, Nuñez et al. (2013b) incorporate "initial enrollment characteristics" as part of LatinX student success, which refers to factors present when students first enroll in higher education. Finally, Crisp et al. (2015) include the ability to transfer to another postsecondary institution as a measure of success, which Nuñez et al. (2013b) do not explicitly address in their definition. While the definitions and indicators offered by Crisp et al. (2015) and Nuñez et al. (2013b) provide valuable theoretical and empirical findings for understanding LatinX student success, Valverde (2002, 2012) shifts the focus to a more practical, applied approach, offering direct guidance to LatinX student and their families as they navigate the educational pipeline from elementary to graduate education.

As previously mentioned, while empirical works exist on LatinX college students, they often focus on academic preparation and persistence, offering little practical guidance for students and families. Valverde (2002, 2012) addresses this gap and takes an applied approach to address the needs of LatinX students. Valverde's (2002, 2012) guide consists of preparing LatinX students and their families for college, navigating admissions, securing financial aid, and succeeding academically. The guide is structured in four sections: preparing for college, navigating campus life, professional testimonials, and a list of top institutions of higher education for Latino students to attend. Valverde's (2002, 2012) guide is unique for a broad audience, including high school students, teachers, counselors, and college outreach personnel. The guide also appeals to various LatinX communities and includes testimonials from successful LatinX professionals in their two- or four-year institutions of higher education pathways. Valverde's (2002, 2012) contribution is invaluable, but as institutions of higher education are constantly changing, a guide of this significance has a limited lifespan. As institutions of higher education continually evolve, with changes in admission policies, graduation requirements, testing, and the rise of online coursework, Valverde's (2002, 2012) guide will need to be regularly updated to remain relevant. Despite this limitation, the guide remains a crucial resource for LatinX students and their families, offering essential tools and motivational support as they navigate the complexities of the higher education landscape.

Overall, research on LatinX student success has developed through theoretical, empirical, and practical approaches. Crisp et al. (2015) and Nuñez et al. (2013b) focus on academic performance, persistence, and institutional support as important indicators impacting LatinX student academic achievement and success. While their work provides significant theoretical and empirical contributions, there is a lack of direct guidance for LatinX students and their families in the academic literature. Valverde (2002, 2012) addresses this gap with a practical step-by-step guide to help LatinX students navigate the educational pipeline from elementary to graduate education. While existing research and practical guides offer valuable perspectives on LatinX student success, the role of institutional types and their actors remains critical in determining these outcomes. To further explore this dynamic, the next section examines key institutional types, particularly public two-year institutions and HSIs, and how institutional actors can cultivate LatinX student success.

LATINX STUDENT SUCCESS—INSTITUTIONAL TYPES AND ACTORS

Community College and Institutional Actors

Public universities educate roughly 70 percent of students in the United States, with a significant proportion coming from underrepresented and economically disadvantaged backgrounds (Carnevale et al., 2019; National Center for Education Statistics, 2020). Public two-year institutions, often referred to as community colleges, are complex organizations where assessing student success is challenging but crucial. Community colleges serve a more diverse population than four-year colleges and universities and offer a broader range of educational programs, including continuing education and technical training for adults. They confer diplomas, associate degrees, and, in some cases, bachelor's degrees, depending on the field of study. Community colleges serve as critical access points to institutions of higher education for economically disadvantaged and underrepresented students (Bailey et al., 2015). However, despite their accessibility, completion rates at community colleges are lower than at other public higher education institutions. Nationally, only about 30 percent of first-time, full-time students entering a two-year community college program graduate within three years (Shapiro et al., 2019).

Empirical research indicates that LatinX students are more inclined to enroll in and attend public two-year colleges as compared with other racial and ethnic groups (Carales, 2020; Kurlaender, 2006). Often, public two-year institutions function as an open-access point for LatinX students who are first-generation, economically disadvantaged, undocumented, and/or adult learners (Dawson et al., 2021). Public two-year institutions provide several vital factors contributing to LatinX student academic achievement and success. Public two-year institutions typically offer lower tuition fees than public four-year institutions, making a college education more financially accessible for many LatinX students (Martinez & Fernández, 2004; Nuñez et al., 2013a, 2013b). Additionally, the closer proximity of public two-year institution campuses to LatinX students' homes reduces the need for extensive travel or relocation. Santiago et al. (2024) found that 79 percent of undergraduate LatinX students lived either off campus or with their parents, a higher proportion than other racial and ethnic groups. Public two-year institutions also provide diverse scheduling options, including evening and online courses, flexible class times, and part-time enrollment, accommodating LatinX students who often work and/or have family commitments (Martinez & Fernández, 2004). Regardless of LatinX's initial college readiness, public two-year institutions offer remedial courses, and they typically maintain open access policies, welcoming LatinX students from a wide range of educational backgrounds (Bailey & Smith Morest, 2006; Dougherty, 1994).

Despite the high enrollment rates of LatinX students in public two-year institutions, the pathway to transfer success and postsecondary degree or credential completion remains complex due to various reasons, including transfer requirements, geographic location, and resources of the institutional type (Bensimon, 2007; Felix, 2020; Perez & Ceja, 2010; Perna et al., 2008a; Stanton-Salazar, 2011; Stanton-Salazar et al., 2000). Crisp and Nora (2010) identify that although over 80 percent of LatinX students at two-year community colleges intend to transfer, less than 25 percent are successfully able to do so. Studies have shown that LatinX students have high aspirations and motivation to transfer to a four-year institution when they enroll at a community college. However, the type of transfer pathway they pursue can significantly hinder their transfer success and postsecondary degree completion (Dowd, 2007; Jain et al., 2020; Pérez & Ceja, 2010).

Jain et al. (2020) argue that student transfers can occur in several forms in higher education. Vertical transfer, the most common, refers to when a student moves from a public two-year institution to a four-year university to pursue a bachelor's degree. In contrast, reverse transfer occurs when a student transfers from a four-year institution to a public two-year institution to complete an associate degree or take more affordable or flexible pathways. Lateral transfer is when a student transfers between institutions at the same level, such as moving from one public two-year institution to another. Lastly, dual credit transfer occurs when high school students earn college credits through dual enrollment programs, which can be transferred to an institution of higher education upon enrollment. In 2024, Excelencia in Education reported that lateral transfer was the most common pathway among LatinX transfer students. Understanding the transfer pathway for LatinX students is critical for institutions of higher education aiming to support LatinX students through structured transfer pathways that lead to higher rates of postsecondary degree completion, academic achievement, and success.

When LatinX students attend public two-year institutions, they might experience obstacles such as enrolling part-time, facing financial hardships, encountering academic challenges, and lacking sufficient access to information and resources. These factors could disrupt, postpone, or hinder their progress toward transferring to a four-year institution and completing a postsecondary degree (Acevedo-Gil et al., 2015; Acevedo-Gil, 2018; Del Real Viramontes, 2021). Part-time enrollment notably stands out as a significant hurdle for LatinX students at public two-year institutions, as research indicates it decreases their likelihood of transferring to four-year institutions (Crisp & Nora, 2010; Del Real Viramontes, 2021; Jain et al., 2020). Part-time students often face longer timelines for completing their postsecondary degrees or credentials and may lack the institutional support to navigate the transfer process effectively (Del Real Viramontes, 2021). While part-time enrollment and other issues pose significant challenges for LatinX students at public two-year institutions, these barriers are compounded by the lack of institutional accountability in supporting student transfers.

Jain et al. (2020) argue that most empirical research on public two-year institutions focuses on the institution's perspective rather than being student-centered and designed to serve students effectively. Jain et al. (2020) argue that institutions often fail to take responsibility for successfully transferring students and cultivating a transfer-receptive culture. Rather than attributing outcomes to only individual actors or choices, public two-year institutions must shift their focus to how broader institutional factors impact student decisions. This shift in perspective is critical due to systematic barriers, such as inadequate advising, limited access to resources, and lack of institutional commitment to transfer pathways, which can significantly decrease LatinX students' ability to transfer successfully. Jain et al. (2011, 2020) conceptualize and ground a transfer-receptive culture in Critical Race Theory, which centralizes the role of race and racism during vertical transfer when a student moves from a public two-year institution to a four-year university to pursue a bachelor's degree. Jain et al. (2011, 2020) define a transfer-receptive culture as an institutional culture that actively supports and facilitates the successful transfer of students from public two-year institutions by providing clear pathways, resources, and an inclusive environment for students. Significant to this definition is that the receiving institution of higher education shares responsibility and accountability in the process with the sending public two-year institution for the success of transfer students. Bridging these two cultures

creates a holistic view of the transfer process and honors student identities. In particular, in a transfer-receptive culture, LatinX students should be
able to identify the institution's commitment to transfer them by assisting
their navigation through the two-year setting, taking the proper coursework,
and applying for and completing a postsecondary degree. Recently, Carales
(2020), using a nationally representative sample of LatinX community college
students, found that:

> Latina/o community college student educational outcomes were found to
> be related to demographic or pre-college variables, including primary lan-
> guage spoken in the home, citizenship status, socioeconomic status, degree
> expectations; college experiences including academic integration, first-year
> college grade point average (GPA), enrollment intensity, co-enrollment; and
> environmental pull factors including the receipt of a federal student loan
> and Pell Grant.
>
> (p. 195)

Carales (2020) emphasizes the critical role of financial aid in supporting
LatinX community college students, addressing college affordability issues, and
enhancing student outcomes and institutional effectiveness through aligned
advising services and programs. A significant component of facilitating a
transfer-receptive culture for LatinX students, based on the findings of Carales
(2020), is the role of institutional actors such as faculty, administrators, and
staff (Barnett, 2010; Chang, 2005; Doran, 2023; Dowd et al., 2013; Nuñez
et al., 2013b; Tovar, 2015; Zalaquett & Lopez, 2006).

Tovar (2015) examined the role of institutional actors such as faculty,
counselors, and support programs and found that validation and caring
interactions from institutional actors positively influence students' intent
to persist and succeed. Tovar (2015) argues that supportive relationships
with faculty and counselors can significantly enhance LatinX students'
sense of belonging and academic self-efficacy, primarily through student
support programs. Alcantar and Hernandez (2020) employ validation
theory (Rendon, 1994) to examine LatinX students attending public two-
year HSIs and their interactions with institutional actors who served as their
faculty when enrolled. Aligned with previous research (Cejda & Rhodes,
2004), Alcantar and Hernandez (2020) found that faculty serve as validating agents for LatinX students, which can contribute to their sense of
belonging, persistence, and academic self-concepts, all positive indicators
associated with student success. According to Doran (2023), research on
HSIs, particularly in the context of public two-year institutions and the role
of institutional actors, has made significant strides in emphasizing support
for LatinX student success. HSIs often implement practices better aimed at

serving LatinX students compared with non-HSIs, though the effectiveness of these practices can vary (Cuellar, 2012; Bensimon et al., 2019; Contreras et al., 2008; Garcia & Hurtado, 2011; Hurtado et al., 2012; Nelson Laird et al., 2007). Aligned with Doran (2023), while research on the institutional actors in public two-year institutions examines the importance of cultivating LatinX student success, it is equally important to examine the broader institutional contexts in which these interactions occur. Hispanic-Serving Institutions are a specific type of Minority-Serving Institution (MSI), with over 40 percent of all HSIs being community colleges (U.S. Department of Education, 2021). In the next section, I define HSIs, explain their federal designation, and discuss their significance within the broader landscape of institutions of higher education in the United States.

Hispanic-Serving Institutions and Institutional Actors

Hispanic-Serving Institutions [14] fall under the broader category of Minority-Serving Institutions (MSIs). MSIs are divided into historically defined and enrollment-defined institutions (NASEM, 2019). The Higher Education Act (HEA) of 1965, signed by President Johnson, established what we now know as MSIs. Although the HEA aimed to strengthen educational resources and provide financial assistance to postsecondary students, it also enabled institutions to offer higher education to historically marginalized students (Higher Education Act of 1965). Issued in 1965, the first designation under the HEA was for Historically Black Colleges and Universities (HBCUs) in 1965. This was followed by Tribal Colleges and Universities (TCUs) through the Tribally Controlled Colleges and Universities Assistance Act of 1978 (Tribally Controlled Community College Assistance Act, 1978). These federal recognitions made institutions eligible for federal grants as part of reauthorizing the Higher Education Act of 1965 and its subsequent versions. Additional MSI designations and their recognition years include Hispanic-Serving Institutions (1992), Alaska Native and Native Hawaiian-Serving Institutions (1998), Asian American and Native American Pacific Islander-Serving Institutions (2007), Predominantly Black Institutions (2008), and Native American-Serving Nontribal Institutions (2008) (Santiago, 2007; U.S. Department of Education, 2021).

Hispanic-Serving Institutions are federally defined as accredited two-year or four-year, private or public, not-for-profit institutions of higher education that enroll at least 25 percent of full-time LatinX students (U.S. Department of Education, n.d.). The number of two- and four-year public institutions of higher education enrolling at least 25 percent LatinX students is increasing, making HSIs one of the fastest-growing MSI sub-groups of U.S. colleges and universities (Excelencia in Education, 2024). In 2022–23, Excelencia in Education reported 600 HSIs across 28 states, including the District of Columbia and Puerto Rico. Additionally, 412 emerging HSIs have LatinX enrollment between 15 percent and 25 percent of their undergraduate student body (Excelencia in Education, 2024). The Office of Postsecondary Education (OPE), a division of the Department of Education, administers grants for MSIs, including HSIs, to enhance educational opportunities for LatinX students and other underrepresented groups. Accredited institutions are eligible to participate if they meet the following conditions: 1) full-time undergraduate student enrollment of at least 25 percent LatinX students and 2) at least 50 percent of students are eligible for need-based financial aid (U.S. Department of Education, 2018; HACU, 2018). Under the Higher Education Opportunity Act, HSIs can qualify for three types of federal funding: HSI STEM (Title III), Developing HSI Grants (Title V-Part A), and Promoting Postbaccalaureate Opportunities for Hispanic Americans (PPOHA) (Title V-Part B). HSI STEM (Title III) funding focuses on increasing the number of LatinX students attaining degrees in STEM fields and/or improving transfer rates or articulation agreements between public two-year and four-year institutions of higher education for STEM (U.S. Department of Education, n.d.). Title V funding supports HSIs in advancing or expanding educational opportunities to improve degree attainment rates for their LatinX students. To maintain eligibility for these grants, HSIs must maintain their LatinX enrollment percentage and demonstrate progress in achieving grant objectives, which vary and are complex to measure. As the number of HSIs continues to grow and federal funding supports their efforts to serve LatinX students, it is critical to examine the distinct challenges these institutions face to effectively meet the needs and the resources for their LatinX student populations.

A significant majority of LatinX undergraduate students, 66 percent, attend HSIs despite these institutions only comprising 18 percent of all colleges and universities in the United States (Excelencia in Education, 2022). Scholarship concerning HSIs has predominantly addressed the educational outcomes of their LatinX student populations (Cuellar, 2015; Nuñez et al., 2010), the cultural dynamics within these institutions (Dayton et al., 2004; Laden, 2001, 2004; Medina & Posadas, 2012), and the impact of these experiences on LatinX students' academic self-perceptions (Cuellar, 2014). HSIs often enroll and graduate students from historically marginalized backgrounds, many of whom are first-generation or come from economically disadvantaged backgrounds upbringings. HSIs disproportionately enroll adult learners and nontraditional students—frequently juggling full-time employment, intermittent college enrollment, the need for developmental education, and commuting from home (Nuñez et al., 2010). Despite federal funding opportunities, HSIs remain widely under-resourced and underfunded, especially as more institutions become HSIs-eligible or emerging. Without sufficient financial support, HSIs will struggle to effectively serve LatinX students who often face financial, academic, and social challenges that require additional institutional resources such as tutoring, counseling, and support programs to support their academic success (Anguiano & Navarro, 2020; HACU, 2021; Malcom et al., 2010; Merisotis & McCarthy, 2005; Nellum & Valle, 2015). Two organizations that are significant in supporting HSIs and LatinX students are Excelencia in Education and Hispanic Association of College & University (HACU), which have been pivotal in developing HSIs, examining how federal funding promotes LatinX success in higher education. Additionally, higher education scholars have examined how institutional actors operationalize the concept of being "Hispanic Serving," how federal designation shapes the organizational culture and functioning of HSIs, and have called for HSI typologies that consider organizational culture and student outcomes (Garcia, 2017; Garcia et al., 2018; Marin & Pereschica, 2017; Nuñez, 2014).

Nuñez (2014) introduced the first typology of HSIs, which has since been expanded to categorize HSIs into six distinct clusters: 1) urban enclave community colleges, 2) rural dispersed community colleges, 3) big systems four-years, 4) small communities four-years, 5) Puerto Rican institutions, and 6) health science schools. Urban enclave community colleges refer to public two-year institutions in urban areas that serve a high proportion of LatinX students, while rural dispersed community colleges serve LatinX students in rural areas. Big-systems four-years are large, four-year institutions that are part of a state or university system, whereas small communities four-years are smaller institutions serving close rural or suburban communities. Puerto Rican institutions refer to institutions of higher education located in Puerto Rico, where the majority of the student body are LatinX. Finally, health science schools are specialized institutions focused on health-related fields such as medical or nursing schools. As a typology framework, Nuñez et al. (2013a) incorporates student enrollment characteristics (such as race and/ or ethnicity, first-generation status, and socioeconomic status) and student-level outcome data to group together similar institutional contexts among the growing number of HSIs, which assists to differentiate the varied institutional contexts within HSI designations. This typology acknowledges the big systems four-year as having the most significant student enrollments of all clusters and provides broad access to students (Nuñez et al., 2013a). However, it is essential to note that access to these institutions, especially R1 four-year institutions, is limited for LatinX students (Mireles-Rios & Garcia, 2019). Based on the Carnegie Classifications of Institutions of Higher Education, an R1 institution refers to having very high research activity and is frequently classified as a selective institution due to its emphasis on research and academic excellence. While LatinX enrollment into R1 four-year insti-tutions grows, LatinX undergraduate students remain underrepresented on these campuses due to factors such as college affordability, geographic prox-imity, and/or campus climate (Mireles-Rios et al., 2024).

Garcia's (2017) typology of HSI organizational culture asks the question, "What does it mean for a postsecondary institution to be Latinx-serving?" (p. 112). Using organizational theory as a lens, Garcia examined the implica-tions of this identity for institutions, emphasizing the importance of under-standing the cultural and operational aspects of serving LatinX students. Garcia (2017) calls attention to how scholars define "Latinx-servingness" and suggests that an institution's *servingness* is not solely determined by the outcomes of its students or an institution's culture but rather the intersection of each. Garcia's (2017) typology considers "legitimized outcomes," which include graduation rates, graduate school enrollment, and employment for LatinX students, how institutional actors experience their environments, and how those lived experiences can help explain an institution's "servingness" (Garcia, 2017). Garcia's (2017) typology has four categories: Latinx-enrolling institutions, Latinx-producing, Latinx-enhancing, and Latinx-serving. Latinx-enrolling institutions enroll the minimum 25 percent requirement of LatinX students to qualify for the HSI federal designation but do not produce equit-able outcomes for this population, nor do they necessarily have a culture that supports their LatinX student population beyond enrollment (Garcia, 2017). Latinx-producing refers to HSIs whose enrollment of LatinX students meets the 25 percent threshold and produce high graduation rates, but may not have a culture that supports the success of these students (Garcia, 2017). Institutions designated as Latinx-enhancing have an organizational iden-tity that meets the federal requirement for enrollment and offers additional resources that support the experiences of LatinX students at that institution (Garcia, 2017). Lastly, the Latinx-serving organizational identity refers to institutions whose enrollment meets the 25 percent LatinX minimum, who fully integrate their mission to serve LatinX students, cultivate an environ-ment that enhances the experiences of their LatinX students, and produce an equitable number of outcomes for their LatinX students compared with the rest of their student body. Extending her work, Garcia (2018) proposes the *Organizational Framework for Decolonizing HSIs*, which accounts for the processes needed to address LatinX student engagement in transforma-tion of organizational culture and complex factors such as the impact of campus climate and addressing the permeation of whiteness. Garcia's (2018) framework outlines nine critical dimensions that institutional actors must address when transforming and implementing efforts to enhance LatinX serv-ingness and student success at HSIs. Garcia (2018), drawing on decolonial and anti-racist ideologies, examines the internal and external characteristics of institutions and identifies nine distinct dimensions:

1. **Purpose Dimension:** HSIs should move beyond traditional outcomes of success like graduate rates to prioritize broader postsecondary goals. This approach emphasizes fostering students' critical and oppositional consciousness and promoting holistic student development.
2. **Mission Dimension:** HSIs' missions should embrace antiracist, antioppressive, and decolonizing ideologies and explicitly incorporate HSI identity into them.
3. **Membership Dimension:** HSIs should foster inclusivity by welcoming members from diverse communities, including students, faculty, staff, alumni, trustees, and community partners. They should work collectively to advance decolonization and liberation.
4. **Technology Dimension:** Educational delivery methods should prioritize the experiences and knowledge of LatinX students. This approach encourages students to explore their identities, challenge oppressive structures, and develop community consciousness.
5. **Governance Dimension:** HSIs should adopt shared, decentralized leadership and decision-making processes, moving away from traditional centralized and bureaucratic structures.
6. **Community Standards Dimension:** Members should participate in developing rules, regulations, and policies. Community standards should complement the decentralized governance structure.
7. **Justice and Accountability Dimension:** Justice within HSIs should be rooted in restorative practices rather than punitive measures like criminal or administrative proceedings.
8. **Incentive Structure Dimension:** HSIs should incentivize faculty and staff to engage in work that enhances racial and cultural understanding.
9. **External Boundary Management Dimension:** HSIs should cultivate relationships with local communities, other HSIs, and organizations like HACU to strengthen their external networks and partnerships.

Taken together, these typologies are significant because they provide a structured way to examine the diverse contexts and challenges within HSIs, moving beyond mere enrollment numbers to consider the cultural and operational factors that impact LatinX student success (Garcia, 2017; Garcia et al., 2018; Nuñez, 2014). Additionally, they assist institutions in evaluating and improving practices for LatinX students, ensuring that servingness is not just about representation but about comprehensive support for academic and personal development. A critical component of successfully implementing these typologies is how the actions of institutional actors such as faculty, administrators, and staff are enacted in defining the success and effectiveness of HSIs in serving LatinX students.

Nuñez et al. (2013a) provide a comprehensive analysis of faculty and administrators within the HSI context. Faculty and administrators at HSIs, particularly those from LatinX racial and ethnic backgrounds, often have a personal investment in their institutions, which can significantly contribute to LatinX student success. The high representation of LatinX faculty and staff promotes inclusive college environments that support postsecondary education and credential completion. When LatinX students see faculty and administrators who reflect their culture, language, and community within their college environment, they find relatable role models. Research indicates that HSI faculty employ effective pedagogical strategies such as class discussions, collaborative learning, reflective thinking, and engaging students as co-creators of knowledge (Hurtado & Ruiz, 2012; Gonzales & Murakami-Ramalho, 2015; Nuñez et al., 2013a, 2013b). Institutional actors must critically examine and understand their own complex identities in relation to the students they serve, as these institutional cultures should embody "innovation, transparency, flexibility, adaptability, and a commitment" to LatinX student success (Nuñez et al., 2013b, p. 90). Garcia and Ramirez (2018) detail how the skill of institutional actors can empower LatinX students through institutional support. Specifically, using the theoretical work of social capital (Stanton-Salazar, 2011), Garcia and Ramirez (2018) found that institutional actors at a public four-year HSIs (i.e., faculty, administrators, staff) use four kinds of social capital: 1) resource agent and political advocate, 2) advocate and networking coach, 3) lobbyist and integrative agent, and 4) bridging agent and institutional broker (Garcia & Ramirez, 2018). A resource agent and political advocate are institutional actors who provide resources to students, such as academic or financial, and advocate for their needs at an institutional or policy level. Advocates and networking coaches are institutional actors who mentor students, advocate for various spaces, and assist them in building social networks that can provide academic and professional opportunities. A lobbyist and integrative agent are institutional actors who actively lobby for institutional change that benefits LatinX students to make them feel integrated into the institution and cultivate a sense of belonging. Finally, a bridging agent and institutional broker are institutional actors who serve as intermediaries between students and the institution and bridge the gaps in understanding and connecting students to critical institutional resources and opportunities. Each role demonstrates how institutional actors can use social capital to empower students, guiding them through academic and non-academic challenges to promote LatinX student academic achievement and success. Garcia and Ramirez (2018) argue that HSIs' institutional actors are crucial in providing tailored support services to LatinX students. Despite extensive research

89

focusing on HSI institutional actors, formal shared-governance structures like governing boards, trustees, faculty senates, and student senates receive scant attention for their roles in contributing to the overall organizational culture. Recently, Garcia (2023) called for greater transformation concerning student support at HSIs, with an emphasis on redistributing power and resources within governance and leadership. Traditionally, formal governance often excludes LatinX students, families, staff, and community members (Garcia, 2023). According to Garcia (2023), HSIs must prioritize racial equity, social justice, and collective liberation by unifying governance and leadership to achieve this transformation. In doing so, an institution's organizational culture can be reimagined by shaping its mission, identity, and purpose while ensuring LatinX students' perspectives are central to curricula, decision-making, and policy. The presence and active involvement of institutional actors are imperative for creating supportive, inclusive environments that assist LatinX students' academic success toward postsecondary degree or credential completion. Overall, HSIs vary widely in size, mission, and student demographics, encompassing diverse institutional types. Despite federal recognition and eligibility for grants aimed at enhancing LatinX student success, HSIs often face resource challenges and how to best serve their LatinX students. In the next section, I conclude the chapter through an examination of social identities that LatinX students bring with them into institutions of higher education, emphasizing the gaps in current research and the need for more inclusive strategies to support the success of all LatinX students.

LATINX STUDENT SUCCESS AND SOCIAL IDENTITIES

For LatinX students, gender differences remain a significant sociocultural factor in their academic achievement and success (Arellano, 2020). Gender among LatinX student success has been a point of exploration focused explicitly on the disproportionately low rate of postsecondary degree or credential completion among LatinX males in comparison with their female counterparts (Sáenz & Ponjuán, 2009). Research on LatinX students and gender viewed from a patriarchal and cisgender lens, meaning a binary, socially constructed framing of male and female in which an individual's gender identity matches the sex assigned at birth, suggests that Latina females are more likely to enroll, persist, and complete a postsecondary degree or credential compared with their male counterparts (Arellano, 2020; Hurtado, 2008; Gonzalez, 2016; Lopez et al., 2020). For Latino males, research suggests that several factors, such as financial barriers (Sáenz & Ponjuán, 2016), not being academically prepared (Sáenz & Ponjuán, 2009), and being pushed out of high school at higher rates than their peers (Garcia et al., 2022) more often prevent them from completing a postsecondary degree or credential compared with their female counterparts.

In any patriarchal system, gender roles matter and directly impact LatinX student success (Gomez Cervantes, 2010; Perez, 2012). For LatinX students, traditional gender roles within LatinX culture and family are described as *machismo* (masculinity) and *marianismo* (femininity) in the field of educational psychology, which higher education research heavily draws from (Hurtado, 1998; Stevens, 1973; Sanchez et al., 2018; Villarreal, 2021; Miville et al., 2017; Castellanos & Gloria, 2007; Rodriguez & Castillo, 2013). Research from elementary to graduate education on *machismo* (masculinity) and *marianismo* (femininity) examines how traditional gender roles, including attitudes, behaviors, values, and beliefs, impact LatinX student academic achievement and success (Hurtado, 1998; Stevens, 1973; Sanchez et al., 2018; Villarreal, 2021; Miville et al., 2017; Castellanos & Gloria, 2007; Rodriguez & Castillo, 2013). For Latino males, machismo refers to qualities such as bravery, reliability, accountability, authority, and the obligation to provide for one's family (Stevens, 1973); whereas, for Latina females, marianismo refers to how they embody the importance of virginity and chastity, as well as spirituality and obedience to males or their families, which is heavily influenced by the Virgin Mary—a foundational figure in Roman Catholicism (Baca Zinn, 1982; Falicov, 1982). Much of educational research has drawn on these and related constructs of gender socialization to explain similarities and differences among LatinX students' academic achievement and success. While social constructions of gender roles are at times helpful, they can also overlook and negate the assets LatinX students and their families possess and draw from such as family, peers, home, and community. To counter the social construction of gender roles among LatinX families and communities, much research has been done on the concepts of *familismo* (family) (Cauce & Domenech-Rodriguez, 2002; Alvarez & Juang, 2010; Martinez, 2013), *respeto* (respect) (Calzada et al., 2010; Lopez et al. 2022), *cariño* (care) (Valenzuela, 1999), and *bien educada/o* (being well educated) (Valdés, 1996; Lopez et al., 2022). These asset-based cultural values provide a holistic understanding of the strengths LatinX students and their families bring to educational institutions, disrupting the limitations of traditional gender role frameworks.

More recently, in higher education research, LatinX students who do not identify within a gender binary but rather through a diverse array of gender identities, gender expressions, and/or sexual orientations are being examined as their perspective and self-identity pertain to their academic achievement and success. Garvey and Dolan (2021) state: "[Student success] literature heteronormatively and cisnormatively flattens students without attending to the unique and identity-specific conditions for QT [Queer and Trans] students . . . [therefore] scholars define student success based on cisgender and heterosexual dominance and identity-neutral politics" (p. 163). Garvey and Dolan (2021) present evidence indicating that students who do not identify within heteronormative and cisgender frameworks have historically been excluded from student success research. Furthermore, the knowledge gap on college students and their academic success becomes even more pronounced when considering intersections of gender identity, gender expression, sexual orientation *and* race, ethnicity, and ethnoracial identity. Over the past 20 years, research examining the experiences of Queer LatinX individuals in higher education has brought several important issues to light (Gonzalez et al., 2023). This body of work addresses the complexities of navigating multiple marginalized identities on and off campus (Peña-Talamantes, 2013). It also emphasizes the experiences and impacts of disclosing non-heteronormative sexualities (Duran & Pérez, 2017; Eaton & Rios, 2017), explores the developmental processes of Queer LatinX college students (Orozco & Perez-Felkner, 2018), and illustrates how Queer LatinX individuals build supportive kinships (Duran et al., 2019; Duran & Pérez, 2019; Hernandez Rivera & Frias, 2021; Revilla, 2010). Emerging from ChicanX Studies, Jotería Studies, which examines Queer LatinX "embodiment of a marginalized identity and a reclamation of spatiality in normalized heteronormative spaces," is newly developing in higher education (see Chapter 4) (Orozco, 2021, p. 179). This research broadens the scope of LatinX student success research in higher education because it challenges traditional heteronormative cisnormative frameworks that have historically dictated the understanding of student achievement and success. Nonetheless, there remains a critical need for studies that explicitly identify, and center, paradigms and frameworks rooted in the knowledge and experiences of Queer and/or Trans-LatinX individuals in student success research (Orozco, 2021) (see Chapters 4 and 5).

Furthermore, it is problematic to treat LatinX students as a homogenous group, as facets of their social identities are multifaceted and dynamic and often intersect with other social identities. Examining LatinX student success at the intersections of gender identity, gender expression, sexual orientation, race, ethnicity, and ethnoracial identity must be approached comprehensively. In higher education research, "culture" is frequently used as a proxy for race, ethnicity, or ethnoracial identity, which complicates the differentiation between systematic oppression and deficit-oriented views of culture. As discussed in Chapter 2, parent–child socialization based on race and ethnicity is complex, contradictory, and non-linear. This complexity similarly applies to LatinX student success concerning race, ethnicity, and ethnoracial identity. Given the high proportion of Mexican American or ChicanX individuals in the United States, much of the higher education research has focused on their experiences (Zerquera et al., 2020). However, it is imperative to expand this research to include the experiences of many other LatinX racial, ethnic, and ethnoracial groups in the context of student success (Gándara & Contreras, 2009; Nuñez, 2014; Hurtado & Sinha,

2016). Extending research to examine how various LatinX subgroups experience academic achievement and success allows for the development of more effective and responsive support systems tailored to the specific needs of these groups.

More recently, research disrupting the homogenous categorizations of race and ethnicity which contribute to anti-Blackness experiences among Afro-LatinX college students is gaining traction in higher education research (Haywood, 2017; Dache et al., 2019a, 2019b; García-Louis & Cortes, 2023). García-Louis (2016) proposed that Afro-LatinX college students encounter a myriad of challenges navigating institutions of higher education cultures *and* racial and/or ethnic barriers, which may complicate their acceptance and perseverance within their own communities and higher education trajectories. In April 2023, the UCLA Latino Policy & Politics Institute released one of the first wide-ranging reports to address the Afro-LatinX population in the United States. The report reveals that Afro-LatinXs, who are considered ethnically LatinX and racially Black, experience significant social inequities compared with their non-Black LatinX peers, especially in occupation placement after postsecondary or credential completion. Despite their higher educational attainment rates compared with the general LatinX population—26 percent of Afro-Latinas and 20 percent of Afro-Latinos have completed a college degree compared with 18 percent and 15 percent of non-Black Latinas and Latinos, respectively—Afro-LatinXs face worse outcomes in areas such as income and homeownership (UCLA LPPI, 2023, p. 5). While this report offers a wide-ranging data portrait of Afro-LatinX postsecondary completion, ongoing research that delves into the unique experiences of this student population concerning academic achievement and student success is needed. Further investigation is required to understand the specific challenges and successes affecting Afro-LatinX students' educational trajectories, addressing the intersectionality of their racial, ethnic, and cultural identities.

Similarly, Indigeneity is often overlooked as it pertains to the LatinX race, ethnicity, and ethnoracial identities, especially regarding the intersections of LatinX academic achievement and student success research in higher education. Blackwell et al. (2017) advocate for a mapping approach that centers on Indigenous migrants from Latin America to redefining Latinidad and Indigeneity in the United States. Blackwell et al. (2017) introduce the concept of Critical Latinx Indigeneities, which, as an analytical framework, recognizes the interconnectedness of various power dynamics and colonial histories of LatinX and Indigenous communities. Blackwell et al. (2017) emphasize that the historical relationship between Latin America and the United States has systematically enforced colonial and racial dominance over Indigenous populations, described as hybrid hegemonies (Blackwell,

2011). Critical Latinx Indigeneities examines these hybrid hegemonies at hemispheric and local levels, examining the impact of settler colonialism displacing, erasing, and eliminating Indigenous people to allow other groups to occupy lands that they previously inhabited (Arvin et al., 2013). To date, and to my knowledge, Sánchez (2020, 2019, 2021) is one of the first scholars in the field of higher education to grapple with how diasporic Indigenous students with ancestral ties to Oaxaca and Guerrero, Mexico, navigate institutions of higher education and the impact on their racial and ethnic identities. Sánchez (2020) found that after enrolling in college, participants' association with their Indigenous ethnic identity strengthened due to their engagement with coursework (Prieto & Villenas, 2012). Culturally responsive courses in Latin American studies offered alternative perspectives on Mexican history, validating indigeneities in their cultural experiences (Sánchez & Machado-Casas, 2009).

Since the 1980s, the Central American population in the United States has grown exponentially but remains underrepresented in research on LatinX academic achievement and student success in higher education (Coronado & Paredes, 2018). Coronado and Paredes (2018) note, "educational research has primarily focused on Mexican/Chicanx student experiences. However, it is also important to address the heterogeneity of the Latinx population by highlighting Central American student experiences" (p. 5). They argue that including Central Americans in higher education research is essential, as immigration issues and policies have profoundly affected their psychosocial, economic, social, political, and educational positioning within the United States (Coronado & Paredes, 2018). Furthermore, Maldonado Dominguez (2019) documents that Central American students at UCLA develop a dual identification as LatinX and U.S. Central American. While Chicanx Studies assisted in mitigating undergraduate LatinX students' emotional isolation in a predominantly white institution, the Mexican dominance faculty representation in the department and curricula limited their full inclusion.

Access to institutions of higher education for undocumented LatinX students varies by state policy. These students may attend institutions of higher education with support from In-state Resident Tuition (ISRT) and state financial aid policies. As of 2024, 24 states and D.C. provide access to ISRT, while nine states actively restrict access, and three prohibit enrollment in public institutions of higher education for undocumented students (Higher Ed Immigration Portal, 2024). Within states, access to ISRT can vary among different higher education systems, and each institution has discretion over implementing these policies (Higher Ed Immigration Portal, 2024). The absence of standardized information on ISRT access poses a significant barrier for undocumented LatinX students, necessitating them to navigate state legislation on an individual basis. Additionally, states such as

California and Texas offer state-issued financial aid, which helps alleviate student financial burdens but still often proves insufficient due to the substantial needs of undocumented LatinX students, who frequently come from economically disadvantaged backgrounds (Bjorklund, 2018; Golash-Boza & Valdez, 2018; Teranishi et al., 2015). Despite benefiting from these supportive policies in several states, LatinX undocumented students continue to encounter specific challenges due to the fragmented and inconsistent nature of these resources. Moreover, the legal status of LatinX undocumented students contributes to them encountering systemic barriers that further complicate their access to and persistence in higher education (Golash-Boza & Valdez, 2018). Like other students with historically disadvantaged or marginalized identities, undocumented LatinX students require assistance navigating the complexities of higher education institutions such as access to financial aid, legal resources, emotional and mental health support, and culturally responsive support services. Furthermore, for LatinX undocumented students, the fragmented nature of immigration policies and institutional support often leaves these students navigating complex and inconsistent systems, exacerbated by race, racism, and white supremacy and a lack of guidance from uninformed institutional actors (Bjorklund, 2018; Castrellón, 2021, 2022; Tapia-Fuselier, 2021). Therefore, LatinX students with undocumented status frequently find themselves needing to ask multiple institutional actors the same questions and receiving conflicting answers (Castrellón, 2021, 2022). They report feeling unsupported once they disclose their undocumented status to institutional actors (Castrellón, 2021; Cisneros & Valdivia, 2020), a decision that is deeply personal and often driven by safety concerns (Abrego, 2008, 2011; Aguilar, 2019; Bjorklund, 2018). In the current political climate, characterized by persistent anti-immigrant sentiments in the aftermath of the Trump presidency, undocumented LatinX students face heightened anxiety about finding trusted allies, which complicates their decision to disclose their legal status to unfamiliar individuals (Abrego, 2008, 2011; Aguilar, 2019; Bjorklund, 2018; Escudero et al., 2019; Hall, 2022; Lachica Buenavista, 2018; Lara, 2023; Muñiz et al., 2018).

In addressing gender identity, gender expression, sexual orientation, race, ethnicity, and ethnoracial identity among LatinX students, higher education institutions can develop interventions and policies that support the holistic success of all LatinX students, ensuring they are not rendered invisible within academic research or discourse. Gender roles, cultural expectations, and intersectional identities play significant roles in shaping these experiences, particularly for subgroups such as Central Americans, Afro-LatinX, and LatinX Indigenous students. Overall, addressing the diverse experiences of LatinX students is crucial for fostering their academic success in higher education.

CONCLUSION

In conclusion, this chapter examines LatinX academic achievement and student success focusing on the critical research of Nuñez et al. (2013b), Crisp et al. (2015), and Valverde (2002, 2012), who define and analyze indicators such as sociocultural factors and academic performance and how they impact post-secondary degree or credential completion. I also address how and why public two-year intuitions and HSIs are vital in providing access to a postsecondary education for LatinX students despite these institutions encountering resource limitations which impact how they serve their students. Finally, this chapter discusses the social identities LatinX students bring with them into institutions of higher education, emphasizing the gaps in current research and the need for more inclusive strategies to support the success of all LatinX students.

DISCUSSION QUESTIONS

Using the content within this chapter, consider the following questions for reflection and discussion:

- How can cultural and historical connections impact students' academic achievement and success? In what ways can institutions of higher education and their actors support LatinX students in connecting to their culture, values, and traditions?
- How can LatinX students balance familial and institutional expectations while pursuing their academic interests?
- How do the social identities of Afro-LatinX and non-binary students influence their navigation of institutions of higher education? What actions can institutions of higher education and their actors take to create supportive environments that promote student success and personal expression for LatinX students with diverse identities?

NOTES

1. I use "their" and "they" as a singular pronoun to promote gender inclusivity and to avoid assumptions about gender based on cisgender and heteronormative discourse.
2. Brooklyn College has a rich history as part of the City of New York City (CUNY) system in New York. Known for its focus on the liberal arts and sciences, the college is also designated as a Hispanic-Serving Institution (HSI), with at least 25 percent of the undergraduate population identified as "Hispanic." This reflects the diverse LatinX population of New York City and the borough of Brooklyn.
3. "Pa'lante" is a song by the band Hurray for the Riff Raff, led by Alynda Segarra, who identifies as Puerto Rican. The band is known for blending folk,

Americana, and indie rock and their commitment to social justice and activism. The song "Pa'lante" is in response to colonization and displacement, especially in the wake of Hurricane Irma and Maria, which devastated the island in 2017. The song serves as an ode to the Puerto Rican diaspora.

4. Similar to Brooklyn College, Hunter College is part of the CUNY system. In 1969, Hunter College students and faculty advocated for the creation of a Puerto Rican Studies Department in direct response to the marginalization of Puerto Rican students and the rise of activism across the nation for civil rights and educational reform.

5. Segarra directly references Pedro Pietri, a well-known Puerto Rican poet, in the spoken word portion of the song, quoting his prolific poem "Puerto Rican Obituary," which documents the Puerto Rican in New York during the 1970s, emphasizing the struggle with low-wage labor, poor living conditions, racism, and the myth of meritocracy.

6. The Young Lords were a Puerto Rican nationalist and civil rights organization founded in Chicago in 1968, which later expanded to New York City. Inspired by the Black Panther Party, the Young Lords advocated for the rights of Puerto Ricans in the United States and on the Island.

7. On September 23, 1969, Pedro Pietri recited "Puerto Rican Obituary" during a rally commemorating El Grito de Lares, a historic revolt against Spanish colonial rule in 1868. The event took place at Saint Mary's Park in the South Bronx.

8. "Non-binary Afro-Nuyorican" refers to an individual who identifies as non-binary in terms of gender, is of African descent and identifies with the LatinX community, and belongs to the Nuyorican community, which consists of Puerto Ricans whose lived experiences are part of the Puerto Rican diaspora in New York City.

9. Founded in 1973, Centro was established in response to the growing demand from Puerto Rican students, faculty, and activists for institutional support and academic resources focused on the Puerto Rican experience. It is considered a hub for research and preservation of Puerto Rican history, culture, and activism.

10. Founded in 1961 by Dr. Antonia Pantoja, ASPIRA was created in New York City to address the educational needs of Puerto Rican students, who were experiencing high push-out rates and injustice in the city's public schools. For more information see: https://aspira.org/about-us/our-founder-dra-antonia-pantoja/

11. Centro's library and archives hold one of the largest collections dedicated to the Puerto Rican diaspora, including historical documents, oral histories, photographs, and other materials. Centro houses the archive of handwritten manuscripts of Pedro Pietri.

12. Elizabeth Acevedo is an award-winning Afro-Dominican author and poet, known for her young adult fiction books *The Poet X* and *With the Fire on High*, which examine identity, culture, and the experiences of Afro-LatinX youth. Gabby Rivera is a Puerto Rican author and comic book writer, they are known for their young adult novel *Juliet Takes a Breath* and for writing Marvel's "America" series, featuring America Chaves, the first LatinX LGBTQ superhero. Rivera's work focuses on queer LatinX identity and feminisms.

13. In this chapter, I use the original authors' terminology in their studies. When I switch to using "LatinX," it signals that I am offering my interpretations, connections, and arguments.

14. Although U.S. federal and state government entities use "Hispanic" in their official definitions and documents, I will use "LatinX" whenever referring to the population, students, and their families.

REFERENCES

Abrego, L. J. (2008). Legitimacy, social identity, and the mobilization of law: The effects of Assembly Bill 540 on undocumented students in California. *Law & Social Inquiry, 33*(3), 709–734.

Abrego, L. J. (2011). Legal consciousness of undocumented Latinos: Fear and stigma as barriers to claims-making for first-and 1.5-generation immigrants. *Law & Society Review, 45*(2), 337–370.

Acevedo-Gil, N. (2018). The role of community colleges in fostering Latina/o educational achievement and socioeconomic mobility. *Community College Journal of Research and Practice, 42*(7–8), 509–515. https://doi.org/10.1080/10668926.2018.1429967

Acevedo-Gil, N., Santos, R. E., Alonso, L., & Solórzano, D. G. (2015). Examining the transfer conditions of Latina/o community college students: A case study of baccalaureate aspirations and limitations. *Journal of Hispanic Higher Education, 14*(1), 17–35. https://doi.org/10.1177/1538192714551085

Aguilar, J. (2019). The effect of Deferred Action for Childhood Arrivals on unauthorized youth: Evidence from California. *Journal of Policy Analysis and Management, 38*(2), 338–366.

Alcantar, C. M., & Hernandez, I. (2020). Validating Latinx students at public two-year Hispanic-serving institutions. *Journal of Diversity in Higher Education, 13*(2), 123–134.

Alvarez, A. N., & Juang, L. P. (2010). Filipino American college students' family conflict and support and their relationships to academic achievement. *Journal of College Student Development, 51*(3), 314–328.

Anguiano, V., & Navarro, A. (2020). Hispanic-serving institutions need $1 billion more in federal funding. *Center for American Progress*. Retrieved from https://www.americanprogress.org/article/hispanic-serving-institutions-need-1-billion-federal-funding/

Arellano, L. (2020). Capitalizing baccalaureate degree attainment: Identifying student and institution level characteristics that ensure success for Latinxs. *The Journal of Higher Education, 91*(4), 588–619.

Arvin, M., Tuck, E., & Morrill, A. (2013). Decolonizing feminism: Challenging connections between settler colonialism and heteropatriarchy. *Feminist Formations, 25*(1), 8–34.

Baca Zinn, M. (1982). Chicano men and masculinity. *Journal of Ethnic Studies, 10*(2), 29–44.

Bailey, T. R., & Smith Morest, V. (2006). *Defending the community college equity agenda*. Johns Hopkins University Press.

Bailey, T. R., Jaggars, S. S., & Jenkins, D. (2015). *Redesigning America's community colleges: A clearer path to student success*. Harvard University Press.

Barnett, E. A. (2010). Validation experiences and persistence among community college students. *The Review of Higher Education*, 34, 193–230. https://doi.org/10.1353/rhe.2010.0019

Bensimon, E. M. (2007). The underestimated significance of practitioner knowledge in the scholarship on student success. *The Review of Higher Education*, 30(4), 441–469. https://doi.org/10.1353/rhe.2007.0032

Bensimon, E. M., Dowd, A. C., & Stanton-Salazar, R. (2019). The role of institutional agents in providing institutional support to Latinx students in STEM. *The Review of Higher Education*. Retrieved from https://muse.jhu.edu/pub/1/article/729358/summary

Bjorklund, P. (2018). Legal status as a social determinant of health for undocumented Latino students: A participatory action research study. *Journal of Adolescence*, 62(3), 37–48.

Blackwell, M. (2011). Geographies of indigeneity: Indigenous migrant women's organizing and translocal politics of place. *Gender, Place & Culture*, 18(5), 668–686.

Blackwell, M., Boj-Lopez, M. A., & Urrieta Jr, L. (2017). Critical Latinx Indigeneities: Unsettling, reimagining, and delinking indigeneity from the nation-state. *Latino Studies*, 15(2), 126–137.

Bourdieu, P. (1986). The forms of capital. In J. G. Richardson (Ed.), *Handbook of theory and research for the sociology of education* (pp. 241–258). Greenwood Press.

Calzada, E. J., Fernandez, Y. P., & Cortes, D. E. (2010). Incorporating the cultural value of respeto into a framework of Latino parenting. *Cultural Diversity and Ethnic Minority Psychology*, 16(1), 77–86.

Carales, V. D. (2020). Examining educational attainment outcomes: A focus on Latina/o community college students. *Community College Review*, 48(2), 195–219.

Carnevale, A. P., Strohl, J., & Gulish, A. (2019). *The overlooked value of certificates and associate's degrees: What students need to know before they go to college.* Georgetown University, Center on Education and the Workforce.

Castellanos, J., & Gloria, A. M. (2007). Research considerations and theoretical application for best practices in higher education: Latina/os achieving success. *Journal of Hispanic Higher Education*, 6(3), 1–22. https://vtechworks.lib.vt.edu/bitstream/handle/10919/83002/ResearchConsiderationsLatinosSuccess.pdf?sequence=1&isAllowed=y

Castrellón, L. E. (2021). Navigating systems of illegality: Institutional actors and the undocumented Latinx student experience. *Review of Higher Education*, 45(2), 181–205.

Castrellón, L. E. (2022). The complexities of disclosing undocumented status: Experiences of Latinx students at four-year public institutions. *Journal of College Student Development*, 63(3), 309–326.

Cauce, A. M., & Domenech-Rodriguez, M. (2002). Latino families: Myths and realities. In J. M. Contreras, K. A. Kerns, & A. M. Neal-Barnett (Eds.), *Latino children and families in the United States: Current research and future directions* (pp. 3–25). Praeger.

Cejda, B. D., & Rhodes, J. H. (2004). Through the pipeline: The role of faculty in promoting associate degree completion among Hispanic students. *Community College Journal of Research and Practice, 28*(3), 249–262.

Chang, J. C. (2005). Faculty-student interaction at the community college: A focus on students of color. *Research in Higher Education, 46,* 769–802. https://doi.org/10.1007/s11162-004-6225-7

Cisneros, J., & Valdivia, C. (2020). Undocumented Latinx students navigating higher education: Disclosure decisions and the role of institutional agents. *Journal of Hispanic Higher Education, 19*(4), 348–362.

Contreras, F., Malcom, L., & Bensimon, E. M. (2008). Hispanic-serving institutions: Closeted identity and the production of equitable outcomes for Latino/a students. In M. Gasman, B. Baez, & C. S. V. Turner (Eds.), *Understanding minority-serving institutions* (pp. 71–90). State University of New York Press.

Coronado, H. M., & Paredes, A. D. (2018). From invisible to visible: Documenting the voices and resilience of Central American students in US schools. *Interactions: UCLA Journal of Education and Information Studies, 15*(1).

Crisp, G., & Nora, A. (2010). Hispanic student success: Factors influencing persistence and transfer in higher education. *Journal of College Student Retention: Research, Theory & Practice, 12*(2), 153–177.

Crisp, G., Taggart, A., & Nora, A. (2015). Student characteristics, pre-college, and environmental factors predicting Latino/a academic success in higher education: A moderated mediation analysis. *Research in Higher Education, 56*(6), 595–645.

Cuellar, M. (2012). *Latina/o student success in higher education: Models of empowerment at Hispanic-serving institutions (HSIs), emerging HSIs, and non-HSIs* (Order No. 3497388).

Cuellar, M. (2014). The impact of Hispanic-serving institutions (HSIs), emerging HSIs, and non-HSIs on Latina/o academic self-concept. *The Review of Higher Education, 37*(4), 499–530.

Cuellar, M. (2015). Latina/o student characteristics and outcomes at four-year Hispanic-serving institutions (HSIs), emerging HSIs, and non-HSIs. In A.-M. Núñez, S. Hurtado, & E. Calderón Galdeano (Eds.), *Hispanic-serving institutions: Advancing research and transformative practice* (pp. 101–120). Routledge.

Dache, A., Haywood, J. C., & King, J. (2019a). AfroLatinx college students' experiences with racism and institutional discrimination. *The Urban Review, 51*(3), 412–431.

Dache, A., Haywood, J. M., & Mislán, C. (2019b). A badge of honor not shame: An AfroLatina theory of Black-imiento for US higher education research. *Journal of Negro Education, 88*(2), 130–145.

Dawson, R. F., Kearney, M. S., & Sullivan, J. X. (2021, April 7). Why expanded student supports can improve community college outcomes and boost skill attainment. *Brookings*. https://www.brookings.edu/blog/brown-center-chalkboard/2021/04/07/why-expanded-student-supports-can-improve-community-college-outcomes-and-boost-skill-attainment/

Dayton, B., Gonzalez-Vasquez, N., Martinez, C. R., & Plum, C. (2004). Hispanic-serving institutions through the eyes of students and administrators. *New Directions for Student Services, 2004*(105), 29–40.

Del Real Viramontes, J. R. (2021). Latina/o transfer students and community cultural wealth: Expanding the transfer receptive culture framework. *Community College Journal of Research and Practice, 45*(12), 855–870.

Doran, E. (2023). Toward a new understanding of Hispanic-serving community colleges. *Community College Review, 51*(2), 285–305.

Dougherty, K. J. (1994). *The contradictory college: The conflicting origins, impacts, and futures of the community college.* State University of New York Press.

Dowd, A. C. (2007). Community colleges as gateways and gatekeepers: Moving beyond the access "saga" toward outcome equity. *Harvard Educational Review, 77*(4), 407–419.

Dowd, A. C., Pak, J. H., & Bensimon, E. M. (2013). The role of institutional agents in promoting transfer access. *Education Policy Analysis Archives, 21*(15), 1–40.

Duran, A., & Pérez, D. II. (2017). Supporting queer Latinx students in higher education. *Journal of Diversity in Higher Education, 10*(1), 66–77.

Duran, A., & Pérez, D. II. (2019). The multiple roles of chosen familia: Examining the interconnections of queer Latino men's community cultural wealth. *International Journal of Qualitative Studies in Education, 32*(1), 67–84.

Duran, A., Rodriguez, F., & Patron, O. E. (2019). Queer love in the lives of gay Latino men in college. *International Journal of Qualitative Studies in Education, 33*(9), 905–920. https://doi.org/10.1080/09518398.2019.1687957

Eaton, A. A., & Rios, D. (2017). Social challenges faced by queer Latino college men: Navigating negative responses to coming out in a double minority sample of emerging adults. *Cultural Diversity and Ethnic Minority Psychology, 23*(4), 457–467. https://doi.org/10.1037/cdp0000134

Excelencia in Education. (2022). *Hispanic-Serving Institutions (HSIs) Infographic: 2020–21.* Washington, D.C.: Excelencia in Education. https://www.edexcelencia.org/research/infographics/hsis-infographic-2020-21

Excelencia in Education. (2024). *Hispanic-Serving Institutions (HSIs): 2022–23.* Washington, D.C.: Excelencia in Education.

Falicov, C. J. (1982). Mexican families. In M. McGoldrick, J. K. Pearce, & J. Giordano (Eds.), *Ethnicity and family therapy* (pp. 134–163). Guilford Press.

Felix, E. R. (2020). Using state-equity reform to improve Latinx student transfer. *Association of Mexican American Educators Journal, 14*(1), 21–48.

Gándara, P., & Contreras, F. (2009). *The Latino education crisis: The consequences of failed social policies.* Harvard University Press.

Garcia, G. A. (2017). What does it mean to be Latinx-serving? Testing the utility of the typology of HSI organizational identities. *Association of Mexican American Educators Journal, 11*(3), 109–138.

Garcia, G. A. (2018). Decolonizing Hispanic-serving institutions: A framework for organizing. *Journal of Hispanic Higher Education, 17*(2), 132–147.

Garcia, G. A. (2023). *Transforming Hispanic-Serving Institutions for equity and justice.* Johns Hopkins University Press.

Garcia, G. A., & Hurtado, S. (2011). Predicting Latina/o academic success: The role of campus climate and faculty interactions. In J. C. Smart & M. B. Paulsen (Eds.), *Higher education: Handbook of theory and research* (Vol. 26, pp. 101–148). Springer.

Garcia, G. A., & Ramirez, J. J. (2018). Institutional agents at a Hispanic-serving institution: Using social capital to empower students. *Urban Education.* Retrieved from https://www.academia.edu/download/47076871/Urban_Education-2015-Garcia-Ramirez.pdf

Garcia, N. M., Ibarra, J. M., Mireles-Rios, R., Rios, V. M., & Maldonado, K. (2022). Advancing QuantCrit to rethink the school-to-prison pipeline for Latinx and Black youth. *Journal of Criminal Justice Education, 33*(2), 269–288.

García-Louis, C. (2016). *Invisible no more: AfroLatina/o undergraduate students' sense of belonging and persistence at a small urban northeastern college* (Publication No. 101) [doctoral dissertation, University of Texas at Austin]. University of Texas Libraries.

García-Louis, C., & Cortes, K. L. (2023). Rejecting Black and rejected back: AfroLatinx college students' experiences with anti-AfroLatinidad. *Journal of Latinos and Education, 22*(1), 182–197.

Garvey, J. C., & Dolan, C. V. (2021). Queer and trans college student success: A comprehensive review and call to action. In M. B. Paulsen (Ed.), *Higher education: Handbook of theory and research: Volume 36* (pp. 161–215). Springer.

Gay, G. (2018). *Culturally responsive teaching: Theory, research, and practice* (3rd ed.). Teachers College Press.

Golash-Boza, T., & Valdez, Z. (2018). Nested contexts of reception: Undocumented students at the University of California, Central. *Sociological Perspectives, 61*(4), 535–552.

Gomez Cervantes, A. (2010). Breaking stereotypes by obtaining a higher education: Latinas' family values and tradition on the school institution. *McNair Scholars Journal, 14*(1), 43–60. https://scholarworks.gvsu.edu/cgi/viewcontent.cgi?article=1237&context=mcnair

Gonzales, L. D., & Murakami-Ramalho, E. (2015). The horizon of possibilities: How HSI faculty can reshape the production and legitimization of knowledge within academia. In J. P. Mendez, F. A. Bonner II, J. Méndez-Negrete, & R. T. Palmer (Eds.), *Hispanic-serving institutions in American higher education: Their origin, and present and future challenges* (pp. 153–172). Stylus Publishing.

Gonzalez, Á. D. J., Orozco, R. C., & Gonzalez, S. A. (2023). Joteando y mariconadas: Theorizing queer pláticas for queer and/or trans Latinx/a/o research. *International Journal of Qualitative Studies in Education, 36*(9), 1741–1756.

Gonzalez, M. J. (2016). Values and gender role orientation in gender role conflict with a sample of Latinas pursuing higher education at a Hispanic Serving Institution [doctoral dissertation]. *University of Georgia.* http://getd.libs.uga.edu/pdfs/gonzalez_marta_j_201612_phd.pdf

Haywood, J. M. (2017). "Latino spaces have always been the most violent": Afro-Latino collegians' experiences with colorism and Black exclusion. *International Journal of Qualitative Studies in Education, 30*(8), 759–782.

Hernandez Rivera, S., & Frias, D. S. (2021). *Iluminando la oscuridad*: Queer Latinas healing in Spanish through *conocimiento*. *Journal of Women and Gender in Higher Education, 14*(1), 5–23.

Higher Ed Immigration Portal. (2024). *State policies on in-state tuition for undocumented students.* Higher Ed Immigration Portal. https://www.higheredimmigrationportal.org/

Higher Education Act of 1965, Pub. L. No. 89–329, 79 Stat. 1219 (1965). https://www.govinfo.gov/content/pkg/STATUTE-79/pdf/STATUTE-79-Pg1219.pdf

Hispanic Association of Colleges and Universities (HACU). (2018). *HSI definition.* Retrieved from https://www.hacu.net/hacu/HSI_Definition1.asp

Hispanic Association of Colleges and Universities (HACU). (2021). *HACU statement on HSI funding allocations in year-end spending and COVID-19 relief bill.* Retrieved from https://www.hacu.net/NewsBot.asp?ID=3273&MODE=VIEW

Hurtado, A. (1998). Sitios y lenguas: Chicanas theorize feminisms. *Hypatia, 13*(2), 134–161.

Hurtado, S. (Ed.). (2008). *Advancing in higher education: A portrait of Latina/o college freshmen at four-year institutions, 1975–2006.* Higher Education Research Institute.

Hurtado, S., & Ruiz, A. (2012). The climate for underrepresented groups and diversity on campus. *Higher Education Research Institute.*

Hurtado, S., & Sinha, M. (2016). More than symbolic moments: The influence of diversity on learning and teaching experiences in higher education. *Association for the Study of Higher Education (ASHE) Higher Education Report.*

Jain, D., Herrera, A., Bernal, S., & Solórzano, D. (2011). Critical race theory and the transfer function: Introducing a transfer receptive culture. *Community College Journal of Research and Practice, 35*(3), 252–266.

Jain, D., Bernal Melendez, S. N., & Herrera, A. R. (2020). *Power to the transfer: Critical race theory and a transfer receptive culture.* Michigan State University Press.

Kurlaender, M. (2006). Choosing community college: Factors affecting Latino college choice. *New Directions for Community Colleges, 2006*(133), 7–16.

Laden, B. V. (2001). Hispanic-serving institutions: Myths and realities. *Peabody Journal of Education, 76*(1), 73–92.

Laden, B. V. (2004). Hispanic-serving institutions: What are they? Where are they? *Community College Journal of Research and Practice, 28*(3), 181–198.

Lopez, C., Vazquez, M., & McCormick, A. S. (2022). Familismo, respeto, and bien educado: Traditional/cultural models and values in Latinos. In M. H. L. B. Shields & H. H. W. Chen (Eds.), *Family literacy practices in Asian and Latinx families: Educational and cultural considerations* (pp. 87–102). Springer International Publishing.

Lopez, D., Ochoa, D., Romero, M., & Parr, K. (2020). Integrating Latinx/Hispanic culture, traditions, and beliefs into effective school psychology practice. *Communique, 48*(4), 1–4. https://www.researchgate.net/profile/Monica-Romero-6/publication/ 348309418_Integrating_LatinxHispanic_culture_traditions_and_beliefs_ into_effective_school_psychology_practice/links/5ff73f4645851553a02adb46/ Integrating-Latinx-Hispanic-culture-traditions-and-beliefs-into-effective-school- psychology-practice.pdf?origin=journalDetail&_tp=eyJwYWdlljoiam91cm5hbE RldGFpbCJ9

Malcom, L. E., Bensimon, E. M., & Davila, B. A. (2010). (Re)constructing Hispanic- serving institutions: Moving beyond numbers toward student success. *Education Policy and Practice Perspectives, 6*(1), 1–12.

Maldonado Dominguez, K. J. (2019). US Central American students in higher educa- tion: Finding a sense of belonging. *Aleph, UCLA Undergraduate Research Journal for the Humanities and Social Sciences, 16*.

Marin, P., & Pereschica, P. (2017). Becoming a Hispanic-serving research institution: Involving graduate students in organizational change. *Association of Mexican American Educators Journal, 11*(3), 154–177.

Martinez, M., & Fernández, E. (2004). Latinos at community colleges. *New Directions for Student Services, 105*, 51–62. https://doi.org/10.1002/ss.116

Martinez, M. A. (2013). (Re) considering the role *familismo* plays in Latina/o high school students' college choices. *The High School Journal, 97*(1), 21–40.

Medina, C. A., & Posadas, C. E. (2012). Hispanic student experiences at a Hispanic- serving institution: Strong voices, key message. *Journal of Latinos and Education, 11*(3), 182–188.

Merisotis, J. P., & McCarthy, K. (2005). Retention and student success at minority- serving institutions. *New Directions for Institutional Research, 2005*(125), 45–58.

Mireles-Rios, R., & Garcia, N. M. (2019). What would your ideal graduate mentoring program look like?: Latina/o student success in higher education. *Journal of Latinos and Education*, 18(4), 376–386.

Mireles-Rios, R., Garcia, N. M., Castro, I. M. J., Hernandez, M., & Cerda, R. (2024). Racial micro-affirmations: Latinx close friendships and ethnic identity development. *Education Sciences*, 14(7), 737.

Miville, M. L., Mendez, N., & Louie, M. (2017). Latina/o gender roles: A content analysis of empirical research from 1982 to 2013. *Journal of Latina/o Psychology*, 5(1), 1–22. https://psycnet.apa.org/record/2016-60838-001

National Academies of Sciences, Engineering, and Medicine (NASEM). (2019). *Minority serving institutions: America's underutilized resource for strengthening the STEM workforce*. The National Academies Press. https://doi.org/10.17226/25257

National Center for Education Statistics. (2020). *The Condition of Education 2020*. U.S. Department of Education. https://nces.ed.gov/programs/coe/indicator_csa.asp

Nellum, C. J., & Valle, K. (2015). *Government investment in public Hispanic-serving institutions*. American Council on Education. Retrieved from https://www.acenet.edu/Documents/Government-Investment-in-Public-Hispanic-Serving-Institutions.pdf

Nelson Laird, T. F., Bridges, B. K., Morelon-Quainoo, C. L., Williams, J. M., & Holmes, M. S. (2007). African American and Hispanic student engagement at minority serving and predominantly White institutions. *Journal of College Student Development*, 48(1), 39–56.

Nuñez, A.-M. (2014). Advancing an intersectionality framework in higher education: Power and Latino postsecondary opportunity. In M. B. Paulsen (Ed.), *Higher education: Handbook of theory and research* (pp. 33–92). Springer.

Nuñez, A.-M., Crisp, G., & Elizondo, D. (2013a). Mapping Hispanic-serving institutions: A typology of institutional diversity. *The Journal of Higher Education*, 87(1), 55–83. https://doi.org/10.1080/00221546.2016.11777368

Nuñez, A.-M., Murakami-Ramalho, E., & Cuero, K. K. (2010). Pedagogy for equity: Teaching in a Hispanic-serving institution. *Innovative Higher Education*, 35(3), 177–190.

Nuñez, A.-M., Hoover, R. E., Pickett, K., Stuart-Carruthers, A. C., & Vázquez, M. (2013b). *Latinos in higher education and Hispanic-serving institutions: Creating conditions for success*. Wiley/Jossey-Bass.

Orozco, R. C. (2021). A futurity of Jotería studies and higher education research: Epistemological and theoretical shifts. In N. Garcia, C. Salinas, & J. Cisneros (Eds.), *Studying Latinx/a/o students in higher education* (pp. 175–187). Routledge. https://doi.org/10.4324/9781003008545-14

Orozco, R. C., & Perez-Felkner, L. (2018). *Ni de aquí, ni de allá*: Conceptualizing the self-authorship experience of gay Latino college men using *conocimiento*. *Journal*

of Latinos and Education, 17(4), 386–394. https://doi.org/10.1080/15348431.2
017.1371018

Peña-Talamantes, A. E. (2013). Empowering the self, creating worlds: Lesbian and
gay Latina/o college students' identity negotiation in figured worlds. *Journal
of College Student Development, 54*(3), 267–282. https://doi.org/10.1353/
csd.2013.0039

Perez, J. J. (2012). The influence of Latino/a gender roles and culture on student achievement and resistance (Doctoral dissertation). *University of North Carolina.* https://
cdr.lib.unc.edu/downloads/pr76f4544

Pérez, P. A., & Ceja, M. (2010). Building a Latina/o student transfer culture: Best
practices and outcomes in transfer to universities. *Journal of Hispanic Higher
Education, 9*(1), 6–21. https://doi.org/10.1177/1538192709350073

Perna, L. W., Rowan-Kenyon, H. T., Thomas, S. L., Bell, A., Anderson, R., & Li, C.
(2008a). The role of college counseling in shaping college opportunity: Variations
across high schools. *The Review of Higher Education, 31*, 131–159. https://doi.
org/10.1353/rhe.0.0025

Perna, L. W., Lundy-Wagner, V., Drezner, N. D., Gasman, M., Yoon, S., Bose, E., &
Gary, S. (2008b). The contributions of HBCUs to the preparation of African
American women for STEM careers: A case study. *Research in Higher Education,
50*(1), 1–23. https://doi.org/10.1007/s11162-008-9101-5

Prieto, L., & Villenas, S. (2012). Reframing the discourse on Latino students. *Journal
of Latinos and Education, 11*(1), 23–40.

Rendon. L. I. (1994). Validating culturally diverse students: Toward a new model of
learning and student development. *Innovative Higher Education, 19*, 33–51.

Revilla, A. T. (2010). Raza womyn—Making it safe to be queer: Student organizations
as retention tools in higher education. *Black Women, Gender & Families, 4*(1),
37–61.

Rodriguez, K. M., & Castillo, L. G. (2013). The influence of marianismo, ganas,
and academic motivation on Latina adolescents' academic achievement inten-
tions. *Journal of Latina/o Psychology, 1*(4), 218–231. https://www.academia.
edu/download/87603922/lat000000820220616-1-649bbr.pdf

Sáenz, V. B., & Ponjuán, L. (2009). The vanishing Latino male in higher education. *Journal of Hispanic Higher Education, 8*(1), 54–89.

Sáenz, V. B., & Ponjuán, L. (2016). *Ensuring the success of Latino males in higher
education: A national imperative.* Stylus Publishing.

Sanchez, D., Smith, L. V., & Adams, W. (2018). Among perceived discrimination, marianismo gender role attitudes, racial-ethnic socialization, coping styles, and mental
health outcomes in Latina college students. *Journal of Latina/o Psychology, 6*(1),
1–14. https://www.ncbi.nlm.nih.gov/pmc/articles/PMC10888508/

Sánchez, G. K. (2019). *Affirming Indigeneity in Public Spaces: Indigenous Mexican
Testimonios About Higher Education* (Doctoral dissertation). The Claremont
Graduate University.

Sánchez, G. K. (2020). Reaffirming Indigenous identity: Understanding experiences of stigmatization and marginalization among Mexican Indigenous college students. *Journal of Latinos and Education*, 19(1), 31–34.

Sánchez, G. K. (2021). "If we don't do it, nobody is going to talk about it": Indigenous students disrupting Latinidad at Hispanic-Serving Institutions. *AERA Open*, 7(1), 1–14.

Sánchez, P., & Machado-Casas, M. (2009). Advancing a critical understanding of race and power in the context of Latino student experiences. *International Journal of Qualitative Studies in Education*, 22(5), 625–642.

Santiago, D., Arroyo, C., & Cuellarsola, L. (April 2024). *Latinos in Higher Education: 2024 Compilation of Fast Facts*. Washington, D.C.: Excelencia in Education.

Shapiro, D., Dundar, A., Wakhungu, P. K., Yuan, X., & Harrell, A. (2019). *Completing college: A national view of student completion rates—Fall 2013 cohort (Signature Report No. 16)*. National Student Clearinghouse Research Center.

Santiago, D. A. (2007). *Choosing Hispanic-serving institutions (HSIs): A closer look at Latino students' college choices*. Excelencia in Education. Retrieved from https://www.edexcelencia.org/research/choosing-hispanic-serving-institutions-hsis-closer-look-latino-students-college-choices

Solórzano, D. G., & Delgado Bernal, D. (2001). Examining transformational resistance through a critical race and LatCrit theory framework: Chicana and Chicano students in an urban context. *Urban Education*, 36(3), 308–342. https://doi.org/10.1177/0042085901363002

Stanton-Salazar, R. D. (2011). A social capital framework for the study of institutional agents and their role in the empowerment of low-status students and youth. *Youth & Society*, 43(3), 1066–1109. https://doi.org/10.1177/0044118X10382877

Stanton-Salazar, R. D., Vasquez, O. A., & Mehan, H. (2000). Engineering academic success through institutional support. *Educational Policy*, 14(3), 333–352. https://doi.org/10.1177/0895904800014003004

Stevens, E. P. (1973). Marianismo: The other face of machismo in Latin America. In A. Pescatello (Ed.), *Female and male in Latin America* (pp. 89–101). University of Pittsburgh Press.

Tapia-Fuselier, N. (2021). Enhancing Institutional Undocu-Competence through Establishing Undocumented Student Resource Centers: A Student-Encompassed Approach. *Journal of College Access*, 6(2), 132–145.

Teranishi, R. T., Suárez-Orozco, C., & Suárez-Orozco, M. M. (2015). In the shadows of the ivory tower: Undocumented undergraduates and the liminal state of immigration reform. *The UndocuScholars Project at the Institute for Immigration, Globalization, and Education, University of California, Los Angeles*.

Tovar, E. (2015). The role of faculty, counselors, and support programs on Latino/a community college students' success and intent to persist. *Community College Review*. https://doi.org/10.1177/0091552115574568

Tribally Controlled Community College Assistance Act of 1978, Pub. L. No. 95–471, 92 Stat. 1325 (1978).

UCLA Latino Policy & Politics Institute (UCLA LPPI). (2023). *The labor market experiences of working-age Afro-Latinxs*. UCLA Latino Policy & Politics Institute. Retrieved from https://latino.ucla.edu/research/afro-latinx-labor-market/

U.S. Department of Education. (n.d.). *Hispanic-Serving Institutions—Science, Technology, Engineering, or Mathematics and Articulation Programs*. Retrieved from https://www.ed.gov/grants-and-programs/grants-special-populations/grants-hispanic-students/hispanic-serving-institutions--science-technology-engineering-or-mathematics-and-articulation-programs

U.S. Department of Education. (2018). *Hispanic-Serving Institutions (HSIs)*. White House Initiative on Educational Equity, Excellence, and Economic Opportunity for Hispanics. Retrieved from https://sites.ed.gov/hispanic-initiative/hispanic-serving-institutions-hsis/

U.S. Department of Education. (2021). *Minority Serving Institutions (MSIs)*. Retrieved from https://www2.ed.gov/about/offices/list/ocr/edlite-minorityinst.html

Valdés, G. (1996). *Con respeto: Bridging the distances between culturally diverse families and schools*. Teachers College Press.

Valenzuela, A. (1999). *Subtractive schooling: U.S.-Mexican youth and the politics of caring*. State University of New York Press.

Valverde, L. A. (2002). *Navigating the college journey: A guide for LatinX students and their families*. Higher Education Press.

Valverde, L. A. (2012). *Success pathways for LatinX students: Before, during, and after college enrollment*. Education Resource Publications.

Villarreal, N. (2021). Marianismo and social support: Predicting achievement motivation and ganas in doctoral Latinas (Doctoral dissertation). *ProQuest Dissertations Publishing*. https://search.proquest.com/openview/d0f559fb7217fef876beaebf6d8cce69/1?pq-origsite=gscholar&cbl=18750&diss=y

Zalaquett, C. P., & Lopez, A. D. (2006). Learning from the stories of successful undergraduate Latina/Latino students: The importance of mentoring. *Mentoring & Tutoring, 14*, 337–353. https://doi.org/10.1080/13611260600635563

Zerquera, D. D., Haywood, J., & Flores, M. D. M. (2020). More than nuance: Measuring race and why disaggregating data matters for addressing educational inequality. *Educational Researcher, 49*(2), 154–164. https://doi.org/10.3102/0013189X20918319

Chapter 4

Critical Perspectives on LatinX Student Success

Asset-Based Theoretical and Methodological
Frameworks from Critical Race Theory and
Chicana Feminisms

YAMARIS: A SENIOR'S URGENT DECISION AMID AFTERSHOCKS OF DISASTER

Yamaris stood frozen in her dorm room, the incessant beeps of the off-the-hook signal echoing like the urgent beat of a distant drum. Each failed attempt to reach her grandparents' landline in the Dominican Republic shot adrenaline through her veins. The stale air hung heavy in her room; she was flush-faced and anxious to hear any connection through the receiver pressed against her ear. In the background, a Spanish news report blared, detailing a natural disaster unfolding in the Dominican Republic. In a serious tone the anchor announced, *"21 muertos después de que las 'lluvias totales más altas de la historia' provocaran inundaciones y deslizamientos de tierra."*[1] Images of streets inundated with people and crumbling hillsides flashed across the screen, particularly from Santo Domingo, where her grandparents lived.

Yamaris paced anxiously, searching frantically under the bed for her shoes. She contemplated rushing to class or heading straight home to Mamí in Washington Heights. Apprehensive, she was torn between her academic responsibilities in her senior year at Columbia University and the overwhelming need to be with her family.[2] Just three years ago, she had endured the isolation of COVID-19[3] in the city, a significant contrast to her quarantined freshman year at home. Completing her bachelor's degree was a personal goal and a promise to her family.[4] Yamaris dreamed of handing her diploma to Mamí, a symbol for their entire community that this academic achievement and success belonged to all of them.

Mamí had bravely immigrated to Manhattan's Washington Heights in the 1980s,[5] driven by a fierce desire to provide Yamaris with greater opportunities than she had known. As a single mother following her husband's early passing, Mamí relied heavily on the involvement of Yamaris's grandparents

DOI: 10.4324/9781003415909-4

in her daughter's upbringing. They lovingly cared for Yamaris while Mamí pursued her career as a hairstylist. By the time they immigrated, Mamí owned her own salon on 173rd St. Despite the physical distance, Mamí ensured Yamaris remained deeply connected to her culture by sending her back to the Dominican Republic every summer to spend time with her grandparents.

Recognized early on as gifted and talented, Yamaris seized the opportunity to take the rigorous Specialized High Schools Admissions Test[6] in eighth grade—a yearly challenge for more than 30,000 eighth and ninth graders in New York. Her hard work paid off with admission to the prestigious High School of American Studies at Lehman College[7] (HSAS), where her lifelong fascination with history found new pathways to be cultivated. When she later applied and was accepted to Columbia University, Yamaris deemed this a natural progression in her academic journey. Determined to delve deeper into her passions, she chose to double-major in history and political science, laying a strong foundation for her aspirations in law.

Still frantic in her dorm room, Yamaris swiftly decided to not attend her morning classes and head to Washington Heights. She caught the express train, her thoughts racing faster than the subway cars. Each station they passed was a blur, her mind preoccupied with scenes of devastation and the safety of her grandparents. Upon arriving, she found Mamí in the living room, surrounded by neighbors, all glued to the ongoing news coverage. The sense of community was palpable, with everyone bringing whatever information, resources, or comfort they could offer. Yamaris hugged her mother tightly, the familiar scent of her perfume momentarily pushing the fear away. Determined to do something constructive, as a McNair Scholar,[8] Yamaris remembered her current undergraduate research project on disaster preparedness.[9] Her academic focus suddenly became personally relevant, providing a unique opportunity to apply her theoretical knowledge to real-world disaster preparedness and response. She reached out to her professor, explaining the situation, and requested they send her the model 0[10] they had produced using an Epistemic Network Analysis.[11] As a research fellow, she had been working with her professor on coding a qualitative dataset of Dominican undergraduates like herself who had experienced COVID-19 and/or other forms of disaster.

Energized by the opportunity to make a meaningful impact, Yamaris spent the next few weeks diving into her model 0s, analyzing data, and connecting with experts. As she gathered insights, Yamaris shared her findings with the Dominican community in Washington Heights, organizing information sessions that helped locals understand the situation and prepare their own response strategies. For example, she explained that Figure 4.1 *Epistemic*

Network Analysis of Dominican Undergraduate Disaster Preparedness Model 0,[12] illustrates the complex web of factors that influenced Dominican undergraduates' experiences during COVID-19. It shows how disaster unpreparedness in social, economic, and academic areas heightened their challenges, while community resilience, familial support, and aspirations for degree completion served as crucial buffers against the pandemic's negative impact.

These sessions also served as fundraisers, generating money, and gathering supplies to send to the affected areas in the Dominican Republic. Through this experience, Yamaris not only fulfilled her academic responsibilities but

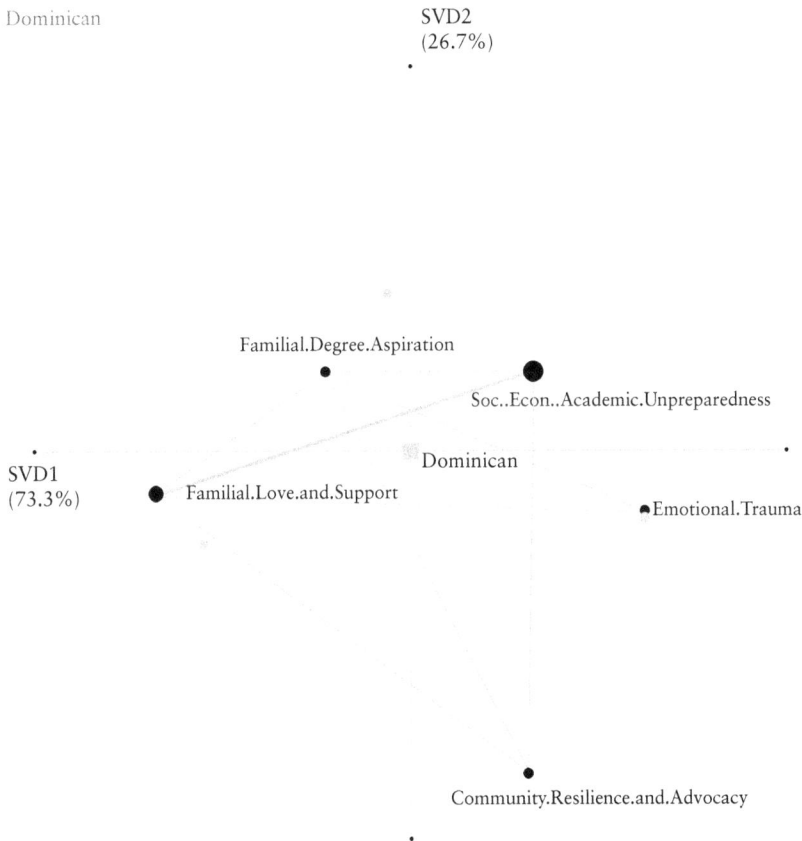

Dominican   SVD2
                                             (26.7%)
                                               .

                    Familial.Degree.Aspiration
                              ●   ●
                                        Soc..Econ..Academic.Unpreparedness

   .   Dominican   .
SVD1
(73.3%)   ● Familial.Love.and.Support
                                                    ● Emotional.Trauma

                                        ●
                          Community.Resilience.and.Advocacy
                                  .

Figure 4.1 This is an example of a Model 0 in an Epistemic Network Analysis in Quantitative Ethnography focusing on Dominican undergraduate students.

also strengthened ties to her community, both locally and abroad. Her efforts culminated in a detailed report that demonstrated effective disaster prepar- edness strategies enacted by undergraduates like herself, mainly providing, receiving, and reinforcing familial love and support as the main source of their resilience when experiencing disasters. Finally, after weeks of anxiously waiting, Yamaris and Mamí received the call they had hoped for. Her grand- parents were safe; their home was damaged, but repairable. The relief was overwhelming and, as they celebrated, Yamaris felt a profound connection between her academic pursuits and personal life, her community's resilience reinforcing her dedication to service through scholarship.

COUNTER-STORY REFLECTION QUESTIONS

- How did Yamaris navigate the challenges posed by the COVID-19 pandemic during her freshman year and subsequent years at Columbia University, and what did she learn from these experiences?
- How could Yamaris leverage her academic achievements and success to community ties to inspire and support others within her com- munity, especially young students aspiring to pursue higher educa- tion?

Over the past 20 years, research in K-12 education focusing on LatinX stu- dents has expanded significantly, employing various theoretical and methodo- logical approaches. However, as a field of study, higher education is still in the early stages of theory development (Crisp et al., 2024). Crisp et al. (2024) state:

> There is no comprehensive list of theories applicable to studying race in a higher education context. Moreover, there is little consistency in how theoretical terms are defined (e.g., framework, lens, model) or distinguished across studies, making it challenging to make decisions about how to appro- priately apply/use a particular theoretical perspective (e.g., aligning theory with epistemology and/or method).
>
> (pp. 4–5)

As briefly discussed in Chapters 2 and 3, the field of higher education often relies heavily on theoretical approaches from psychology and later from educational psychology to describe the experiences of undergraduate students in higher education (Astin, 1993; Chickering, 1969; Erikson, 1959, 1994; Marcia, 1966; Perry, 1968). Namely, student development theories examine how students grow and change during their undergraduate careers. More specifically, these theories describe the cognitive, psychosocial, moral, and social processes involved in identity development within college environments. All these factors can contribute to undergraduate students' academic achievement and success. However, the earliest student development theories were primarily based on white, male, cisgender, Christian students attending Ivy League institutions (Garcia & Mireles-Rios, 2019; Patton et al., 2016). To counter these early notions, Jones and Stewart (2016) provide a detailed genealogy of student development theories and propose a contemporary rethinking of this area of study as a concept.

According to Jones and Stewart (2016), student development theories can be categorized into three waves: "foundational theories rooted in psychology and human development, a shift to including diverse populations and social identities, and applying critical perspectives in understanding student development" (pp. 17–18). While studies in the first wave laid the groundwork and were hence considered "foundational," it was not until the early 1990s, or the second wave, that racial and ethnic student identity development models began addressing the unique experiences of LatinX students—Latino student identity development (Ferdman & Gallegos, 2001, 2012; Torres, 1999, 2003; Torres & Hernandez, 2007). Currently, there is an unfolding shift in student development theories and higher education as a field to consider the third wave. Garvey et al. (2019) posit "it is how one uses theory, and not necessarily the theory itself, that enacts a more socially just environment for students' learning and development" (p. 4). This perspective underscores the importance of understanding theory within academic disciplines, the researchers (theorists), and the underlying philosophical assumptions that inform epistemological perspectives. For Torres et al. (2009), contemporary discussions on racial and ethnic student development emphasize the potential of critical and post-structural theories to transform power systems. Jones and Stewart (2016) argue that the third wave of student development theory focuses on critical and poststructuralist perspectives applied to studying racial and ethnic student populations. These include and are not limited to Critical Race Theory (Bell, 1995; Delgado & Crenshaw, 1993), Queer Theory (Sedgwick, 2008), Black Feminist Thought—intersectionality (Collins, 1999; Crenshaw, 1989), and Chicana/Latina Feminist Thought (Delgado Bernal et al., 2006). Central to these theoretical frameworks are achieving social justice and transforming the material conditions of marginalized populations within higher education.

In this chapter, as a scholar trained in ethnic studies and education, I examine asset-based theoretical frameworks[13] in Critical Race Theory and Chicana/Latina Feminist Thought to hold institutions of higher education and their actors accountable for their role in reproducing white supremacy, racism, and other forms of systemic oppression. To do this, I first briefly review the prevalence of theoretical frameworks extensively utilized in higher education research to examine LatinX academic achievement and success. These include Latino student identity development (Ferdman & Gallegos, 2001; Torres, 1999, 2003; Torres & Hernandez, 2007), forms of capital (Bourdieu, 1986), and funds of knowledge (González et al., 2005; Moll, 1992; Vélez-Ibañez, 1988; Vélez-Ibañez & Greenberg, 1992b). Next, I focus on the emergence of Critical Race Theory in education (CRT) (Ladson-Billings & Tate, 1995; Solórzano, 1997), and the groundbreaking framework informed by CRT, Community Cultural Wealth (Yosso, 2005a, 2005b). My shift to the sub-fields of CRT and theoretical tools applicable to LatinX academic achievement and success follows. I then turn to Chicana feminisms in education (Delgado Bernal et al., 2006) and the seminal framework Chicana Feminist Epistemology (Delgado Bernal, 1998) in education and next provide other Chicana feminist theoretical tools that have been implemented to theorize LatinX academic achievement and success at the intersections of identity, sexuality, embodied knowledge, resistance, healing, transformation, and empowerment (Castillo, 1994; Fregoso, 2003; Hurtado, 1998; Pérez, 1999; Sandoval, 2000).

In analyzing CRT and Chicana feminisms in education, I bridge theory and methods, naming methodologies widely used in these fields. I then introduce Critical Race Feminista Methodologies to higher education, drawing on scholars who have integrated CRT and Chicana feminist theories (Delgado Bernal & Alemán, 2017; Delgado Bernal et al., 2018). Understanding how these methodologies have been theorized in qualitative research reveals possibilities for their application in quantitative work. Finally, I address how quantitative approaches that claim objectivity through statistics have historically mischaracterized LatinX academic achievement and success by placing the blame on individuals navigating oppressive systems rather than acknowledging systemic oppression (Garcia et al., 2023). I conclude the chapter by engaging with data and presenting what I conceptualize, define, and empirically apply as a Critical Race Feminista Quantitative Ethnography Praxis.

PREVALENT THEORETICAL FRAMEWORKS ON LATINX STUDENT SUCCESS

LatinX Student Identity Development

Research on LatinX student identity development has examined how these students interpret their racial and ethnic identities within academic environments (Torres et al., 2019). Foundational studies in student identity development concerning LatinX students have mainly centered on aspects of racial and ethnic identity before later incorporating additional factors like gender, socioeconomic status, generational differences, and immigration status (Torres et al., 2019). Namely, Torres[14] (1999) offered one of the first models, *The Bicultural Orientation Model*, to assess the cultural orientation of "Hispanic" college students. This model evaluates Hispanic students' acculturation and ethnic identity levels to determine their cultural orientation. Students with high acculturation and ethnic identity are categorized as bicultural, enabling them to navigate Hispanic and white cultural contexts. Conversely, those with low ethnic identity are described as having an Anglo orientation, aligning more with white culture. Students who exhibit low levels of both acculturation and ethnic identity are considered to have a marginal orientation (i.e., identity crisis) due to not fully identifying with either culture. Meanwhile, those with low acculturation but high ethnic identity are placed in a Hispanic orientation. In the early 2000s, Torres (2003, 2004, 2011; Torres & Hernandez, 2007) updated her work to account for various LatinX sub-ethnic groups, societal and institutional contexts, and how interpersonal and intrapersonal interactions impact LatinX perceptions of themselves and the broader world. In this line, Torres et al. (2019) propose *A Lifespan Model of Latinx Ethnic Identity Development*, accounting for various statuses and behaviors that influence the ethnic identity formation and development of LatinX college students over the course of entering college into their adulthood. This model argues that LatinX ethnic identity is not static but rather fluid based on the environment in which these individuals find themselves and how they develop their sense of self (Torres et al., 2019).

Furthermore, in exploring the identity development of LatinX students, Ferdman and Gallegos (2001) propose *A Model of Latino Identity Development*, which examines Latino and Latina racial identity orientations rather than ethnic identity. This model requires a deep understanding of the combined racial and cultural factors shaping the experiences of Latino/a people in the United States. It outlines six distinct orientations, ranging from Latino-integrated, Latino-identified (Racial/Raza), subgroup identified, Latino as other, undifferentiation/denial, and white identified. This range of orientations depicts a progression from an identity closely aligned with whiteness to a more integrated Latino identity, influenced by various social and cultural factors. Extending their previous work (Ferdman & Gallegos, 2001), Gallegos and Ferdman (2012) propose *The Model of Latina and Latino Ethnoracial Orientations* to understand and challenge how Latinos view themselves in a U.S. society that conflates racial and ethnic categories, where individuals might not fit into the Black/white racial binary due to varying skin pigmentation and distinct histories, and how Latinos respond to these socially constructed categories. Gallegos and Ferdman (2012) articulate that, for Latinos in the United States, using race and ethnicity interchangeably is problematic and has the potential to lead to erasure of culture, history, language, generational context, and national origins. It is important to note that their model is neither linear nor recurring but is instead dependent on the context of interactions with individuals and their environments—what they refer to as a lens. Gallegos and Ferdman (2012) provide six orientations that assist Latinos to internally process who they are in the context of society, how U.S. society perceives who they are, and how race/racial constructs interact with these processes. The orientations, as outlined by Gallegos and Ferdman (2012), are: undifferentiated, white identified, Latino as "other," sub-group identified, Latino identified, and Latino integrated. Higher education research supports these outlined stages of ethnoracial identity evolution among LatinX college students. For example, Rivas-Drake et al. (2014) observed that LatinX students typically engage in periods of exploration and affirmation of their ethnoracial identity during their college experience. Similarly, Umaña-Taylor and Guimond (2010) highlight the importance of nurturing campus climates and culturally responsive programs in promoting healthy ethnoracial identity development in LatinX students. It is crucial to recognize the variability in how individuals experience these stages, with some undergoing them simultaneously or in other ways. Furthermore, intersecting identities like gender and socioeconomic status are critical in the formation of ethnoracial identity journeys of LatinX college students (Phinney & Alipuria, 1990).

Overall, much of the research on LatinX identity development has focused on ethnicity, tending to overlook the role of white supremacy and systematic oppression to focus instead on the challenges encountered rather than on mechanisms that disrupt and dismantle these conceptions (Azmitia et al., 2023; Kolluri, 2023). A critical viewpoint on LatinX racial and ethnic identity student development models suggests that they oversimplify the complex and contextual nature of identity, framing it as linear stages to be achieved rather than as a nuanced interplay with white supremacy, racism, and other forms of systematic oppression. As discussed in Chapters 1 and 2, the social construction of LatinX race, ethnicity, and ethnoracial identities in the United States is complex and in contention. These identities are influenced by historical, political, and cultural contexts, including institutions of higher education; all these contexts intersect and are often manifested at the expense of LatinX students, families, and communities.

Forms of Capital

French Sociologist Pierre Bourdieu (1973, 1986) focuses on the characteristics of culture, its reproduction and transformation, its relationship to social stratification, and how it contributes to the reproduction of inequities and exertion of power. He is extensively recognized and referenced for his theories on social reproduction and his concepts of cultural[15] and social capital. Bourdieu (1973) argues that social reproduction[16] was grounded in a logic of domination that is manifested in societies and their structures (e.g., law or education). Social reproduction involves the transmission of cultural, structural, and ecological traits that are passed down or inherited from one generation to the next within societies. Bourdieu refers to this transmission of characteristics as "capital" across generations. According to Bourdieu (1973, 1986), the forms of capital involved in social reproduction are economic, symbolic, cultural, and social. These forms of capital are interconnected, and inform and transform into one another under specific circumstances. He argues that the upper and middle classes' knowledge, skills, and cultural practices are viewed as valuable assets within a society and that "capital" is maintained through hierarchical structures. Bourdieu (1986) defines and explains the forms of capital interconnectedness:

> Depending on the field in which it functions, and at the cost of the more or less expensive transformations which are the precondition for its efficacy in the field in question, capital can present itself in three fundamental guises: as economic capital, which is immediately and directly convertible into money and may be institutionalized in the form of property rights; as cultural capital, which is convertible, in certain conditions, into economic capital and may be institutionalized in the form of educational qualifications; and as social capital, made up of social obligations ("connections"), which is convertible, in certain conditions, into economic capital and may be institutionalized in the form of a title of nobility.
>
> (p. 16)

While not explicitly articulated in the excerpt, Bourdieu (1986) argues that symbolic capital is power that is not inherent in an object or resource but is nonetheless attributed to it by people through the process of their own social recognition or misrecognition. Put simply, any form of capital becomes symbolic capital when it is recognized and valued by a society. To reiterate, as discussed by Bourdieu (1973, 1986), social capital is based on resources allocated to group membership, relationships, and networks (connections) that maintain influence. Cultural capital is how families inherit and preserve habits, dispositions, and preferences. In the field of higher education research, Bourdieu's concepts of cultural and social capital[17] gained traction in the late 1980s and early 1990s to explain topics such as student retention and transitions (Tierney, 1999; Walpole, 2003), college choice and access (Freeman, 1997; Nora, 2004; Pascarella et al., 2004; Perna, 2000), academic achievement and success

(Cabrera & La Nasa, 2001; Davies & Guppy, 1997; DiMaggio & Mohr, 1985; Horvat, 2001; McDonough, 1997; Steelman & Powell, 1989), and the impact of socioeconomic background on postsecondary degree or credential completion (McDonough, 1997; McDonough et al., 1999; Winkle-Wagner, 2010). This is significant because economic capital was no longer the only form of capital that could be employed to explain postsecondary degree or credential completion. Instead, the focus on capital shifted to examining how college students from diverse social and cultural backgrounds navigate institutions of higher education, irrespective of their socioeconomic status. Despite higher education scholars employing social and cultural capital theoretical frameworks to analyze college students, the traditional image of a student has predominantly centered around white, male, middle-class norms, setting this identity as the standard against which LatinX social and cultural forms of capital have been considered subordinate (Yosso, 2005a, 2005b).

The white-racial framing of institutions of higher education around white norms perpetuates devaluation of LatinX students' cultural capital, effectively normalizing knowledge, skills, and experiences associated with whiteness (Ayala, 2016; Barajas & Ronnkvist, 2007; Gonzalez, 2012). Moreover, as demonstrated in Chapters 2 and 3, academic achievement and student success are inherently engrained in white culture and values, reproducing white supremacy and racism and ultimately positioning these norms as the standard for success, thereby expecting LatinX students to assimilate into the dominant group by progressing toward postsecondary degree or credential completion (Valenzuela, 1999; Yosso, 2005a, 2005b). To challenge and disrupt these deficit perspectives of LatinX students, scholars have theorized and empirically documented other forms of capital such as community cultural wealth (Yosso, 2005a, 2005b), intercultural capital (Nuñez, 2009), racial and/or ethnic empowerment capital (Ayala & Contreras, 2019), and spiritual capital (Pérez Huber, 2009), with each form related to the assets LatinX students bring with them into institutions of higher education. These other forms of capital, as they relate to LatinX students, demonstrate the skills, abilities, and knowledge utilized by these students in pursuing academic achievement and success. This line of inquiry has continued to evolve, influencing policies and practices aimed at reducing inequities for LatinX students' postsecondary degree or credential completion and improving their outcomes. Overall, for LatinX students in higher education, empirical studies have found that their familial experiences and social and cultural capital have substantially impacted their postsecondary degree or credential aspirations, persistence, and completion starting from elementary to graduate education experiences.

Funds of Knowledge

Drawing from Wolf's (1966) notion of a micro-economy of the home and "funds" (e.g., funds of rent, replacement funds, social funds), anthropologist Vélez-Ibañez's (1988) ethnographic study of economically disadvantaged Mexican communities, in Mexico and the United States, found that they use funds to create systems and practices to support survival, and these systems often involve maintaining extensive networks for exchange between households. Since Vélez-Ibañez's (1988) foundational study, working groups of anthropology and education scholars at the University of Arizona have collaborated on various projects to examine the potential of funds of knowledge in the context of education. Leading scholars within these groups, in addition to Vélez-Ibañez's, were Luis Moll, Norma González and James Greenberg (Hogg, 2011). In particular, Vélez-Ibañez's and Greenberg (1992a) conducted a comparative study[18] on U.S. Mexican, Puerto Rican, and Cuban households to further conceptualize the funds of knowledge that challenge and disrupt deficit theorizing of underachievement in educational institutions among LatinX students and their families. Their study focuses on a case study of the Mexican sub-sample in which they examined the experiences of working-class Mexican American families in Tucson, Arizona, and defined funds of knowledge as a way to name the rich knowledge and practices possessed by Mexican American families and their communities that assist them in their day-to-day lives (Vélez-Ibañez's & Greenberg, 1992a). Vélez-Ibañez's and Greenberg (1992a) state:

> Although small prestations are a constant feature of exchange relations, as they are reciprocal, they balance out, are of less importance economically than is the exchange of information, and special funds of knowledge. Indeed, help in finding jobs, housing, better deals on goods and services, and assistance in dealings with institutions and government agencies is of far greater significance to survival than are the material types of aid these households usually provide each other.
>
> (p. 22)

Based on this understanding, funds of knowledge are mainly concerned with how communities, such as Mexican American families, exchange everyday practical information and assistance, which is more vital to their survival than exchanging small material goods. From there, Vélez-Ibañez and Greenberg (1992b) examine how educational reforms and public schooling fail to acknowledge and utilize the valuable and strategic cultural practices that U.S. Mexican American children bring into the classroom. Extending

119

this work, Moll (1992) defines funds of knowledge as "historically accumulated and culturally developed bodies of knowledge and skills essential for household or individual functioning and well-being" (p. 133). Funds of knowledge are acquired through historical and life experiences, power relations, labor histories, household activities, and social interactions (González et al., 2005; González & Moll, 2002; Mwangi, 2018).

In her 2007 presidential address to the Association for the Study of Higher Education (ASHE), Estela Bensimon urged higher education scholars and practitioners to apply funds of knowledge to their work. She highlighted a significant gap in research and practice regarding how institutional actors' knowledge, beliefs, experiences, education, and self-confidence influence students' academic achievement and success (Bensimon, 2007; Kiyama, 2008; Rios-Aguilar & Kiyama, 2012). Consisting of beliefs, attitudes, understandings, and practices (Bensimon, 2007), funds of knowledge vary and apply to a range of topics such as farming, animals, construction, trade, business, finance, military, and college conceptions (Gonzalez et al., 2005; Kiyama, 2010). This information can be acquired and transmitted through social networks, which serve as conduits for information (Kiyama, 2010). Kiyama and Rios-Aguilar (2018a) explore the strategies of LatinX students, their families, and communities through a funds of knowledge perspective, which provides a culturally inclusive and relevant approach that assists students in navigating their daily lives. However, institutions of higher education and their actors often overlook these strengths (Rodriguez, 2013).

Kiyama and Rios-Aguilar (2018a), leading scholars in studying LatinX college students, funds of knowledge, and student success, offer a thorough review of research on BIPOC students in higher education. For LatinX students, their families, and communities, funds of knowledge, as an interconnected theoretical framework, operates from an asset-based perspective and acknowledges all three as competent and possessing valuable strengths, knowledge, and skill sets (Gonzalez et al., 2005; Kiyama et al., 2018a, 2018b;). To overcome the deficit labeling of LatinX students, their families, and communities, funds of knowledge identify and integrate home practices to transform institutions' formal and informal spaces of higher education contexts by acknowledging that families pushed to the margins have had to provide for themselves, which has required them to learn to cope and resist with various aspects of daily life (Kiyama, 2011; Kiyama et al., 2018a, 2018b; Vélez-Ibañez & Greenberg, 1992b). Concerning LatinX students, scholarship has mainly focused on college access and transitions to college with a need for "the development and understanding of funds of knowledge to also include subgroups of Latina/o students and other ethnic minority, immigrant, and low-income families" (Rios-Aguilar & Kiyama, 2012, p. 13). Overall, the theoretical application of funds of knowledge to examine LatinX academic achievement and student success calls on institutions of higher education and their actors to recognize and build upon the inherent strengths of LatinX students and their families.

THE EMERGENCE AND IMPACT OF CRITICAL RACE THEORY

Critical Race Theory in Education

Critical Race Theory (CRT) emerged post-Civil Rights Movement as legal scholars, attorneys, and activists noted a downturn in social justice and equity in the United States (Delgado, 1984). Broadly, CRT is a movement within legal studies to address oppression, power, and privilege to drive societal and individual transformation (Solórzano & Delgado Bernal, 2001). In the 1970s, prominent legal scholars such as Derrick Bell, Richard Delgado, Mari Matsuda, and Kimberle Crenshaw[19] formalized CRT within the legal field, drawing on influences from critical legal studies, radical feminism, Eurocentric philosophy, and the American radical tradition (Delgado & Stefancic, 2012). These scholars critically examined how legal systems perpetuate racism and white supremacy, and their impact on the material realities of people of color. This foundational critique was extended into the field of education by Ladson-Billings and Tate (1995), leading scholars in applying CRT to explore how race, racism, and white supremacy are deeply embedded in educational contexts. Subsequently, Solórzano (1997) utilized CRT to investigate racial stereotyping in teacher education. Since these seminal contributions, the application of CRT in education has evolved, addressing the nuances of race, ethnicity, and other social identities through various sub-fields such as TribalCrit (Brayboy, 2005), QueerCrit (Valdes, 1998), BlackCrit (Roberts, 1998; Dumas & Ross, 2016), DisCrit (Annamma et al., 2013), UndocuCrit (Aguilar, 2019), LatCrit (Solórzano & Yosso, 2001; Solórzano & Delgado Bernal, 2001), Critical Race Feminisms (Wing, 1997), MultiCrit (Harris, 2016), Critical Whiteness Studies (Matias et al., 2014), and AsianCrit (Museus & Iftikar, 2013).

In educational settings, CRT examines the development of race and ethnic student identities within higher education and student affairs, actively recognizing the contributions and capabilities that LatinX students and their families bring to higher education institutions (Yosso, 2005a, 2005b; Solórzano et al., 2000). Critical Race Theory offers a macro and a micro view of how systems, particularly higher education, either privilege or oppress various student groups, influencing individual and systemic outcomes (Zamudio et al., 2011; Patton et al., 2015). It critically analyzes the conditions that BIPOC students and their families face as they navigate higher education toward academic achievement and student success (Harper & Nichols, 2008; Patton et al., 2015). According to Solórzano (1997), the core tenets of CRT in education are:

1. **The centrality of race and racism and their intersection with other forms of oppression.** Race and racism are viewed as pervasive elements in studying oppression in education among BIPOC communities, intersecting with classism, sexism, and/or other forms of oppression.
2. **A challenge to the dominant ideology.** CRT questions the educational system's reliance on notions of objectivity, meritocracy, and color-evasive practices, recognizing how race, racism, and white supremacy contribute to structural barriers against BIPOC communities.
3. **A commitment to a social justice framework.** Grounded in community struggles and activism, CRT aims for social justice, equity, and inclusion, promoting transformative and liberatory outcomes.
4. **The centrality of experiential knowledge.** CRT values the lived experiences and inherent strengths of BIPOC communities, which challenge dominant narratives and bring marginalized voices to the forefront.
5. **An interdisciplinary perspective.** CRT critiques ahistorical approaches and studies race, racism, and white supremacy through interdisciplinary theory and methods in education and beyond, drawing upon fields like sociology, feminist studies, and history to comprehensively analyze these issues.

After the publication of Solórzano's (1997) seminal piece, a group of graduate students, Octavio Villalpando, Tara J. Yosso, Dolores Delgado Bernal, Miguel Ceja[20] (now well-known and established scholars), and several more at the University of California, Los Angeles (UCLA) initiated groundbreaking studies employing CRT to explore racial differences and their effects on the academic achievement and postsecondary success of BIPOC students—in particular ChicanX and LatinX students. These foundational studies emerged in the late 1990s into the early 2000s, spanned elementary to graduate education, and were concerned with issues of and not limited to race and gender microaggressions (Solórzano, 1998), marginality and oppositional behavior (Solórzano & Villalpando, 1998), data disaggregation of academic achievement and success across the LatinX educational pipeline (Yosso, 2005a), Chicana/o education and CRT (Yosso et al., 2009), transformational resistance (Solórzano & Delgado Bernal, 2001), campus climate (Solórzano et al., 2000), critical race methodology—counter-storytelling (Solórzano & Yosso, 2002), qualitative research (Lynn et al., 2002), affirmative action

(Solórzano & Yosso, 2002), academic achievement and success (Villalpando, 2003), community college pathways to the doctorate (Solórzano et al., 2000), and community cultural wealth (Yosso, 2005a, 2005b).[21]

From there, in the field of higher education, Harper (2012), at the time, identified that only five empirical studies existed across seven major higher education and student affairs journals that employed CRT to examine the impact of racism and white supremacy at individual and institutional levels. Patton et al. (2015) argue that while CRT had a presence in higher education research, it was underutilized and widely neglected in the field in thoroughly exploring issues related to racism and white supremacy as it pertains to BIPOC college students. Therefore, Patton et al. (2015) demonstrate that using CRT to examine college access and admissions, theories of college student development, and college student engagement can serve as a tool to deepen the understanding of institutions of higher education, their actors, and researchers of systematic inequities and the lived experiences of BIPOC students. Since 2015, CRT, its sub-field LatCrit, and related theoretical frameworks focusing on LatinX academic achievement and success have flourished in higher education. Yosso's *Community Cultural Wealth* framework (2005a, 2005b), one of the most widely cited and extensively employed, has been used for nearly two decades to explain the inherent assets that LatinX students possess and draw upon for academic achievement and student success in higher education. In the following sections, I first explain how CRT informed the conceptualization of *Community Cultural Wealth*. From there, and from my viewpoint as a Critical Race Feminista scholar in higher education, I then outline the most significant CRT contributions to studying LatinX academic achievement and success in higher education. Currently, some of these contributions are widely adopted, while others remain underutilized within higher education research.

COMMUNITY CULTURAL WEALTH

Often misinterpreted as a critique rather than an expansion of traditional Bordieuan cultural capital theory, Yosso (2005a, 2005b) drew parallels between Bourdieu's (Bourdieu & Passeron, 1977) and Oliver and Shapiro's (1995) views of income, noting that both focus on a limited range of assets and characteristics, which were attentively aligned with white, middle-class values. This traditional view of cultural capital is more restrictive than the broader concept of wealth, which includes an individual's accumulated assets and resources. However, Yosso (2005a) uses CRT to broaden this traditional perspective. Yosso (2005a, 2005b) integrates the five tenets of CRT in education to present a framework that acknowledges and elucidates the epistemologies and practices of BIPOC communities. In doing so, Yosso (2005a, 2005b) advocates for a significant shift from conventional deficit-focused models to an approach that recognizes the community cultural wealth that BIPOC students contribute to educational environments. She contends that research often overlooks the diverse array of knowledge, skills, abilities, and networks that BIPOC students, families, and communities employ to navigate and resist both macro- and micro-level oppressions, particularly in educational contexts (Yosso, 2005a, 2005b). Yosso identifies and describes six types of capital that inform one another:

1. **Familial Capital** is the rich knowledge nurtured among family members that embodies a sense of community history, memory, and cultural intuition. Familial ties extend beyond blood relations to encompass any deep, nurturing relationships.
2. **Linguistic Capital** encompasses the intellectual and social skills acquired through communication experiences in multiple languages and/or styles. This form of capital is not limited to multilingualism but includes various modes of expression like art, music, and poetry.
3. **Social Capital** comprises the networks and community resources that BIPOC communities create to thrive within social structures.
4. **Navigational Capital** involves the abilities required to maneuver through social institutions, despite these institutions not being designed with BIPOC communities in mind.
5. **Resistance Capital** includes the knowledge and skills cultivated through oppositional actions that challenge and defy inequities, allowing BIPOC communities to preserve and promote their cultural identities.
6. **Aspirational Capital** is the capacity to hold onto hopes and dreams for the future, despite facing subtle or overt obstacles. These aspirations are nurtured and sustained within BIPOC communities.

In exploring the application of community cultural wealth among LatinX students in higher education, researchers have examined specific subgroups, including undocumented Chicana students (Pérez Huber, 2009), Mexican American PhD graduates (Espino, 2014), Queer Latino men (Duran & Pérez, 2017, 2019), Latino male community college students (Sáenz et al., 2018), and immigrant students (Purgason et al., 2020). Furthering this inquiry, scholars such as Rendón et al. (2014) have identified additional forms of capital—including *ganas* (determination), ethnic consciousness, spirituality/faith, and pluriversal cultural wealth—within these communities. These assets, termed "ventajas," enhance LatinX students' perseverance and community contributions. In complement, other studies have expanded the framework to include spiritual capital and other, varied capitals derived from maternal influences that support LatinX academic achievement and success in higher education research (Pérez Huber, 2009; Ballysingh, 2021).

LATCRIT

Emerging from LatCrit in the legal tradition (Montoya & Valdes, 2008), Delgado and Stefancic (2012) argue that LatCrit has four key themes: immigration, language, differential racialization, and the Black/white-race binary, whereas Haney López (1997) views LatCrit as accounting for factors such as national origin, class, gender identity, and various forms of identities that impact an individual's experiences with U.S. colonialism and imperialism (Cha´vez-Moreno, 2023). When LatCrit first emerged in legal scholarship, the field's primary emphasis was on LatinX race or ethnicity framed within the existing Black/white racial binary, a focus that continues to the present day as documented in Chapter 1 (Cha´vez-Moreno, 2023). In the field of education, Solórzano and Delgado Bernal (2001) were two of the first scholars to formally identify CRT and LatCrit, reemphasizing the previously detailed five main tenets of CRT. They defined LatCrit as being "coalitional Latina/ Latino pan-ethnicity and addresses[ing] issues often ignored by critical race theorists such as language, immigration, ethnicity, culture, identity, phenotype, and sexuality" (Solórzano & Delgado Bernal, 2001, p. 311). Therefore, within education, LatCrit functions as a CRT sub-field that examines the experiences of LatinX students, families, and communities that have influenced their trajectories in the United States within the larger structural and sociocultural landscape (Solo´rzano & Delgado Bernal, 2001; Solo´rzano & Yosso, 2001). LatCrit enables higher education researchers to better articulate the experiences of LatinX students, families, and communities, and is mainly concerned with immigration status, language, ethnicity, culture, identity, and phenotype (Solo´rzano & Delgado Bernal, 2001). Since its emergence, foundational and notable studies on LatinX academic achievement and success in higher education research have focused on addressing the academic and sociocultural needs of LatinX college students (Villalpando, 2003, 2004), transformational resistance (Solórzano & Delgado Bernal, 2001), counter-storytelling (Solórzano & Yosso, 2002), undocumented students (Aguilar, 2019; Pérez Huber, 2009), and racial microaffirmations (Rolo´n-Dow & Davison, 2021; Solórzano & Pérez Huber, 2020). In the next subsections, I examine theoretical tools drawn from the intersections of CRT and LatCrit to examine LatinX academic achievement and success.

Transformational Resistance

Drawing from CRT and LatCrit, Solórzano and Delgado Bernal (2001) advocate for a shift in educational research to consider a wider array of resistance behaviors that not only address the immediate challenges faced by working-class students but also have the potential to lead to social transformation. They argue that, for far too long, resistance models have focused on oppositional behaviors rather than transformational behaviors. In using CRT and LatCrit, they develop a more nuanced framework that considers race and gender consciousness and how they impact the resistance behaviors of Chicana and Chicano students.[22] Solórzano and Delgado Bernal (2001) identify four types of oppositional resistance that LatinX students enact: 1) reactionary behavior, 2) self-defeating resistance, 3) conformist resistance, and 4) transformational resistance. Among students, reactionary behavior refers to those who act out or display disorderly behavior without understanding the reasons behind their actions, lacking both a critique of their social conditions and an awareness of social justice. Self-defeating resistance describes students critiquing their social conditions while lacking the motivation or concern to engage in social justice efforts. Conformist resistance occurs when students engage in social justice but simultaneously comply with and internalize oppressive systems. Transformational resistance surpasses these forms as it concerns students critiquing their oppression and actively seeking social justice to change their social conditions (Solórzano & Delgado Bernal, 2001). Therefore, transformational resistance can be defined as liberatory action employed by LatinX students, families, and communities who are conscious of the dynamics of structural oppression and remain deeply committed to social justice (Covarrubias & Revilla, 2003; Bernal, 1997; Solórzano & Villalpando, 1998; Solórzano & Delgado Bernal, 2001). Scholars have considered the extent to which mentors (Revilla, 2004) and co-curricular affinity organizations (Harper & Quaye, 2007; Solórzano & Delgado Bernal, 2001) cultivate resistance within BIPOC students. However, little to no research exists in the field of higher education that examines LatinX students' transformational resistance among different racial or ethnic sub-groups and other identities on their pathways to academic achievement and success.

Critical Race-Gendered Epistemologies

Delgado Bernal (2002) integrates CRT and LatCrit to conceptualize what she terms critical race-gendered epistemologies. This concept critiques dominant narratives that often negatively portray LatinX students, their families, and communities and instead advocates for recognition of their complex roles as both creators and carriers of knowledge. In using CRT and LatCrit, which are foundational to her argument, she asserts that systemic racism and white supremacy are embedded within societal structures such as the legal and educational systems (Bell, 1995; Crenshaw et al., 1995; Solórzano, 1998).

Delgado Bernal (2002) expands these theories to emphasize that critical race-gendered epistemologies are influenced by the interplay of race and gender, leading to diverse and culturally specific ways of knowing. She states,

> there is not just one raced-gendered epistemology but many that each speaks to culturally specific ways of positioning between a raced epistemology that omits the influence of gender on knowledge production and a white feminist epistemology that does not account for race.
>
> (p. 107)

In applying these concepts to higher education, Delgado Bernal (2002) shows how critical race-gendered epistemologies can be used to challenge conventional academic norms and to better understand how LatinX students manage their identities within both educational institutions and their personal lives. In the field of higher education, Espino (2012) draws from critical race-gendered epistemologies to theorize a critical race epistemology in higher education to examine her "methodological approach to analyzing participants educational narratives" (p. 32). In 2020, my colleague and I situated critical raced-gendered epistemologies in higher education research to center our father–daughter relationships with our Chicano fathers and how institutions of higher education play a role in influencing how these pieces of knowledge are shaped in college-choice processes (Garcia & Mireles-Rios, 2020). We found that as Chicana daughters, we were marginalized due to our race and gender in navigating institutions of higher education, while our fathers were privileged in these spaces due to their gender, but not their race. In our households, we have had to negotiate the power dynamics of female–male relationships with our fathers. Our social positions created institutional and personal nuances that, as daughters, we had to negotiate and confront with our fathers during our college-choice processes. Critical race-gendered epistemologies granted us a framework to view and name these nuances (Garcia & Mireles-Rios, 2020). Similar to transformational resistance, critical race-gendered epistemologies are underutilized in examining LatinX academic achievement and success.

Racist Nativism

Grounded in LatCrit, Pérez Huber et al.'s (2008) concept of racist nativism explores how race and racism affect the lives of LatinX individuals through frameworks that analyze anti-immigrant sentiment, xenophobia, and colonization as forms of racism in the United States. This perspective historically frames BIPOC communities, particularly LatinX communities, as "foreigners" and perpetual outsiders (Pérez Huber et al., 2008). Pérez Huber et al. (2008)

state, "the assigning of values to real or imagined differences to justify the superiority of the native, who is to be perceived as white, over that of the non-native, who are perceived to be People and Immigrants of Color, and thereby defend the right of whites, or the natives, to dominance" (p. 43). Racist nativism manifests in microaggressions—subtle, cumulative verbal and non-verbal assaults based on race and perceived immigration status, which serve to alienate those who do not conform to white hegemonic norms, and particularly impacts undocumented LatinX students, families, and communities (Pérez Huber, 2010, 2011). The application of racist nativism as a theoretical framework is still not fully explored in the field of higher education research. This is particularly true in studies across various LatinX racial or ethnic sub-groups and other identities and their pathways to academic achievement and success. Most existing research tends to focus on undocumented Mexican students (Muñoz, 2013; Muñoz et al., 2018; Pérez Huber, 2010, 2011; Ramirez, 2021).

UndocuCrit

Stemming from CRT, LatCrit, and TribalCrit, which all examine white supremacy, racism, and subordination of BIPOC communities, UndocuCrit builds upon these frameworks to specifically address the experiences of undocumented students and their families (Brayboy, 2005; Crenshaw et al., 1995; Delgado Bernal, 2002; Ladson-Billings & Tate, 1995). This approach not only reflects a shift in perspective compared with traditional views on undocumented immigrants but a call for more intricate theories to understand undocumented lives (Gonzales, 2012). As a theoretical framework, UndocuCrit puts forth four central tenets that emphasize the voices and struggles of undocumented immigrants and their families, while critiquing systemic forces that dispossess and marginalize these communities (Aguilar, 2019): 1) pervasive fear within immigrant communities, 2) varied realities shaped by liminality, 3) value of parental sacrifices as a form of capital, and mentorship through acompañamiento, which embodies academic support, redemption, and 4) community engagement (Aguilar 2019, 2021). UndocuCrit is an emerging theoretical framework and has not been applied fully to explore the experiences of undocumented LatinX student racial or ethnic sub-groups and other identities of academic achievement or success in the field of higher education research.

CRITICAL RACE METHODOLOGIES

As discussed in Chapter 1, I engage a critical race methodology in framing the counter-stories for this book. In education, CRT is predominately used as a theoretical framework to help educational researchers identify white supremacy and racism, and comprehend the social contexts that give rise to both. Historically, educational researchers have relied on Eurocentric and Western paradigms in their research processes, which disregard the experiences and knowledge of LatinX students, their families, and communities. Solórzano and Yosso (2002) emphasize the importance of developing critical race methodologies that draw on knowledge generated and sustained within BIPOC communities. Therefore, a critical race methodology challenges and disrupts Western and Eurocentric research paradigms by highlighting the racialized, gendered, and class-based experiences of BIPOC communities, considering these experiences as sources of strength (Solórzano & Yosso, 2002). Critical Race Theory research in education often employs qualitative methods to document the intricate effects of race, racism, and white supremacy on BIPOC communities (DeCuir-Gunby et al., 2019; Lynn et al., 2002). While this approach is prevalent in CRT scholarship, it is essential to recognize the boundaries of qualitative research (DeCuir-Gunby et al., 2019; Parker & Lynn, 2002). Currently, there is a move toward employing CRT in quantitative analysis to address white supremacy and racism within quantitative methodologies (Garcia et al., 2018). Over the past two decades, critical race methodologies have emerged, such as, but not limited to: Critical Race Grounded Theory (Malagón et al., 2009), Critical Race Counter-Storytelling (Solórzano & Yosso, 2002), Critical Race Testimonios (Huber, 2008), Critical Race Participatory Research (Torre, 2009), Critical Race Oral Histories (Aguilar, 2013), Critical Race Urban Ethnography (Duncan, 2002), Critical Race Spatial Analysis (Ve´lez & Solo´rzano, 2017), Critical Race Media Literacies (Yosso, 2020), CRitT Walking (Hughes & Giles, 2010), Critical Race Mixed Methods (DeCuir-Gunby & Walker-DeVose, 2013; Garcia & Mayorga, 2018), Critical Race Quantitative Intersectionality (Covarrubias & Vélez, 2013), and QuantCrit (Garcia et al., 2018; Gillborn et al., 2018). While counter-storytelling has been significantly used in higher education to examine LatinX academic achievement and success, the field at large needs greater implementation of critical race methodologies.

THE EMERGENCE AND IMPACT OF CHICANA FEMINISMS

Chicana Feminisms

The Civil Rights Movement, shaped by the experiences of Black and African Americans, inspired Mexican Americans in the Southwest, known as *el movimento*, to advocate for labor rights, economic equality, educational equity, and political autonomy (Acuña, 1972; Muñoz, 1989). Cultural nationalism initially unified ChicanX communities during the 1960s and 1970s, although leadership was predominantly male, marginalizing women's roles and perspectives. This oversight prompted the rise of Chicana feminisms, which critiqued sexism, racism, and classism within cultural and social frameworks (Anzaldúa, 1987; Blackwell, 2011; Espinoza, 1999; García, 1989; Segura & Pesquera, 1988). Grounded in U.S. Third World Feminisms of Color of the 1960s–1970s, Chicana feminists emphasized their struggles as working-class Women of Color and challenged the mainstream white feminist movement's failure to address their unique challenges (Glenn, 1992; Ruíz & Chavez, 2008).

Therefore, Chicana feminist theories utilize personal experiences to examine, critique, and confront systemic injustices while examining identity, sexuality, embodied knowledge, resistance, healing, transformation, and empowerment (Castillo, 1994; Fregoso, 2003; Hurtado, 1998; Pérez, 1999; Sandoval, 2000). Additionally, these theories emphasize the importance of developing research methodologies that are feminist, aiming to critically address oppression within historical contexts of colonialism, patriarchy, and white supremacy (Alarcón, 1991; Anzaldúa & Moraga, 1981; Anzaldúa, 1987; Castillo, 1994; Fregoso, 2003; Hurtado, 1998; Pérez, 1999; Sandoval, 2000). Scholars, including Gloria E. Anzaldúa, Cherríe Moraga, Emma Pérez, Chela Sandoval, and Aida Hurtado, along with many others, have been instrumental in informing Chicana feminist perspectives in education (Delgado Bernal et al., 2006). In the late 1990s and early 2000s, Chicana scholars in education began to develop and expand this work into educational research (Delgado Bernal, 1998; Delgado Bernal et al., 2006, Villenas, 1996). In the following sections, I provide an overview of foundational Chicana feminist theoretical tools from my perspective as a Critical Race Feminista scholar in higher education. I then discuss how these foundational theories have influenced Delgado Bernal's (1998) concept of a Chicana feminist epistemology in education, with a particular focus on cultural intuition. Next, I shift to examining Chicana feminist theories specific to higher education research that have been used to study LatinX academic achievement and success in higher education.

FOUNDATIONAL CHICANA FEMINIST THEORETICAL TOOLS

Borderlands

Anzaldúa (1987) uses the concept of borderlands to describe both physical (geopolitical) and metaphorical (development of consciousness) spaces. She utilizes the U.S.–Mexico borderlands to illustrate a liminal space where cultures and nations clash yet coexist. This space, marked by marginalization and power dynamics related to race, class, gender, sexuality, and disability, is a third space for examining self, communities, and identity formation.

130

Mestiza Consciousness

The term "mestiza" or "mestizaje" refers to blending two distinct cultures, particularly Indigenous and Spanish cultures, in the context of ChicanX identity. According to Anzaldúa (1987), mestiza consciousness embodies a "consciousness of duality," embracing ambiguity and contradictions and operating in a "pluralistic mode" (pp. 59, 101). Anzaldúa stresses that mestiza consciousness is not just a fusion of conflicting identities but the creation of a "third element" (p. 102). This consciousness transcends existing identities to represent the emergence of a new, third identity.

Conocimiento

Anzaldúa (2002) offers the theoretical framework of conocimiento (knowledge/consciousness) as a "holistic epistemology that incorporates self-reflection, imagination, intuition, sensory experiences, outward-directed action, and social-justice concerns" (p. 10). She posits that achieving conocimiento involves an interconnected journey through seven pathways of awareness that are not linear, but rather progressive: 1) El Arrebato, 2) Nepantla, 3) Coatlicue state, 4) el compromiso, 5) putting Coyolxauhqui together, 6) the blow-up, and 7) shifting realities (spiritual activism). The pathways of conocimiento are personal and collective, occurring in informal spaces like the home and embracing knowledge beyond traditional educational institutions (Anzaldúa, 1987; Delgado Bernal et al., 2006). Unlike mestiza consciousness, conocimiento addresses spirituality and relationality.

Nepantla

Anzaldúa (2015) uses the Nahuatl word "nepantla," meaning the in-between or middle. She describes living in nepantla as a space of tension, contradictions, and ambiguity. Being in nepantla involves a space of self-identification and negotiation between realities shifting toward transformation (Anzaldúa, 1987).

Nos/ortas

Anzaldúa's (1987, 2015) notion of *nos/ortas* (us/others) highlights the deep interconnectedness of individuals and communities whose lives and experiences are interwoven. Individuals exist in relation to one another, in a shared space, where actions and experiences impact one another. She states, "I use the word nos/ortas to illustrate how we're in each other's world, how we're each affected by the other, and how we're all dependent on the other" (Anzaldúa,

2015, p. 268). *Nos/ortas* is a theory that allows for intersubjectivity, underscoring our differences that have the potential to generate connections not previously discernable.

Decolonial Imaginary and Sitios y Lenguas

Pérez (1999) introduces the decolonial imaginary as a third space to resist and subvert colonialism and its methodological assumptions of "objectivity." This imaginary is a "rupturing space" that bridges the colonial and post-colonial periods, recovering what has been "unspoken" and "unseen" in colonial contexts (Pérez, 1999, p. 6). By recovering oral histories through the decolonial imaginary, Pérez (1998) highlights *sitios y lenguas* as tools to reject colonial ideology and its by-products. Pérez (1998) advocates for *sitios y lenguas* (spaces and discourses) that "[reject] colonial ideology and the by-products of colonialism and capitalist patriarchy—sexism, racism, homophobia" (p. 161). Further, Pérez (1998) asserts that Women of Color, especially Chicana lesbians, have long created their own *sitios y lenguas* to counter ahistoricism and provide a history from the margins.

Theories in the Flesh

Moraga conceptualizes theories in the flesh as a form of embodied knowledge. The body is central to generating knowledge based on lived experiences. Moraga states, "A theory in the flesh means one where the physical realities of our lives—our skin color, the land or concrete we grew up on, our sexual longings—all fuse to create a politics born out of necessity" (Anzaldúa & Moraga, 1981, p. 23). Theories in the flesh are deeply rooted in everyday experiences and seek to create political and social transformation based on these embodied realities.

Bodymindspirit

Chicana feminist scholarship challenges dominant Western paradigms that separate the physical (body), psychological (mind), and metaphysical (spirit), a consequence of colonial logic, patriarchy, and white supremacy. Lara (2002) unites these entities under the concept of bodymindspirit, which mitigates the fragmentation caused by colonial and enlightenment philosophies that claim objectivity and that sources of knowledge should not be dichotomized between the mind and body (Anzaldúa & Moraga, 1981; Lara, 2002). Chicana feminists reclaim the integration of bodymindspirit as a source of knowledge grounded in lived experiences of race, gender, class, sexuality, and other identities.

CHICANA FEMINIST TOOLS IN EDUCATION

Chicana Epistemology in Education

In her groundbreaking 1998 work, Dolores Delgado Bernal introduced a Chicana Feminist Epistemology (CFE) to educational research, positioning it as a bridge linking Chicana Feminist Theories with educational research and enriching theoretical frameworks (Delgado Bernal, 2001). Chicana feminist epistemologies draw from the traditions of Black, Native American, and Chicana feminists aiming to transcend the qualitative versus quantitative research paradigm debate. Instead, CFE emphasizes the importance of "whose experiences and realities form the foundation of knowledge" and serves as a tool for Chicanas to examine the world and their intersecting social identities within academia and beyond. (Delgado Bernal, 1998, p. 558). A CFE in educational research challenges and disrupts notions of "objectivity" and universal truth in the research process (Delgado Bernal, 1998). Instead, CFE acts as a transformative catalyst, revealing the diverse knowledge and strengths derived from Chicana experiences influenced by intersecting systems of power, such as racism, sexism, and classism. In 2006, Delgado Bernal collaborated with other influential Chicana educational feminists—Elenes, Godinez, and Villenas—to publish the first edited volume on Chicana/Latina Feminista perspectives on pedagogy and epistemology in education. They asked, "How can we shift the terms by which we approach Chicana/Latina schooling and education from one of deficit to one of complexity, strength, and hope?" (Delgado Bernal et al., 2006, p. 4). Therefore, a Chicana Feminist Epistemology is rooted in the experiences of Chicana/Latinas as holders and generators of knowledge (Delgado Bernal, 1998). Furthermore, CFE challenges the supposed neutrality of traditional research methodologies by fostering collaborative relationships between researchers and collaborators (i.e., participants), making the research process accessible and allowing for collective knowledge creation (Cervantes-Soon, 2014). A CFE approach not only shifts power dynamics but also deepens the theoretical and practical impacts of research in education.[23]

Cultural Intuition

Stemming from a CFE, Delgado Bernal (1998) conceptualized cultural intuition for educational researchers to name the varying degrees of sensitivity they possess in the research process. Cultural intuition is a subjective standpoint and draws upon subjectivity as a source of strength. Therefore, cultural intuition draws from sources in the research process: personal experience, collective experience, professional experience, communal memory, the existing literature on a topic, and the analytical research process itself (Delgado Bernal, 1998, 2016). In engaging in their cultural intuition as LatinX researchers in higher education, scholars have revisited (Calderón et al., 2012) this seminal work to examine undocumented Chicana students (Pérez Huber, 2009), spirituality (Díaz Soto et al., 2009), queer professional and activist communities (Revilla, 2010), scholar-practitioners (Rocha et al., 2024), embodied experiences of land and place (Calderón, 2014), conceptualizing innovative methodologies (Espino et al., 2012; Malagón et al., 2009; Flores, 2017; Garcia et al., 2023; Gonzalez et al., 2023), and many more works that document LatinX student pathways to academic achievement and success.

Pedagogies of the Home

Building on ethnographic research that highlighted Mexicano/Latino teaching and learning in the home as strengths (Delgado Gaitan, 1990; Suárez-Orozco & Suárez-Orozco, 1995; González et al., 1995) and the feminista scholarship of Gloria Anzaldúa (1987), Delgado Bernal (2001) introduced the concept of pedagogies of the home. This concept emphasizes the mestiza consciousness of Chicana first-generation college students in California who navigate the borderlands between home and educational institutions. Anzaldúa (1987) describes mestiza consciousness as embracing duality, ambiguity, and contradictions. Delgado Bernal (2001) identifies bilingualism, biculturalism, commitment to communities, and spiritualities as key elements through which these students resist and navigate higher education. Bilingualism, for instance, serves as a form of cultural self-affirmation and resistance against English-only norms in academia. Biculturalism enables students to balance Mexicano and American cultures, fostering resilience and a tolerance for ambiguity. Their commitment to communities provides social support and motivation, while spiritualities offer internal and familial strength.

Delgado Bernal's (2001) concept of pedagogies of the home offers higher education institutions and their actors a nuanced understanding of race, class, gender, and sexuality. By (re)centering LatinX students, their families, and communities as active contributors to educational trajectories, institutions can develop strategies for academic achievement and student success, shifting the focus from failure to cultural knowledge within these households. Extending this concept, higher education scholars Castillo-Montoya and Torres-Guzmán (2012) incorporate elements specific to the Puerto Rican experience, such as lucha (the struggle or fight), to explain the resistance strategies taught in Puerto Rican households. In 2019, I extended the work of Castillo-Montoya and Torres-Guzmán (2012) and further explored how intergenerational Puerto Rican college-educated families co-construct cultural knowledge to combat racism in higher education through their use of *sin pelos en la lengua* (without mincing words), contradictions among college completers, and *pa'lante siempre pa'lante* (always moving forward) as strategies employed in navigating higher education (Garcia, 2019). Finally, in remembering and revisiting pedagogies of the home among ChicanX college-educated families, Delgado Bernal and I found that (re)making home, (re)covering tensions, and (re)claiming and (re)learning of cultural knowledge were the strategies embraced by two successive generations of college completers (Garcia & Delgado Bernal, 2021). Overall, these studies collectively underscore that pedagogies of the home remain vital for the LatinX academic achievement and success offering implications for K-12 education, higher education, and policy development.

Consejos

Delgado-Gaitan (1994), a pioneering Chicana feminist scholar, was among the first to explore *consejos* in educational research, describing them as cultural narratives filled with "nurturing advice" (p. 298). *Consejos* often occur intergenerationally among LatinX elders and parents to transmit knowledge, wisdom, values, and attitudes among children and young adults (Castillo-Montoya & Torres-Guzmán, 2012). In the field of higher education, Espino (2016) examin how Mexican American women PhDs engaged in *consejos* to navigate institutions of higher education while simultaneously negotiating race and gendered expectations among their families. Espino (2016) found that Mexican American women who earned PhDs employed passed down *consejos*, especially among women and family members, and using this cultural knowledge allowed them to transverse institutions of higher education. Sánchez and Hernández (2021) further extend *consejos* to *consejitos* among leadership practice in institutions of higher education. They argue that often *consejos* occur among family members and kin with power differentials, which limits the co-creation of knowledge as these encounters are not dialogical but instead rely on relationship-specific interactions. They conceptualize *consejitos as* "smaller affirmations for the everyday . . . [and]are co-constructed between peers, with each person responding to the other, and often occur in serendipitous moments" (p. 82). Overall, For LatinX academic achievement and success, recognizing and integrating *consejos* and *consejitos* can be instrumental, and more higher education research should engage this as a theoretical framework.

Epistemology of the Brown Body

Cruz (2001) employs Chicana feminist epistemology to emphasize the consistent absence of brown bodies in early feminist theory. She highlights the physical body as a vital source of knowledge, asserting that,

Each component of the brown body has its own story to tell—the lesbian mouth, the bent back in the fields, the dismembered daughter—and its deconstruction is a necessary process of reclaiming and reimagining the histories and forms of agencies of women who are unrepresented and unheard.

(Cruz, 2001, p. 66)

The longstanding separation between body and mind, or theory and experience, has dominated educational research, leading to an epistemological divide between white feminists and Women of Color feminists. Cruz (2001) further elaborates on this by presenting an epistemology of the brown body through what she calls "messy" texts—narratives that capture and validate the complex realities of their lives. Writing about brown bodies and asserting their histories while acknowledging the historical, social, and cultural actions imprinted on them is inherently messy and ambiguous.

Joteria

In 2014, *Aztlán* published a dossier led and edited by Michael Hames-García, who describes Jotería Studies as an "emergent formation [being developed by] a new generation of multigendered queer Chicana@s and Latin@s, trained and nurtured by women of color feminisms and feminists . . . among trans* and cisgendered people of color who have fought and loved in coalition, inclusion, and multiplicity" (Hames-Garcia, 2014, p. 138). The subfield of Jotería Studies within ChicanX Studies emerged in the early 2000s, although its roots extend back several decades prior to its formal recognition in academia. Revilla et al. (2021) translate *jotería* to queerness, and Salas-SantaCruz (2021) argues that Jotería Studies draws heavily on the work of queer Chicana/Latina feminists such as Anzaldúa (1987), Moraga (1983), and Lugones (2003), who examined how colonialism affects people's lives and developed a way of thinking that considers multiple intersecting aspects of identity and oppression, rather than just focusing on one. As stated in Chapter 2, over the past 20 years, research on the experiences of Queer LatinX individuals in higher education has illuminated several key issues (Gonzalez et al., 2023). This body of work addresses the complexities of navigating multiple marginalized identities on and off the campus (Peña-Talamantes, 2013). Such research emphasizes the experiences and impacts of disclosing non-heteronormative sexualities (Duran & Pérez, 2017; Eaton & Rios, 2017), explores the developmental processes of Queer LatinX college students (Orozco & Perez-Felkner, 2018), and demonstrates how Queer LatinX individuals build supportive kinships (Duran et al., 2019; Duran & Pérez, 2019; Hernandez Rivera & Frias, 2021; Revilla, 2010). Orozco (2021) identifies four themes regarding the literature on Queer LatinX students, Jotería, and higher education: 1) Jotería as an explicit and implicit identity, 2) living multiple and contradictory truths as Jotería, 3) developing a Jotería identity consciousness, and 4) building a Jotería kinship. Jotería is an emerging theoretical framework in the field of higher education research that holds significant promise for examining Queer LatinX college students' academic achievement and success.

CHICANA FEMINIST METHODOLOGIES

According to Saavedra and Pérez (2012), Chicana feminist methodologies are not merely tools; they challenge Eurocentric and Western research paradigms that often separate the bodymindspirit. They call for integrating embodied knowledge and advocate for subjectivity as a source of strength in the research process. For two decades, Chicana feminist scholars in education have developed qualitative research approaches to disrupt structural oppression and honor the knowledge of Chicana/Latina researchers and research collaborators. Examples of these methodologies include, but are not limited to: *convivencia* (Trinidad Galván, 2011), *pláticas* (Delgado Bernal et al., 2023; Fierros & Bernal, 2016; Flores Carmona et al., 2021), walking *pláticas* (Gaxiola Serrano, 2019), Queer *pláticas* (Gonzalez et al., 2023), *testimonio* (Delgado Bernal et al., 2012; Pérez Huber, 2009; Pérez Huber & Cueva, 2012), *pláticas ~testimonios* (Flores Carmona et al., 2021), Chicana feminist participatory research (Sánchez, 2009; López et al., 2020). Chicana feminist ethnography (Téllez, 2005), Chicana feminist cartography (Vélez et al., 2021), and Chicana feminist mixed methods (Canales, 2013; Garcia & Ramirez, 2021). These qualitative methodological tools have opened possibilities for incorporating Chicana feminist approaches into quantitative research to create transformative practices. In 2022, my colleagues and I (Garcia et al., 2023) argued that Chicana Feminist Epistemology (CFE) and cultural intuition offer an insightful pathway for developing innovative quantitative research methodologies that challenge the embedded normalization of power within quantitative inquiry—Critical Race Feminista Quantitative Praxis in education. In higher education research, *testimonio* and *pláticas* have been widely used to examine LatinX academic achievement and student success. Taken together, Chicana feminist methodologies in the higher education research can potentially integrate the bodymindspirit in the research process, acknowledging LatinX students' embodied experiences and the importance of emotional and spiritual well-being in academic achievement and student success. In the following sections, I define Critical Race Feminist Methodologies in educational research and explain how my collaborative work on Critical Race Feminista Quantitative Praxis has contributed to my conceptualizing what I call a Critical Race Feminista Quantitative Ethnography Praxis.

CRITICAL RACE FEMINISTA METHODOLOGIES IN EDUCATIONAL RESEARCH

Delgado Bernal and Alemán (2017) and Delgado Bernal et al. (2018) have developed Critical Race Feminista Methodology by interlocking CRT and Chicana feminist theories. In this chapter, I demonstrate that CRT and Chicana feminisms have extensive intellectual bodies of scholarship that center asset-based theoretical and methodological contributions in examining LatinX students' academic achievement and success. In engaging in a Critical Race Feminista Methodology, this intellectual genealogy should be honored and well documented (Pérez Huber et al., 2024). Thus, a Critical Race Feminista Methodology (CRFM) represents an anti-colonial praxis integrating theory, qualitative research methods, and critical consciousness. Delgado Bernal et al. (2018) state that:

> a critical race feminista methodology is one that seeks to disrupt traditional research paradigms that (re)produce systemic oppression through an intentional praxis to build and create theoretical and methodological strategies that sustain our humanity and honor those with whom we engage in the research process.
>
> (p. 119)

Pérez Huber et al. (2024) argue that there is no single approach to engaging in a critical race feminist methodology, but there are three main guiding principles: 1) methodological nepantla, 2) a commitment to *convivir/convivencia* (co-existing), and 3) healing, and intergenerationality. Alemán et al. (2013) use the concept of *nepantla* to describe a methodological process that embraces the complexity, contradictions, and tensions within a critical race praxis. For them, critical race theories help uncover racist structures, policies, and discourses, while *nepantla* represents a space where practical application and theoretical considerations intersect and sometimes conflict, requiring researchers to navigate ambiguity effectively. Trinidad Galván (2011) uses *convivir/convivencia* to discuss the coexistence and reciprocity of a true connection that is essential in building relationships between researchers and co-creators of knowledge (participants). For Pérez Huber et al. (2024), this is intimately tied to "practices of reciprocity, reflexivity, and shared vulnerability" in the research process that allows researchers to heal from the harm caused by racism and white supremacy (p. 1265). Finally, Pérez Huber et al. (2024) center on intergenerationality to honor their intellectual genealogy, but also the methodological possibilities of Critical Race Feminista Methodology (CRFM) advancing through "intergenerational sharing of stories, ideas, reflections, and dreams" (p. 1265). In our collaborative research (Garcia et al., 2023),

138

we utilized a CRFM to examine the enduring application of descriptive statistics in quantitative research, which has historically perpetuated deficit narratives impacting the academic achievement and success of LatinX students, their families, and communities. Our investigation necessitated an acknowledgment of the eugenic origins of quantitative methods (Zuberi, 2001) and a continuous reflection on their use in educational research, which has often misrepresented rather than elucidated the academic achievement and success of LatinX communities. We articulated a Critical Race Feminista Quantitative Ethnography Praxis (CRF Quant Praxis) as follows:

> a generative space of methodological nepantla that allows us to recognize and contend with the tensions and contradictions inherent in quantifying the experiences of Communities of Color. In this space, we engage our cultural intuitions to theorize how to quantitatively examine our experiences, which are shaped by systems of oppression and imbued by collective memory, community histories, and sites of resistance.
>
> (Garcia et al., 2023, p. 6)

Collectively, the significance of this methodology for LatinX academic achievement and success lies in its potential to disrupt deficit narratives and nurture a more nuanced and empowering understanding of LatinX students, their families, and communities. By centering the voices and experiences of those traditionally marginalized in research, CRFM and CRF Quant Praxis not only contribute to academic scholarship (in this case the field of higher education) but also serve as tools for social justice, advocating for the humanity and dignity of LatinX communities in higher education contexts. In the following section, I conclude this chapter by introducing what I conceptualize, define, and empirically apply as a Critical Race Feminista Quantitative Ethnography Praxis.

TOWARD A CRITICAL RACE FEMINISTA QUANTITATIVE ETHNOGRAPHY PRAXIS

I began this chapter with a critical race counter-story of Yamaris using Quantitative Ethnography (QE) as a methodology and Epistemic Network Analysis (ENA) to examine an *Epistemic Network Analysis of Dominican Undergraduate Disaster Preparedness Model 0* (Figure 4.1). Quantitative Ethnography (QE) is a convergence research approach that integrates (a) rich qualitative analysis with (b) quantitative and computational models (Shaffer, 2017), ENA is a method used in QE (Shaffer, 2017) to measure and visualize the connections among coded elements in data. It is often used to analyze qualitative data such as interviews, observations, and written texts.

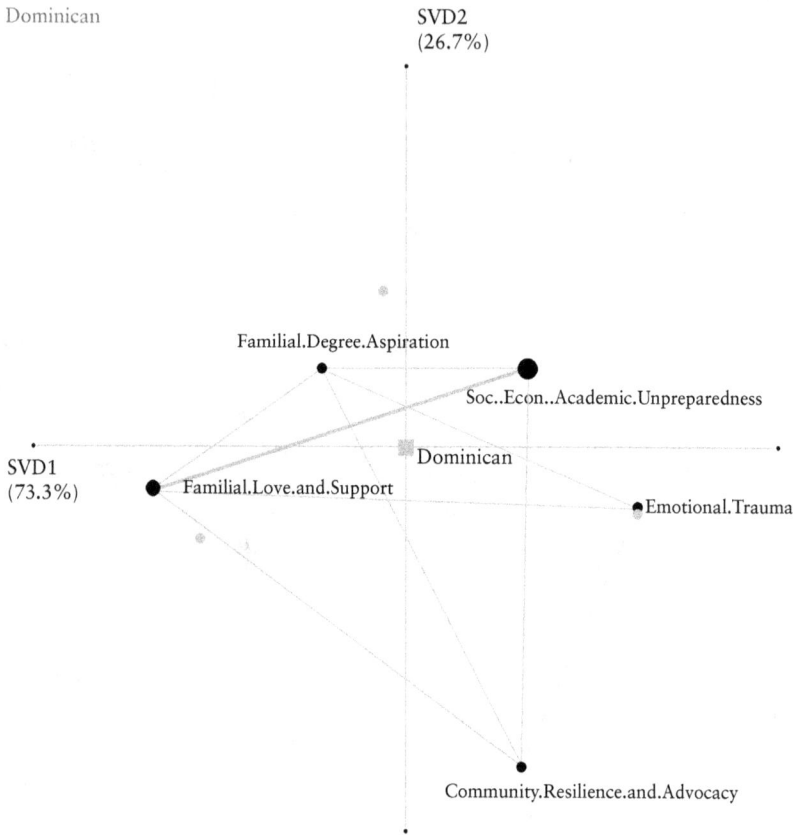

Figure 4.1 This is an example of a Model 0 in an Epistemic Network Analysis in Quantitative Ethnography focusing on Dominican undergraduate students.

As seen at the beginning of this chapter, Figure 4.1 *Epistemic Network Analysis of Dominican Undergraduate Disaster Preparedness Model 0*, this model 0 is a visual representation of qualitative codes in a network that shaped Dominican undergraduates'[24] experiences during COVID-19. It reveals how social, economic, and academic unpreparedness amplified their challenges, while community resilience, familial support, and aspirations for degree completion acted as vital resources against the pandemic's adverse effects. Each labeled point (node) represents a code identified in the data. In this model, the nodes include: Community.Resilience.and.Advocacy, Soc..Econ.Academic. Unpreparedness, Familial.Degree.Aspiration, Familial.Love.and.Support, and Emotional.Trauma. The lines (edges) connecting the nodes represent the strength and frequency of co-occurrence between the codes. Thicker lines indicate stronger or more frequent connections, showing how often these codes are discussed in the data. The point labeled "Dominican" is the centroid or the mean point representing the aggregate position of all the coded data points related to Dominican co-creators of knowledge or themes. It shows the central tendency of how these codes are interconnected for this particular group. For example, the proximity of nodes (i.e., code) and the thickness of the edges (lines) can be interpreted to understand the relationships among different codes. In this case, "Soc..Econ..Academic.Unpreparedness" is closely connected to "Familial.Degree.Aspiration" and "Familial.Love.and.Support," suggesting an important overlap in discussions about socioeconomic and academic challenges with familial support and aspirations among Dominican undergraduates. Distinct to ENA is the ability to run a quantitative analysis of different networks, such as comparing the networks of varied groups or conditions. The differences between the positions of centroids, the strength of connections, or the overall structure of networks can be tested for statistical significance.

While the statistical significance is important, I am more interested in the relationship between ENA, the visualization of model 0, and how storytelling (e.g., critical race counter-stories) can be used to represent and discuss race and other intersectional identities in various discourses pertaining to LatinX students' academic achievement and success. Therefore, I put forth a Critical Race Feminista Quantitative Ethnography Praxis (CRF+QE Praxis) as a methodological approach for a more complete and accurate depiction of the complexities surrounding LatinX academic achievement and success in institutions of higher education. This approach is important for LatinX students' academic achievement and success in higher education because it leverages the strengths of qualitative and quantitative analysis and critical race counter-storytelling to create a more comprehensive, inclusive, and accurate representation of LatinX students' higher education experiences.

A CRF+QE Praxis integrates the insights of Critical Race Feminista Methodologies with the analytical capabilities of Quantitative Ethnography (QE), specifically utilizing Epistemic Network Analysis (ENA). CRF+QE Praxis combines Critical Race Feminista Methodologies and Quantitative Ethnography. Critical Race Feminista Methodologies are grounded in CRT and Chicana feminisms, focusing on issues of race, gender, and their intersections. Alternatively, quantitative ethnography involves analyzing structured data to understand cultural patterns, utilizing tools like Epistemic Network Analysis (ENA) to map and analyze connections within discourse. Therefore, a CRF+QE Praxis embraces methodological nepantla as a state of in-betweenness where educational researchers navigate and reconcile different, often conflicting, epistemologies and methodologies to create a transformative space in broadly quantifying every discourse of the experiences of LatinX students, their families, and communities. A CRF+QE Praxis emphasizes the positionality and reflexivity of educational researchers that challenge colonial logic embedded within qualitative and quantitative methods, data, and analyses, focusing on disrupting ideologies of racism, white supremacy, and patriarchy.

CRF+QE Praxis leverages ENA to model and visualize the structure of connections between elements of discourse within LatinX students, their families, and communities. It aims to disrupt white supremacy racism, and patriarchy while centering embodied knowledge from those who live on the margins and confront daily structural violence, oppression, and power. By quantifying the co-concurrence or *convivencia* (co-existing) of meaningful discourse features, ENA facilitates a deeper understanding of how LatinX students, their families, and communities engage with and transform these features through everyday experiences and interactions.

CRF+QE Praxis seeks to achieve a liberatory praxis that brings epistemological wholeness to qualitative and quantitative analyses, enhancing collaboration, shared vulnerability, human connectedness, and opportunities for communal healing. Ultimately, CRF+QE Praxis aims to reorient qualitative and quantitative research toward improving the material conditions of LatinX students, their families, and communities by transforming it into a tool for liberation and holistic understanding. To effectively demonstrate CRF+QE Praxis in the construction and application of a model 0, in the case of Dominican undergraduates, I put forth the following tenets:

1. **Inter-centricity of Race and Racism**: The ENA model visualizes how themes like "Community.Resilience.and.Advocacy" intersect with "Soc..Econ..Academic.Unpreparedness" and other familial and emotional themes. By considering the inter-centricity of race and racism, it is possible to analyze how the racialized experiences of Dominican undergraduate students intersect with issues of class, gender, and other social identifiers. For example, the connection between "Soc.. Econ..Academic.Unpreparedness" and "Familial.Degree.Aspiration" may reflect the compounded effects of racial and socioeconomic challenges faced by Dominican undergraduate students and their families, examining how these experiences are not isolated but interwoven with their racial identities.

2. **Challenge to Dominant Learning Analytics Ideologies**: The ENA model serves as a tool to challenge dominant ideologies in learning analytics that often claim to be neutral and objective. By explicitly naming and visualizing themes related to racialized experiences, this analysis counters the "intentionality of omission" in traditional learning analytics enabling the analysis to reveal not only what is said but also what is omitted (Yosso, 2020, p. 8). The presence of themes like "Emotional.Trauma" and "Community.Resilience.and.Advocacy"

stresses the need to acknowledge and address the impacts of racialized discourses, rather than perpetuating the myth of meritocracy and neutrality in higher education data.

3. **Commitment to Social Justice**: Using ENA as a method within a social justice framework allows us to expose the negative effects of racialized representation. The visualization highlights how Dominican undergraduates navigate and resist systemic barriers through community resilience and familial support, demonstrating the potential of ENA to reveal both the challenges and strengths within LatinX communities. The strong connections between familial and socioeconomic codes reflect the community's collective efforts to overcome systemic inequities.

4. **Centrality of Experiential Knowledge**: Dominican undergraduate students' experiential knowledge is central to decoding this ENA model. The codes and connections are not mere abstract concepts; they are grounded in Dominican undergraduate students' lived experiences. These insights, in turn, reveal how these individuals perceive and respond to their socio-academic environments by employing counter-storytelling techniques. For instance, understanding the theme of "Familial.Love.and.Support" requires acknowledging the cultural and emotional contexts unique to Dominican families and communities, which may differ significantly from dominant cultural narratives.

5. **Interdisciplinary Perspective**: A multi-method approach, including ENA and other Critical Race Feminista methodologies like counter-storytelling, enriches our understanding of race and racism. CRF+QE Praxis allows us to move beyond traditional methods and engage with theories that capture the complexities of racialized experiences. The visualization can be further complemented by counter-storytelling that provides richer context and a deeper understanding of the codes. For example, counter-stories about "Community.Resilience.and. Advocacy" can illustrate how collective action and advocacy are crucial for navigating white supremacy, racism, and other forms of systematic oppression.

Overall, CRF+QE Praxis is a transformative methodological approach for advancing LatinX academic achievement and success in higher education research. Using Quantitative Ethnography and Epistemic Network Analysis, a CRF+QE Praxis illustrates how model can visually and effectively offer valuable insights into the systemic challenges and strengths that shape the educational pathways of LatinX students—in this case, Dominican undergraduate students—providing a comprehensive framework for promoting their academic achievement and success in higher education.

CONCLUSION

This chapter highlights the evolution of theoretical frameworks in higher education research, particularly those that examine LatinX academic achievement and success. While foundational student development theories laid important groundwork, they often centered on white, male, cisgender, Christian experiences, overlooking the diverse and complex realities of LatinX students. The emergence of Critical Race Theory (CRT) and Chicana/Latina Feminist Thought has provided more nuanced and justice-oriented perspectives that challenge systemic oppression in higher education. By integrating these critical frameworks with methodological approaches such as Critical Race Feminista Methodologies, this chapter underscores the importance of bridging theory and methods to more accurately represent and support LatinX students. Furthermore, it calls for a reexamination of quantitative research practices, advocating for approaches that recognize and address the systemic barriers faced by LatinX students rather than perpetuating deficit-based narratives. Ultimately, this chapter proposes a Critical Race Feminista Quantitative Ethnography Praxis as a transformative tool for advancing equity and accountability in higher education research and practice.

DISCUSSION QUESTIONS

Using the content within this chapter, consider the following questions for reflection and discussion:

- How does the integration of Critical Race Feminista Quantitative Ethnography Praxis (CRF+QE Praxis) challenge traditional theoretical frameworks and methodologies in higher education research, and in what ways can this approach more accurately capture the lived experiences of LatinX students, their families, and communities?
- In what ways can the visualization of interconnections between themes such as community resilience, familial support, and academic unpreparedness through ENA inform the development of more effective support systems and policies for LatinX students' academic achievement and success?
- How does the emphasis on counter-storytelling within CRF+QE Praxis contribute to a deeper understanding of the intersectional identities of LatinX students, and what impact might this have on their academic achievement and success?

NOTES

1. Translation in English: "Dominican Republic—21 Dead After "Highest Ever Rainfall Total" Triggers Floods and Landslides." This was reported by FloodList, and the article can be found here: https://floodlist.com/america/floods-november-2023-jamaica-dominicanrepublic-haiti. This occurred on November 23, 2023.
2. For a novel study on the experiences of second-generation Caribbean youth and urban education in New York, please refer to: Lopez, N. (2020). *Hopeful girls, troubled boys: Race and gender disparity in urban education.* Routledge.
3. Inevitably, COVID-19 has changed the landscape of higher education, especially for LatinX students, furthering disparities and only widening their educational opportunities in K-20+ contexts (Garcia & Danek, 2023).
4. Please refer to: Huber, L. P., Vélez, V. N., & Solórzano, D. (2023). More than "papelitos": A QuantCrit counterstory to critique Latina/o degree value and occupational prestige. In N. M. Garcia, N. López, & V. N. Vélez (Eds.), *QuantCrit: An antiracist quantitative approach to educational inquiry* (pp. 60–82). Routledge.
5. By the 1980s, Dominicans had become one of the largest immigrant groups in New York City, particularly in neighborhoods such as Washington Heights in Manhattan. This influx, sometimes referred to as the "Dominican wave," significantly shaped the city's cultural and social landscape, contributing to the vibrant Dominican community that remains a vital part of New York's identity today. Please refer to: Hernández, R. (2002). *The mobility of workers under advanced capitalism: Dominican migration to the United States.* Columbia University Press.
6. This exam is used by the New York City Department of Education to determine admission to eight of the city's nine specialized high schools. These schools are highly competitive and are known for their rigorous academic programs. The SHSAT is the sole criterion for admission to these schools, meaning that a student's performance on this test is the only factor considered for acceptance. The test is typically taken by eighth and ninth graders interested in attending a specialized high school.
7. This is one of the high schools that use the SHSAT for admissions.
8. The Ronald E. McNair Post-Baccalaureate Achievement Program, commonly known as the McNair Program, is a federally funded initiative designed to prepare undergraduate students from underrepresented groups for doctoral studies. Named after Dr. Ronald E. McNair, a physicist and NASA astronaut who tragically died in the Space Shuttle Challenger explosion in 1986, the program is part of the TRIO programs funded by the U.S. Department of Education. I am a proud alum of the program and have served as the faculty advisor at Rutgers for it. This critical race counter-story is based on the many Dominican undergraduates I have worked with in the McNair program.
9. I collected qualitative data as part of a larger study focusing on LatinX undergraduates who had or were currently experiencing a disaster from 2019 through 2021. Co-creators of knowledge were eligible if they met the following criteria: 1) identified as a LatinX college student who had experienced a disaster (e.g., hurricane, pandemic, earthquake, wildfires), 2) currently resided in the United States, and 3) currently enrolled at an accredited not-for-profit institution of higher education in the United States.

10. In an Epistemic Network Analysis, a model 0 is a baseline model to measure the significance of connections or interactions observed in qualitative data.

11. Epistemic Network Analysis is a method used in Quantitative Ethnography (Shaffer, 2017) to measure and visualize the connections among coded elements in data. It is often employed to analyze qualitative data such as interviews, observations, and written texts. This model is specifically labeled for "Dominican," suggesting it represents connections within data related to Dominican participants who experienced disaster. I explain what the model represents later in the chapter, but how I understand ENA begins with critical race counter-storytelling. Please refer to: Shaffer, D. W. (2017). *Quantitative ethnography*. Cathcart Press.

12. I am indebted to Dr. Brendan Eagan, the Associate Director for Partnerships and Community Engagement in the Epistemic Analytics lab at the University of Wisconsin—Madison who attended one of my lectures on QuantCrit and encouraged me to think about Quantitative Ethnography (QE) and ENA. Since our first meeting, he has introduced me to a beautiful, very giving, supportive research community to continue my work. In the summer of 2023, I became a QE fellow and have been learning this methodology. Since that time, I have been working closely with Dr. David Shaffer and Dr. Adaurennaya Onyewuenyi to think through an application of critical theories to ENA. I especially want to thank Alexander Tan, undergraduate researcher at the lab, for transforming my data, generating model 0s, and talking me through their meaning.

13. I acknowledge that this chapter addresses theoretical and methodological approaches covered by decades of research across various academic disciplines. It is intended to offer a general overview and does not represent a comprehensive review.

14. In this chapter, I use the terminology that the original authors used in their studies. When I switch to using "LatinX," it signals that I am offering my own interpretations, connections, and arguments.

15. Bourdieu and Passeron's (1977) concept and theory of cultural capital is further expanded and discussed regarding education, culture, and society. See Bourdieu, P., & Passeron, J. C. (1977). *Reproduction in education, society, and culture*. Sage.

16. Bourdieu's social reproduction theory identifies social capital, cultural capital, habitus, and the field as the main components of this theory. I only explain and examine social and cultural capital for this book since it is mainly used in higher education research on LatinX student success.

17. For a comprehensive analysis of social and cultural capital in higher education, see Winkle-Wagner, R. (2010). *Cultural capital: The promises and pitfalls in education research*: *AEHE, Volume 36, Number 1*. John Wiley & Sons.

18. In my own empirical investigation of the literature, I found that two publications emerged in 1992 by Vélez-Ibañez and Greenberg. The first study was interested in examining the differences and similarities between not only Mexicans but also Puerto Ricans and Cubans. Vélez-Ibañez and Greenberg (1992a) use statistical portraits of each group to discuss their "appropriate historical, regional, and ecological niche in order to decipher the paradoxes and contradictions of relations between education, occupation, income, and schooling performance, and completion" (p. 1). The second study examined how educational reforms and public schools often dismiss the strategic and cultural

resources—funds of knowledge—U.S. Mexican American children possess in classroom settings. It is important to document this intellectual genealogy, as I found in my research within the higher education literature that there is a lack of acknowledging the first study, which could be one of the first studies to urge the disaggregation of statistical data to account for the heterogenous experiences of LatinX sub racial and ethnic-populations in education. See Vélez-Ibañez, C. G., and Greenberg, J. B. (1992a, January 27). Schooling processes among US Mexicans, Puerto Ricans, and Cubans: A comparative, distributive, and case study approach, https://eric.ed.gov/?id=ED347022 and Vélez-Ibañez, C. G., & Greenberg, J. B. (1992b). Formation and transformation of funds of knowledge among U.S.-Mexican households. *Anthropology and Education Quarterly, 23*(4), 313–335. https://doi.org/10.1525/aeq.1992.23.4.05x1582v

19. I acknowledge that I have not provided an in-depth overview of CRT in law. Despite this shortcoming, there is a plethora of rich research and literature in the field of law that individuals interested in using CRT should critically examine and understand.

20. As an advisee of Solórzano, I have come to understand the lineage of research produced through the Research Apprenticeship Course (RAC) at UCLA. Personally, I benefited from firsthand training by Delgado Bernal and Villalpando at the University of Utah during my undergraduate studies and later as a master's student at the University of California, Santa Barbara, under the guidance of Yosso. There are many more from the RAC that have helped me develop into a Critical Race Feminista scholar. This intergenerational mentorship is detailed extensively by Solórzano; for more information, see Solórzano, D. G. (2024a). My journey to this place called the RAC: Reflections on a movement in critical race thought and critical race hope in higher education. In M. C. Ledesma, V. Johnson Ojeda, S. R. Coon, & L. Parker (Eds.), *Critical Race Theory and Qualitative Methods* (pp. 87–98). Routledge, and Solórzano, D. G. (2024b). My journey in the tall grass of resistance and refusal: from race, ethnic, and gender studies to Freirean critical pedagogy to critical race theory to the RAC. In K. Watson, N. Cisneros, L. Pérez Huber, & V. Vélez (Eds.), *Handbook of Race and Refusal in Higher Education* (pp. 25–41). Edward Elgar Publishing.

21. I recognize that a substantial body of CRT scholarship, particularly by Ladson-Billings, Tate, and other graduate students at the University of Wisconsin, has been produced over the decades. My goal here is to trace the intellectual genealogy that has positioned LatinX students as central subjects of research within higher education through a CRT lens.

22. In their original conceptualizations, Solórzano and Delgado Bernal (2001) derived their findings from the Chicana and Chicano student resistance.

23. For an in-depth analysis of CFE in higher education see: García, C. T. (2023). Chicana feminist epistemology in higher education. In *Oxford Research Encyclopedia of Education.*

24. I collected qualitative data as part of a larger study focusing on LatinX undergraduates who had or were currently experiencing a disaster from 2019 through 2021. Co-creators of knowledge were eligible if they met the following criteria: 1) identified as a Latinx college student who had experienced a disaster (e.g., hurricane, pandemic, earthquake, wildfires), 2) currently resided in the United States, and 3) currently enrolled at an accredited not-for-profit institution of higher education in the United States. This is a sub-sample of the Dominican students who participated.

REFERENCES

Acuña, R. (1972). *Occupied America: A history of Chicanos*. Harper & Row.

Aguilar, C. (2019). Undocumented critical theory. *Cultural Studies ↔ Critical Methodologies, 19*(3), 152–160.

Aguilar, C. (2021). Undocumented critical theory in education. In N. M. Garcia, C. Salinas Jr., & J. Cisneros (Eds.), *Studying Latinx/a/o students in higher education* (pp. 149–163). Routledge.

Aguilar, J. M. (2013). *¡Sí se pudo!: A critical race history of the movements for Chicana and Chicano studies at UCLA, 1990–1993* (Publication No. 3595375) [Doctoral dissertation, University of California, Los Angeles]. ProQuest Dissertations & Theses.

Alarcón, N. (1991). The theoretical subject(s) of *This bridge called my back* and Anglo-American feminism. In H. Calderón & J. D. Saldivar (Eds.), *Criticism in the borderlands: Studies in Chicano literature, culture, and ideology* (pp. 28–45). Duke University Press.

Alemán Jr., E., Delgado Bernal, D., & Mendoza, S. (2013). Critical race methodological tensions: Nepantla in our community-based praxis. In M. Lynn & A. D. Dixson (Eds.), *Handbook of critical race theory in education* (pp. 345–358). Routledge.

Annamma, S. A., Connor, D., & Ferri, B. (2013). Dis/ability critical race studies (DisCrit): Theorizing at the intersections of race and dis/ability. *Race Ethnicity and Education, 16*(1), 1–31.

Anzaldúa, G. (1987). *Borderlands/La frontera: The new mestiza*. Aunt Lute Books.

Anzaldúa, G. (2015). *Light in the dark/Luz en lo oscuro: Rewriting identity, spirituality, reality*. Duke University Press.

Anzaldúa, G., & Moraga, C. (1981). This bridge called my back. *New York: Kitchen Table*.

Anzaldúa, G. E. (2002). Now let us shift . . . the path of conocimiento . . . inner work, public acts. In G. Anzaldúa & A. Keating (Eds.), *This bridge we call home: Radical visions for transformation* (pp. 530–538). Routledge.

Astin, A. W. (1993). Diversity and multiculturalism on the campus: How are students affected? *Change: The Magazine of Higher Learning, 25*(2), 44–49. https://doi.org/10.1080/00091383.1993.9940617

Ayala, M. I. (2016, April). Navigating the higher education space: An examination of Latino college students. Presented at the American Educational Research Association World Education Research Association 2016 Focal Meeting, Washington, DC.

Ayala, M. I., & Contreras, S. M. (2019). It's capital! Understanding Latina/o presence in higher education. *Sociology of Race and Ethnicity, 5*(2), 229–243. https://doi.org/10.1177/2332649218757803

Azmitia, M., Garcia Peraza, P. D., & Casanova, S. (2023). Social identities and inter-sectionality: A conversation about the what and the how of development. *Annual Review of Developmental Psychology*, *5*(1), 169–191.

Ballysingh, T. A. (2021). Aspirational and high-achieving Latino college men who strive "por mi madre": Toward a proposed model of maternal cultural wealth. *Journal of Hispanic Higher Education*, *20*(4), 347–364.

Barajas, H., & Ronnkvist, A. (2007). Racialized space: Framing Latino and Latina experience in public schools. *Teachers College Record*, *109*(6), 1517–1538. https://doi.org/10.1177/016146810710900605

Bell, D. A. (1995). Who's afraid of critical race theory. *University of Illinois Law Review*, *4*, 893–910.

Bensimon, E. M. (2007). The underestimated significance of practitioner knowledge in the scholarship of student success. *The Review of Higher Education*, *30*(4), 441–469. https://doi.org/10.1353/rhe.2007.0032

Bernal, D. D. (1997). *Chicana school resistance and grassroots leadership: Providing an alternative history of the 1968 East Los Angeles blowouts*. University of California, Los Angeles.

Bernal, D. D., Huber, L. P., & Malagón, M. C. (2018). Bridging theories to name and claim a critical race feminista methodology. In J. T. DeCuir-Gunby, T. K. Chapman, & P. A. Schutz (Eds.), *Understanding critical race research methods and methodologies: Lessons from the field* (pp. 109–121). Routledge.

Blackwell, M. (2011). *¡Chicana power! Contested histories of feminism in the Chicano movement*. University of Texas Press.

Bourdieu, P. (1973). The three forms of theoretical knowledge. *Social Science Information*, *12*(1), 53–80.

Bourdieu, P. (1986). The forms of capital. In J. G. Richardson (Ed.), *Handbook of theory and research for the sociology of education* (pp. 241–258). Greenwood Press.

Bourdieu, P., & Passeron, J. C. (1977). *Reproduction in education, society, and culture*. Sage.

Brayboy, B. M. J. (2005). Toward a tribal critical race theory in education. *The Urban Review*, *37*(5), 425–446.

Cabrera, A. F., & La Nasa, S. M. (2001). On the path to college: Three critical tasks facing America's disadvantaged. *Research in Higher Education*, *42*(2), 119–149.

Calderón, D. (2014). Anticolonial methodologies in education: Embodying land and indigeneity in Chicana feminisms. *Journal of Latino/Latin American Studies*, *6*(2), 81–96.

Calderón, D., Delgado Bernal, D., Huber, L. P., Malagón, M., & Vélez, V. N. (2012). A Chicana feminist epistemology revisited: Cultivating ideas a generation later. *Harvard Educational Review*, *82*(4), 513–539. https://doi.org/10.17763/haer.82.4.l518621577461p68

Canales, G. (2013). Transformative, mixed methods checklist for psychological research with Mexican Americans. *Journal of Mixed Methods Research*, 7(1), 6–21. https://doi.org/10.1177/1558689812446022

Castillo, A. (1994). *Massacre of the dreamers: Essays on Xicanisma*. University of New Mexico Press.

Castillo-Montoya, M., & Torres-Guzmán, M. (2012). Thriving in our identity and in the academy: Latina epistemology as a core resource. *Harvard Educational Review*, 82(4), 540–558.

Cervantes-Soon, C. (2014). The US-Mexico border-crossing Chicana researcher: Theory in the flesh and the politics of identity in critical ethnography. *Journal of Latino/Latin American Studies*, 6(2), 97–112.

Chávez-Moreno, L. C. (2023). Examining race in LatCrit: A systematic review of Latinx critical race theory in education. *Review of Educational Research*. https://doi.org/10.3102/00346543231192685

Chickering, A. W. (1969). *Education and identity*. Jossey-Bass.

Collins, P. H. (1999). Moving beyond gender: Intersectionality and scientific knowledge. In M. M. Ferree, J. Lober, & B. B. Hess (Eds.), *Revisioning gender* (pp. 261–284). Sage.

Covarrubias, A., & Revilla, A. T. (2003). Agencies of transformational resistance. *Florida Law Review*, 55(3), 459–488.

Covarrubias, A., & Vélez, V. (2013). Critical race quantitative intersectionality: An anti-racist research paradigm that refuses to "let the numbers speak for themselves." In M. Lynn & A. D. Dixson (Eds.), *Handbook of critical race theory in education* (pp. 290–306). Routledge.

Crenshaw, K. (1989). Demarginalizing the intersection of race and sex: A black feminist critique of antidiscrimination doctrine, feminist theory and antiracist politics. *University of Chicago Legal Forum*, 140, 139–167.

Crenshaw, K., Gotanda, N., Peller, G., & Thomas, K. (Eds.). (1995). *Critical race theory: The key writings that formed the movement*. The New Press.

Crisp, G., Alcázar, L., Sherman, J. R., Schaffer-Enomoto, J., & Rooney, N. (2024). Systematic review of theoretical perspectives guiding the study of race and racism in higher education journals. *Innovative Higher Education*, 49(2), 247–269. https://doi.org/10.1007/s10755-023-09694-1

Cruz, C. (2001). Toward an epistemology of a brown body. *International Journal of Qualitative Studies in Education*, 14(5), 657–669.

Davies, S., & Guppy, N. (1997). Fields of study, college selectivity, and student inequalities in higher education. *Social Forces*, 75(4), 1413–1438.

DeCuir-Gunby, J. T., & Walker-DeVose, D. C. (2013). Expanding the counterstory: The potential for critical race mixed methods studies in education. In M. Lynn & A. D. Dixson (Eds.), *Handbook of critical race theory in education* (pp. 268–279). Routledge.

DeCuir-Gunby, J. T., Chapman, T., & Schutz, P. A. (2019). *Understanding critical race research methods and methodologies*. Routledge.

Delgado, R. (1984). The imperial scholar: Reflections on a review of civil rights literature. *University of Pennsylvania Law Review, 132*, 561–578.

Delgado, R., & Crenshaw, K. (1993). *Words that wound: Critical race theory, assaultive speech, and the first amendment*. Westview Press.

Delgado, R., & Stefancic, J. (2012). *Critical race theory: An introduction*. New York University Press.

Delgado Bernal, D. (1998). Using a Chicana feminist epistemology in educational research. *Harvard Educational Review, 68*(4), 555–583.

Delgado Bernal, D. (2001). Learning and living pedagogies of the home: The mestiza consciousness of Chicana students. *International Journal of Qualitative Studies in Education, 14*(5), 623–639.

Delgado Bernal, D. (2002). Critical race theory, Latino critical theory, and critical raced-gendered epistemologies: Recognizing students of color as holders and creators of knowledge. *Qualitative Inquiry, 8*(1), 105–126.

Delgado Bernal, D. (2016). *Cultural intuition: Then, now, and into the future*. University of Utah. Research Brief, Center for Critical Race Studies at UCLA, Issue No. 1.

Delgado Bernal, D., & Alemán, E. (2017). *Transforming educational pathways for Chicana/o students: A critical race feminista praxis*. Teachers College Press.

Delgado Bernal, D., Burciaga, R., & Flores Carmona, J. (2012). Chicana/Latina testimonios: Mapping the methodological, pedagogical, and political. *Equity & Excellence in Education, 45*(3), 363–372. https://doi.org/10.1080/10665684.2012.698149

Delgado Bernal, D., Pérez Huber, L., & Malagón, M. C. (2018). Bridging theories to name and claim a critical race feminista methodology. In J. T. DeCuir-Gunby, T. K. Chapman, & P. A. Schutz (Eds.), *Understanding critical race research methods and methodologies: Lessons from the field* (pp. 13–27). Routledge.

Delgado Bernal, D., Elenes, C. A., Godinez, F. E., & Villenas, S. (Eds.). (2006). *Chicana/Latina education in everyday life: Feminista perspectives on pedagogy and epistemology*. State University of New York Press.

Delgado Bernal, D., Flores, A. I., Gaxiola Serrano, T. J., & Morales, S. (2023). An introduction: Chicana/Latina feminista pláticas in educational research. *International Journal of Qualitative Studies in Education, 36*(9), 1627–1630.

Delgado-Gaitan, C. (1990). *Literacy for empowerment: The role of parents in children's education*. Routledge.

Delgado-Gaitan, C. (1994). Consejos: The power of cultural narratives. *Anthropology & Education Quarterly, 25*(3), 298–316.

Díaz Soto, L., Cervantes-Soon, C., Villarreal, E., & Campos, E. E. (2009). The Chicana sacred space: A communal circle of compromise for educational researchers. *Harvard Educational Review, 79*(4), 755–775.

DiMaggio, P., & Mohr, J. (1985). Cultural capital, educational attainment and marital selection. *American Journal of Sociology*, *90*(6), 1231–1985.

Dumas, M. J., & Ross, K. M. (2016). "Be real black for me": Imagining BlackCrit in education. Urban Education, *51*(4), 415–442.

Duncan, G. A. (2002). Critical race theory and method: Rendering race in urban ethnographic research. *Qualitative Inquiry*, *8*(1), 85–104. https://doi.org/10.1177/107780040200800106

Duran, A., & Pérez, D. II. (2017). Supporting queer Latinx students in higher education. *Journal of Diversity in Higher Education*, *10*(1), 66–77.

Duran, A., & Pérez, D. II. (2019). The multiple roles of chosen familia: Examining the interconnections of queer Latino men's community cultural wealth. International Journal of Qualitative Studies in Education, *32*(1), 67–84.

Duran, A., Rodriguez, F., & Patron, O. E. (2019). Queer love in the lives of gay Latino men in college. *International Journal of Qualitative Studies in Education*, *33*(9), 905–920. https://doi.org/10.1080/09518398.2019.1687957

Eaton, A. A., & Rios, D. (2017). Social challenges faced by queer Latino college men: Navigating negative responses to coming out in a double minority sample of emerging adults. *Cultural Diversity and Ethnic Minority Psychology*, *23*(4), 457–467. https://doi.org/10.1037/cdp0000134

Erikson, E. H. (1959). Identity and the life cycle: Selected papers. *Psychological Issues*, *1*, 1–171.

Erikson, E. H. (1994). *Identity and the life cycle*. W.W. Norton & Company.

Espino, M. M. (2012). Seeking the "truth" in the stories we tell: The role of critical race epistemology in higher education research. *Review of Higher Education*, *36*(1), 31–67.

Espino, M. M. (2014). Exploring the role of community cultural wealth in graduate school access and persistence for Mexican American PhDs. *American Journal of Education*, *120*(4), 545–574.

Espino, M. M. (2016). "Get a degree in case he leaves you": Consejos for Mexican American women PhDs. *Harvard Educational Review*, *86*(2), 183–205.

Espino, M. M., Vega, I. I., Rendón, L. I., Ranero, J. J., & Muñiz, M. M. (2012). The process of reflexión in bridging testimonios across lived experience. *Equity and Excellence in Education*, *45*(3), 444–459.

Espinoza, D. (1999). Chicanas in the US: Multiple identities. *Resources for Gender and Women's Studies*, *21*(1), 6.

Ferdman, B. M., & Gallegos, P. V. (2001). Racial identity development and Latinos in the United States. In C. L. Wijeyesinghe & B. W. Jackson III (Eds.), *New perspectives on racial identity development: A theoretical and practical anthology* (pp. 32–66). New York University Press.

Ferdman, B. M., & Gallegos, P. V. (2012). Latina and Latino ethnoracial identity orientations: A dynamic and developmental perspective. In C. L. Wijeyesinghe & B. W. Jackson III (Eds.), *New perspectives on racial identity development: Integrating emerging frameworks* (2nd ed., pp. 51–80). New York University Press.

Fierros, C. O., & Bernal, D. D. (2016). Vamos a platicar: The contours of pláticas as Chicana/Latina feminist methodology. *Chicana/Latina Studies*, 98–121.

Flores, A. I. (2017). The muxerista portraitist: Engaging portraiture and Chicana feminist theories in qualitative research. *Chicana/Latina Studies*, 17(1), 60–93.

Flores Carmona, J., Hamzeh, M., Delgado Bernal, D., & Hassan Zareer, I. (2021). Theorizing knowledge with pláticas: Moving toward transformative qualitative inquiries. *Qualitative Inquiry*, 27(10), 1213–1220. https://doi.org/10.1177/10778004211021813

Freeman, K. (1997). Increasing African Americans' participation in higher education: African American high-school students' perspectives. *Journal of Higher Education*, 68(5), 523–551.

Fregoso, R. L. (2003). *MeXicana encounters: The making of social identities on the borderlands*. University of California Press.

Gallegos, P. V., & Ferdman, B. M. (2012). Latina and Latino ethnoracial identity orientations: A dynamic and developmental perspective. *New Perspectives on Racial Identity Development: Integrating Emerging Frameworks*, 2, 51–80.

García, A. M. (1989). *Chicana feminist thought: The basic historical writings*. Routledge.

García, C. T. (2023). Chicana Feminist Epistemology in higher education. In *Oxford Research Encyclopedia of Education*.

Garcia, G. A., & Ramirez, J. J. (2021). Proposing a methodological borderland: Combining Chicana feminist theory with transformative mixed methods research. *Journal of Mixed Methods Research*, 15(2), 240–260. https://doi.org/10.1177/1558689820954023

Garcia, N. M. (2019). Pa'lante, siempre pa'lante: Pedagogies of the home among Puerto Rican college educated families. *International Journal of Qualitative Studies in Education*, 32(6), 576–590. https://doi.org/10.1080/09518398.2019 .1609116

Garcia, N. M., & Danek, V. (2023). Shelter from the storm: Disaster capitalism and Puerto Rican undergraduates in post-Hurricane María stateside higher education. *Teachers College Record*, 125(4), 182–211.

Garcia, N. M., & Delgado Bernal, D. (2021). Remembering and revisiting pedagogies of the home. *American Educational Research Journal*, 58(3), 567–601.

Garcia, N. M., & Mayorga, O. J. (2018). The threat of unexamined secondary data: A critical race transformative convergent mixed methods. *Race Ethnicity and Education*, 21(2), 231–252.

Garcia, N.M. & Mireles-Rios, R. (2019). Historical development of multiculturalism and diversity in student affairs practice. In N. Zhang & M. Howard- Hamilton (Eds.), *Multicultural and diversity issues in student affairs practice: A professional competency-based approach* (pp. 42–61). Charles C. Thomas.

Garcia, N. M., & Mireles-Rios, R. (2020). "You were going to go to college": The role of Chicano fathers' involvement in Chicana daughters' college choice. *American Educational Research Journal, 57*(5), 2059–2088.

Garcia, N. M., López, N., & Vélez, V. N. (2018). QuantCrit: Rectifying quantitative methods through critical *race theory. Race Ethnicity and Education, 21*(2), 149–157.

Garcia, N. M., & Vélez, V. N., & Huber, L. P. (2023). Can numbers be gender and race conscious? Advocating for a critical race feminista quantitative praxis in education. *Equity & Excellence in Education, 56*(1–2), 190–205.

Garvey, J. C., Harris, J. C., Means, D. R., Perez, R. J., & Porter, C. J. (Eds.). (2019). Case studies for student development theory: Advancing social justice and inclusion in higher education. Routledge.

Gaxiola Serrano, T. J. (2019). *Las enseñanzas de la línea: Sense of self and academic experiences of Latina/o/x community college students in the Tijuana-San Diego borderlands* (Unpublished doctoral dissertation). University of California, Los Angeles. Retrieved from https://escholarship.org/uc/item/0kg0x55f

Gillborn, D., Warmington, P., & Demack, S. (2018). QuantCrit: Education, policy, "Big Data" and principles for a critical race theory of statistics. *Race Ethnicity and Education, 21*(2), 158–179.

Glenn, E. N. (1992). From servitude to service work: Historical continuities in the racial division of paid reproductive labor. *Signs: Journal of Women in Culture and Society, 18*(1), 1–43.

Gonzalez, Á. D. J., Orozco, R. C., & Gonzalez, S. A. (2023). Joteando y mariconadas: Theorizing queer pláticas for queer and/or trans Latinx/a/o research. *International Journal of Qualitative Studies in Education, 36*(9), 1741–1756. https://doi.org/1 0.1080/09518398.2023.2181433

Gonzalez, L. D. (2012). Stories of success: Latinas redefining cultural capital. *Journal of Latinos and Education, 11*(2), 124–138. https://doi.org/10.1080/15348431.2 012.659566

González, N., & Moll, L. C. (2002). Cruzando El Puente: Building bridges to funds of knowledge. *Educational Policy, 16*(4), 623–641. https://doi. org/10.1177/0895904802016004009

González, N., Moll, L. C., & Amanti, C. (Eds.). (2005). *Funds of knowledge: Theorizing practices in households, communities, and classrooms.* Lawrence Erlbaum Associates. https://doi.org/10.4324/9781410613462

González, N., Moll., L. C., Tenery, M. F., Rivera, A., Rendon, P., González, R., & Amanti, C. (1995). Funds of knowledge for teaching Latino households. *Urban Education, 29*(4), 443–470.

Hames-García, M. (2014). Jotería studies, or the political is personal. *Aztlán: A Journal of Chicano Studies*, 39(1), 135–141. Retrieved from https://www.chicano.ucla.edu/files/Aztlan_39.1_Hames-Garcia.pdf

Haney López, I. F. (1997). Race, ethnicity, erasure: The salience of race to LatCrit theory. *California Law Review*, 85(3), 1143–1211.

Harper, S. R. (2006). Reconceptualizing reactive policy responses to Black male college achievement: Implications from a national study. *Journal of Student Affairs Research and Practice*, 47(1), 123–145.

Harper, S. R. (2012). Race without Racism: How Higher Education Researchers Minimize Racist Institutional Norms. *The Review of Higher Education*, 36(1), 9–29. https://dx.doi.org/10.1353/rhe.2012.0047

Harper, S. R., & Nichols, A. H. (2008). "Are they not all the same?" Racial heterogeneity among Black male undergraduates. *Journal of College Student Development*, 49(3), 127–144.

Harper, S. R., & Quaye, S. J. (2007). Student organizations as venues for Black identity expression and development among African American male student leaders. *Journal of College Student Development*, 48(2), 127–144.

Harris, J. C. (2016). Toward a critical multiracial theory in education. *International Journal of Qualitative Studies in Education*, 29(6), 795–813.

Hernández, R. (2002). *The mobility of workers under advanced capitalism: Dominican migration to the United States*. Columbia University Press.

Hernandez Rivera, S., & Frias, D. S. (2021). Iluminando la oscuridad: Queer Latinas healing in Spanish through conocimiento. *Journal of Women and Gender in Higher Education*, 14(1), 5–23.

Hogg, L. (2011). Funds of knowledge: An investigation of coherence within the literature. *Teaching and Teacher Education*, 27, 666–677. https://doi.org/10.1016/j.tate.2010.11.005

Horvat, E. M. (2001). Understanding equity and access in higher education: The potential contribution of Pierre Bourdieu. In J. C. Smart (Ed.), *Higher education: Handbook of theory and practice*. Agathon.

Huber, L. P. (2008). Building critical race methodologies in educational research: A research note on critical race testimonio. *FIU Law Review*, 4, 159.

Huber, L. P., Vélez, V. N., & Solórzano, D. (2023). More than "papelitos": A QuantCrit counterstory to critique Latina/o degree value and occupational prestige. In N. M. Garcia, N. López, & V. N. Vélez (Eds.), *QuantCrit: An antiracist quantitative approach to educational inquiry* (pp. 60–82). Routledge.

Hughes, R., & Giles, M. (2010). CRiT walking in higher education: Activating critical race theory in the academy. *Race Ethnicity and Education*, 13(1), 41–57. https://doi.org/10.1080/13613320903549685

Hurtado, S. (1998). *The color of privilege: Three blasphemies on race and feminism*. University of Michigan Press.

Jones, S. R., & Stewart, D.-L. (2016). Evolution of student development theory. *New Directions for Student Services, 2016*(154), 17–28.

Kiyama, J. M. (2008). *Funds of knowledge and college ideologies: Lived experiences among Mexican-American families* [unpublished doctoral dissertation]. The University of Arizona.

Kiyama, J. M. (2010). College aspirations and limitations: The role of educational ideologies and funds of knowledge in Mexican American families. *American Educational Research Journal, 47*(2), 330–356.

Kiyama, J. M. (2011). Family lessons and funds of knowledge: College-going paths in Mexican American families. *Journal of Latinos and Education, 10*(1), 23–42. https://doi.org/10.1080/15348431.2011.531656

Kiyama, J. M., Rios-Aguilar, C., & Deil-Amen, R. (2018a). Funds of knowledge as a culturally responsive pedagogy in higher education. In J. M. Kiyama & C. Rios-Aguilar (Eds.), *Funds of knowledge in higher education: Honoring students' cultural experiences and resources as strengths* (pp. 175–188). Routledge. https://doi.org/10.4324/9781315447322

Kiyama, J. M., Rios-Aguilar, C., & Sarubbi, M. (2018b). A review of existing research on funds of knowledge and the forms of capital. In J. M. Kiyama & C. Rios-Aguilar (Eds.), *Funds of knowledge in higher education: Honoring students' cultural experiences and resources as strengths* (pp. 24–47). Routledge. https://doi.org/10.4324/9781315447322-3

Kolluri, S. (2023). Patchwork capital and postsecondary success: Latinx students from high school to college. *Race Ethnicity and Education, 26*(6), 793–813.

Ladson-Billings, G., & Tate, W. F. (1995). Toward a critical race theory of education. *Teachers College Record, 97*(1), 47–68.

Lara, I. (2002). Healing sueños for academia. In G. E. Anzaldúa & A. Keating (Eds.), *This bridge we call home: Radical visions for transformation* (pp. 433–438). Routledge.

Lopez, N. (2020). *Hopeful girls, troubled boys: Race and gender disparity in urban education.* Routledge.

Lopez, R. M., Valdez, E. C., Pacheco, H. S., Honey, M. L., & Jones, R. (2020). Bridging silos in higher education: Using Chicana feminist participatory action research to foster Latina resilience. *International Journal of Qualitative Studies in Education, 33*(8), 872–886. https://doi.org/10.1080/09518398.2020.1735566

Lugones, M. (2003). The inseparability of race, class, and gender in Latino studies. *Latino Studies, 1*(2), 329–329.

Lynn, M., Yosso, T. J., Solórzano, D. G., & Parker, L. (2002). Critical race theory and education: Qualitative research in the new millennium. *Qualitative Inquiry, 8*(1), 3–6.

Malagon, M. C., Huber, L. P., & Velez, V. N. (2009). Our experiences, our methods: Using grounded theory to inform a critical race theory methodology. *Seattle Journal for Social Justice, 8*, 253.

Marcia, J. E. (1966). Development and validation of ego-identity status. *Journal of Personality and Social Psychology, 3*(5), 551–558. https://doi.org/10.1037/h0023281

Matias, C. E., Viesca, K. M., Garrison-Wade, D. F., Tandon, M., & Galindo, R. (2014). "What is critical whiteness doing in a nice field like critical race theory?" Applying CRT and CWS to understand the white imaginations of white teacher candidates. *Equity & Excellence in Education, 47*(3), 289–304.

McDonough, P. M. (1997). *Choosing colleges: How social class and schools structure opportunity.* State University of New York Press.

McDonough, P. M., Ventresca, M., & Outcalt, C. (1999). Field of dreams: Understanding sociohistorical changes in college access, 1965–1995. *Higher Education: Handbook of Theory and Research, 14.*

Moll, L. C. (1992). Funds of knowledge for teaching: Using a qualitative approach to connect homes and classrooms. *Theory into Practice, 31*(2), 132–141.

Montoya, M. E., & Valdes, F. (2008). "Latina/os" and Latina/o legal studies: A critical and self-critical review of LatCrit theory and legal models of knowledge production. *FIU Law Review, 4*(1), 187–211.

Moraga, C. (1983). La guera. In C. Moraga & G. Anzaldúa (Eds.), *This bridge called my back: Writings by radical women of color* (2nd ed., pp. 27–34). Kitchen Table: Women of Color Press.

Muñoz, C. (1989). *Youth, identity, power: The Chicano movement.* Verso.

Muñoz, S. M. (2013). "I just can't stand being like this anymore": Dilemmas, stressors, and motivators for undocumented Mexican women in higher education. *Journal of Student Affairs Research and Practice, 50*(3), 233–249. https://doi.org/10.1515/jsarp-2013-0018

Muñoz, S. M., Vigil, D., Jach, E., & Rodriguez-Gutierrez, M. (2018). Unpacking resilience and trauma: Examining the "Trump effect" in higher education for undocumented Latinx college students. *Association of Mexican American Educators Journal, 12*(3), 33–52.

Museus, S. D., & Iftikar, J. (2013). An Asian Critical theory (AsianCrit) framework. *Asian American Students in Higher Education,* 18–29.

Nora, A. (2004). The role of habitus and cultural capital in choosing a college, transitioning from high school to higher education, and persisting in college among minority and non- minority students. *Journal of Hispanic Higher Education, 2*(3), 180–208.

Nuñez, A. M. (2009). Modeling the effects of diversity experiences and multiple capitals on Latina/o college students' academic self-confidence. *Journal of Hispanic Higher Education, 8*(2), 179–196.

Oliver, M., & Shapiro, T. (1995). *Black wealth/White wealth: a new perspective on racial inequality.* Routledge.

Orozco, R. C. (2021). A futurity of Jotería studies and higher education research: Epistemological and theoretical shifts. In N. Garcia, C. Salinas, & J. Cisneros

(Eds.), *Studying Latinx/a/o students in higher education* (pp. 175–187). Routledge. https://doi.org/10.4324/9781003008545-14

Orozco, R. C., & Perez-Felkner, L. (2018). *Ni de aquí, ni de allá*: Conceptualizing the self-authorship experience of gay Latino college men using *conocimiento*. Journal of Latinos and Education, 17(4), 386–394. https://doi.org/10.1080/15348431.2 017.1371018

Parker, L., & Lynn, M. (2002). What's race got to do with it? Critical race theory's conflicts with and connections to qualitative research methodology and epistemology. *Qualitative Inquiry, 8*(1), 7–22.

Pascarella, E. T., Pierson, C. T., Wolniak, G. C, and Terenzini, P. T. (2004). First-generation college students: Additional evidence on college experiences and outcomes. *Journal of Higher Education, 75*(3), 249–284.

Patton, L. D., Harper, S. R., & Harris, J. (2015). Using critical race theory to (re) interpret widely studied topics related to students in US higher education. *Critical Approaches to the Study of Higher Education*, 193–219.

Patton, L. D., Renn, K. A., Guido, F. M., & Quaye, S. J. (2016). *Student development in college: Theory, research, and practice* (3rd ed.). Jossey-Bass.

Peña-Talamantes, A. E. (2013). Empowering the self, creating worlds: Lesbian and gay Latina/o college students' identity negotiation in figured worlds. *Journal of College Student Development, 54*(3), 267–282. https://doi.org/10.1353/ csd.2013.0039

Pérez, E. (1998). Irigaray's female symbolic in the making of Chicana lesbian *sitios y lenguas* (sites and discourses). In C. Trujillo (Ed.), *Living Chicana theory* (pp. 87–101). Third Woman Press.

Pérez, E. (1999). *The decolonial imaginary: Writing Chicanas into history*. Indiana University Press.

Pérez Huber, L. (2009). Challenging racist nativist framing: Acknowledging the community cultural wealth of undocumented Chicana college students to reframe the immigration debate. *Harvard Educational Review, 79*(4), 704–730.

Pérez Huber, L. (2010). Using Latina/o critical race theory (LatCrit) and racist nativism to explore intersectionality in the educational experiences of undocumented Chicana college students. *Educational Foundations, 24*, 77–96.

Pérez Huber, L (2011). Discourses of racist nativism in California public education: English dominance as racist nativist microaggressions. *Educational Studies, 47*(4), 379–401.

Pérez Huber, L., & Cueva, B. M. (2012). Chicana/Latina testimonios on effects and responses to microaggressions. *Equity & Excellence in Education, 45*(3), 392–410.

Pérez Huber, L., Vélez, V. N., & Malagón, M. C. (2024). Charting methodological imaginaries: Critical Race Feminista Methodologies in educational research. *International Journal of Qualitative Studies in Education, 37*(5), 1263–1271.

Pérez Huber, L., Benavides López, C., Malagón, M. C., Velez, V. N., & Solórzano, D. G. (2008). Getting beyond the "symptom," acknowledging the "disease": Theorizing racist nativism. *Contemporary Justice Review*, *11*(1), 39–51.

Perna, L. W. (2000). Differences in the decision to attend college among African Americans, Hispanics, and Whites. *Journal of Higher Education*, *71*(2), 117–141.

Perry, W. G. (1968). *Forms of intellectual and ethical development in the college years: A scheme*. Holt, Rinehart and Winston.

Phinney, J. S., & Alipuria, L. L. (1990). Ethnic identity in college students from four ethnic groups. *Journal of Adolescence*, *13*(2), 171–183.

Purgason, L. L., Honer, R., & Gaul, I. (2020). Capitalizing on cultural assets: Community cultural wealth and immigrant-origin students. *Professional School Counseling*, *24*(1), 2156759X20973651. https://doi.org/10.1177/2156759X20973651

Ramirez, B. R. (2021). Racist nativism in the college access experiences of undocumented Latinx students. *Journal of College Access*, *6*(2), 6.

Rendón, L. I., Nora, A., & Kanagala, V. (2014). Ventajas/assets y conocimientos/knowledge: Leveraging Latin@ strengths to foster student success. *Center for Research and Policy in Education, The University of Texas at San Antonio*.

Revilla, A. T. (2004). Muxerista pedagogy: Raza womyn teaching social justice through student activism. *The High School Journal*, *87*(4), 80–94.

Revilla, A. T. (2010). Raza womyn—Making it safe to be queer: Student organizations as retention tools in higher education. *Black Women, Gender and Families*, *4*(1), 37–61.

Revilla, A. T., Nuñez, J., Blanco, J. M. S., & Gonzalez, S. A. (2021). Radical Joteria-Muxerista love in the classroom: Brown queer feminist strategies for social transformation. In J. M. Kiyama & C. Rios-Aguilar (Eds.), *Handbook of Latinos and education* (pp. 22–34). Routledge.

Rios-Aguilar, C., & Kiyama, J. M. (2012). Funds of knowledge: An approach to studying Latina (o) students' transition to college. *Journal of Latinos and Education*, *11*(1), 2–16.

Rivas-Drake, D., Seaton, E. K., Markstrom, C. A., Quintana, S. M., Syed, M., Lee, R. M., & French, S. E. (2014). Ethnic and racial identity in adolescence: Implications for psychosocial, academic, and health outcomes. *Child Development*, *85*(1), 40–57.

Roberts, D. E. (1998). BlackCrit theory and the problem of essentialism. *University of Miami Law Review*, *53*, 855.

Rocha, J., Coronella, T., Reyes, M., & Romasanta, L. (2024). The value of scholar-practitioner cultural intuition in transforming educational systems. *International Journal of Qualitative Studies in Education*, *37*(6), 1752–1771.

Rodriguez, G. M. (2013). Power and agency in education: Exploring the pedagogical dimensions of funds of knowledge. *Review of Research in Education*, *37*(1), 87–120.

Rolón-Dow, R., & Davison, A. (2021). Theorizing racial microaffirmations: A critical race/LatCrit approach. *Race Ethnicity and Education, 24*(2), 245–261.

Ruíz, V., & Chávez, J. R. (Eds.). (2008). *Memories and migrations: mapping Boricua and Chicana histories.* University of Illinois Press.

Saavedra, C. M., & Pérez, M. S. (2012). Chicana and Black feminisms: Testimonios of theory, identity, and multiculturalism. *Equity & Excellence in Education, 45*(3), 430–443. https://doi.org/10.1080/10665684.2012.681970

Sáenz, V. B., García-Louis, C., Drake, A. P., & Guida, T. (2018). Leveraging their family capital: How Latino males successfully navigate the community college. *Community College Review, 46*(1), 40–61. https://doi.org/10.1177/0091552117743567

Salas-SantaCruz, O. (2021). Jotería literacies and coalitional possibilities. In A. Cortez & M. Lizárraga (Eds.), *Language, literacy, youth, and culture: Encyclopedia of social justice in education.* Bloomsbury.

Sánchez, N. C., & Hernández, E. (2021). Consejitos as a counter-hegemonic peer leadership practice. In N. M. Garcia, C. Salinas, & J. Cisneros (Eds.), *Studying Latinx/a/o students in higher education* (pp. 79–90). Routledge.

Sánchez, P. (2009). Chicana feminist strategies in a participatory action research project with transnational Latina youth. *New Directions for Youth Development, 2009*(123), 83–97. https://doi.org/10.1002/yd.316

Sandoval, C. (2000). *Methodology of the oppressed.* University of Minnesota Press.

Sedgwick, E. K. (2008). *Epistemology of the closet* (2nd ed.). University of California Press.

Segura, D. A., & Pesquera, B. M. (1988). Beyond indifference and antipathy: The Chicana movement and Chicana feminist discourse. *Aztlán: A Journal of Chicano Studies, 19*(2), 69–92.

Shaffer, D. W. (2017). *Quantitative ethnography.* Cathcart Press.

Solórzano, D. G. (1997). Images and words that wound: Critical race theory, racial stereotyping, and teacher education. *Teacher Education Quarterly, 24*(3), 5–19. https://www.jstor.org/stable/23478088

Solórzano, D. G. (1998). Critical race theory, race and gender microaggressions, and the experience of Chicana and Chicano scholars. *International Journal of Qualitative Studies in Education, 11*(1), 121–136.

Solórzano, D. G. (2024a). My journey to this place called the RAC: Reflections on a movement in critical race thought and critical race hope in higher education. In M. C. Ledesma, V. Johnson Ojeda, S. R. Coon, & L. Parker (Eds.), *Critical Race Theory and Qualitative Methods* (pp. 87–98). Routledge.

Solórzano, D. G. (2024b). My journey in the tall grass of resistance and refusal: from race, ethnic, and gender studies to Freirean critical pedagogy to critical race theory to the RAC. In K. Watson, N. Cisneros, L. Pérez Huber, & V. Vélez

(Eds.), *Handbook of Race and Refusal in Higher Education* (pp. 25–41). Edward Elgar Publishing.

Solórzano, D. G., & Delgado Bernal, D. (2001). Examining transformational resistance through a critical race and LatCrit theory framework: Chicana and Chicano students in an urban context. *Urban Education, 36*(3), 308–342. https://doi.org/10.1177/0042085901363002

Solórzano, D. G., & Pérez Huber, L. (2020). *Racial microaggressions: Using critical race theory to respond to everyday racism.* Teachers College Press.

Solórzano D. G., & Villalpando O. (1998). Critical race theory, marginality, and the experience of minority students in higher education. In C. Torres & T. Mitchell (Eds.), *Emerging issues in the sociology of education: Comparative perspectives* (pp. 211–224). SUNY Press.

Solórzano, D. G., & Yosso, T. J. (2001). Critical race and LatCrit theory and method: Counter-storytelling—Chicana and Chicano graduate school experiences. *International Journal of Qualitative Studies in Education, 14*(4), 471–495. https://doi.org/10.1080/09518390110063365

Solórzano, D. G., & Yosso, T. J. (2002). Critical race methodology: Counter-storytelling as an analytical framework for education research. *Qualitative Inquiry, 8*(1), 23–44. https://doi.org/10.1177/107780040200800103

Solorzano, D., Ceja, M., & Yosso, T. (2000). Critical race theory, racial microaggressions, and campus racial climate: The experiences of African American college students. *Journal of Negro Education, 69*(1/2), 60–73.

Steelman, L. C., & Powell, B. (1989). Acquiring capital for college: The constraints of family configuration. *American Sociological Review, 54*(5), 844–855.

Suárez-Orozco, C., & Suárez-Orozco, M. M. (1995). *Transformations: Immigration, family life, and achievement motivation among Latino adolescents.* Stanford University Press.

Téllez, M. (2005). Doing research at the borderlands: Notes from a Chicana feminist ethnographer. *Chicana/Latina Studies, 4*(2), 46–70. https://doi.org/10.2307/23014465

Tierney, W. G. (1999). Models of minority college-going and retention: Cultural integrity versus cultural suicide. *Journal of Negro Education, 68*, 80–91.

Torre, M. E. (2009). Participatory action research and critical race theory: Fueling spaces for nos-ortas to research. *The Urban Review, 41*(1), 106–120. https://doi.org/10.1007/s11256-008-0097-7

Torres, V. (1999). Validation of a bicultural orientation model for Hispanic college students. *Journal of College Student Development, 40*(3), 285–298.

Torres, V. (2003). Influences on ethnic identity development of Latino college students in the first two years of college. *Journal of College Student Development, 44*(4), 532–547.

Torres, V. (2004). Reconstructing Latino identity: The influence of cognitive development on the ethnic identity process of Latino students. *Journal of College Student Development, 45*(3), 333–347.

Torres, V. (2011). Using student development theories to explain student outcomes. In J. C. Smart (Ed.), *Higher education: Handbook of theory and research: Volume 26* (pp. 425–448). Springer Netherlands.

Torres, V., & Hernandez, E. (2007). The influence of ethnic identity on self-authorship: A longitudinal study of Latino/a college students. *Journal of College Student Development, 48*(5), 558–573.

Torres, V., Hernández, E., & Martínez, S. (2019). *Understanding the Latinx experience: Developmental and contextual influences.* Routledge.

Torres, V., Jones, S. R., & Renn, K. A. (2009). Identity development theories in student affairs: Origins, current status, and new approaches. *Journal of College Student Development, 50*(6), 577–596.

Trinidad Galván, R. (2011). Chicana transborder vivencias and autoherteorías: Reflections from the field. *Qualitative Inquiry, 17*(6), 552–557. https://doi.org/10.1177/1077800411409888

Umaña-Taylor, A. J., & Guimond, A. B. (2010). Ethnic and racial identity during adolescence and into young adulthood: An integrated conceptualization. *Child Development Perspectives, 4*(2), 99–105.

Valdes, F. (1998). Theorizing OutCrit theories: Coalitional method and comparative jurisprudential experience—RaceCrits, QueerCrits, and LatCrits. *University of Miami Law Review, 53*, 1265.

Valenzuela, A. (1999). *Subtractive schooling: US-Mexican youth and the politics of caring.* State University of New York Press.

Vélez, V. N., & Solórzano, D. G. (2017). Critical race spatial analysis: Conceptualizing GIS as a tool for critical race research in education. In D. G. Solórzano & V. N. Vélez (Eds.), *Critical race spatial analysis* (pp. 8–31). Routledge.

Vélez, V. N., Torres, D. P., & Jaramillo, D. L. (2021). Trenzudas, truchas, and traviesas: Mapping higher education through a Chicana feminist cartography. In J. M. Kiyama & C. Rios-Aguilar (Eds.), *Studying Latinx/a/o students in higher education* (pp. 106–120). Routledge.

Vélez-Ibañez, C. G. (1988). Networks of exchange among Mexicans in the U.S. and Mexico: Local level mediating responses to national and international transformations. *Urban Anthropology, 17*(1), 27–51.

Vélez-Ibañez, C. G., & Greenberg, J. B. (1992a, January 27). Schooling processes among US Mexicans, Puerto Ricans, and Cubans: A comparative, distributive, and ca-se study approach, https://eric.ed.gov/?id=ED347022

Ve´lez-Iban~ez, C. G., & Greenberg, J. B. (1992b). Formation and transformation of funds of knowledge among U.S.-Mexican households. *Anthropology and Education Quarterly, 23*(4), 313–335. https://doi.org/10.1525/aeq.1992.23.4.05x1582v

Villalpando, O. (2003). Self-segregation or self-preservation? A critical race theory and Latina/o critical theory analysis of a study of Chicana/o college students. *International Journal of Qualitative Studies in Education*, 16(5), 619–646. https://doi.org/10.1080/0951839032000142922

Villalpando, O. (2004). Practical considerations of critical race theory and Latino critical theory for Latino college students. *New Directions for Student Services*, 2004(105), 41–50. https://doi.org/10.1002/ss.115

Villenas, S. (1996). The colonizer/colonized Chicana ethnographer: Identity, marginalization, and co-optation in the field. *Harvard Educational Review*, 66(4), 711–731.

Walpole, M. (2003). Socioeconomic status and college: How SES affects college experiences and outcomes. *Review of Higher Education*, 1(27), 45–73.

Wing, A. K. (Ed.). (1997). *Critical race feminism: A reader*. NYU Press.

Winkle-Wagner, R. (2010). *Cultural capital: The promises and pitfalls in education research: AEHE, Volume 36, Number 1*. John Wiley & Sons.

Wolf, E. R. (1966). *Peasants*. Prentice-Hall.

Yosso, T. J. (2005a). *Critical race counterstories along the Chicana/Chicano educational pipeline*. Routledge.

Yosso, T. J. (2005b). Whose culture has capital? A critical race theory discussion of community cultural wealth. *Race Ethnicity and Education*, 8(1), 69–91. https://doi.org/10.1080/1361332052000341006

Yosso, T. J. (2020). Critical race media literacy for these urgent times. *International Journal of Multicultural Education*, 22(2), 5–13. https://doi.org/10.18251/ijme.v22i2.2685

Yosso, T. J., Smith, W. A., Ceja, M., & Solórzano, D. G. (2009). Critical race theory, racial microaggressions, and campus racial climate for Latina/o undergraduates. *Harvard Educational Review*, 79(4), 659–691. https://doi.org/10.17763/haer.79.4.m6867014157m707l

Zamudio, M., Russell, C., Rios, F., & Bridgeman, J. L. (2011). *Critical race theory matters: Education and ideology*. Routledge.

Zuberi, T. (2001). *Thicker than blood: How racial statistics lie*. University of Minnesota Press.

Chapter 5

LatinX Intergenerational Bendiciones Framework for Student Success

FELIX: DEFYING ERASURE IN THE FACE OF ANTI-DIVERSITY, EQUITY, AND INCLUSION LEGISLATION

Felix, a Bolivian student in Georgia,[1] traveled an educational journey that had been anything but easy. He was one of many undocumented LatinX students[2] facing the harsh realities of anti-Diversity, Equity, and Inclusion (DEI) and anti-Critical Race Theory (CRT) legislation[3] sweeping through the South. For Felix, education had always been his sanctuary, a place where he could dream. His parents had sacrificed everything to bring him to the United States, hoping he could pursue his education *con muchas bendiciones*.[4] But as he navigated the educational system, he quickly realized that the promise of opportunity was met with obstacles designed to keep students like him from meeting their full potential.

The nation's current wave of ant-DEI legislation was a stark reminder of this. As of 2022, "divisive concepts and ideologies"[5] referring to Critical Race Theory was now a banned subject in K-12 education, and any attempt to discuss systemic racism or the contributions of Black, Indigenous, or People of Color communities was met with consequences such as the elimination of funding and resources. Diversity programs were on the verge of being dissolved throughout all public universities and colleges. As undergraduate sophomores, Felix and his friends refused to be silenced. They saw these measures for what they were: a deliberate attempt to erase their stories and invalidate their experiences. They formed a group called "Voces Unidas."[6] This support network of undocumented students and allies was determined to fight back. Felix found himself stepping into a leadership role, driven by a deep sense of responsibility to his community. One evening, as the group gathered in a dimly lit room at the local community center, Felix addressed them with a passion he had not known he possessed. "We cannot let them erase us," he said, his voice steady but filled with integrity. "Our stories matter. Our history matters. We have to push back with knowledge and as a collective."

DOI: 10.4324/9781003415909-5

The group created a counter-curriculum for the general public, a series of workshops and seminars covering the banned DEI topics. They invited professors, activists, and community leaders to speak, ensuring that discriminatory policies would not dictate their education.[7] Felix spearheaded the project, meticulously organizing events and spreading the word through personal and professional networks.[8] The group's resistance became a beacon of hope for the undocumented community across the state, symbolizing resilience in the face of oppression. Felix knew the fight against white supremacy, racism, and oppressive legislation was far from over. But he also knew that he and other undocumented students had the power to make a difference, to challenge the reproduction of white supremacy and racism that sought to define their lives. And together, they would ensure that their stories would never be silenced.

COUNTER-STORY REFLECTION QUESTIONS

- How do anti-DEI and anti-Critical Race Theory laws impact the educational opportunities and psychological well-being of undocumented LatinX students like Felix in institutions of higher education?
- In what ways does Felix's leadership and the formation of "Voces Unidas" challenge anti-DEI efforts and the attempt to erase the contributions and experiences of LatinX communities within the educational system?
- What strategies can institutional actors, students, and communities employ to counteract the effects of legislation that seeks to suppress discussions of race, identity, and systemic inequities in institutions of higher education?

Today, the racial climate of institutions of higher education across the United States reflects a tension between progress and significant setbacks. More than half of states have introduced anti-DEI legislation, which seeks to limit or ultimately ban DEI initiatives in institutions of higher education (Chronicle Staff, 2024). *The Chronicle of Higher Education* has implemented a tracking system to document these legislative developments as the impact of these laws continues to unfold rapidly. Anti-DEI laws propose eliminating DEI offices and positions, DEI training, curriculum content in courses and books (e.g., Critical Race Theory), DEI criteria in hiring and admissions, and related funding (Chronicle Staff, 2024). States like Florida, Texas, Georgia, and Utah have successfully implemented anti-DEI legislation. As a Critical Race Feminista scholar born and raised in Utah, this especially hits home as I witnessed House Bill 261, "Equity Opportunity Initiatives," shut down all the campus culture centers at the University of Utah, where I first learned, developed, and began

165

to understand what it meant to be a Student of Color and what success meant beyond a simple metric.

Most recently, on June 29, 2023, the Supreme Court ruled (6–3) in favor of *Students for Fair Admissions, Inc. v. President* and *Fellows of Harvard College and Students for Fair Admissions, Inc. v. University of North Carolina,* effectively dismantling race-conscious admissions and affirmative action programs throughout the nation. Affirmative action is just one example of what Bell (1992) refers to as the notion of racial realism, which acknowledges the permeance of racism; the goal is not racial equity, but rather "efforts we hail as successful will produce no more than temporary 'peaks of progress,' short-loved victories that slide into irrelevance as racial patterns adapt in ways that maintain white dominance" (p. 373). In this context, Bell's (1992) insight "that the struggle for freedom is, at bottom, a manifestation of our humanity that survives and grows stronger through resistance to oppression even if that oppression is never overcome" becomes especially poignant (p. 378). In the case of LatinX student academic achievement and success, racial realism examines how white supremacy and racism continue to shape institutional structures, as seen in institutions of higher education across the nation, where the devaluation of LatinX culture and the normalization of white cultural norms further embed racial disparities and expectations of assimilation. As documented throughout this book, the definition of student success is widely debated and in contention within the field of higher education research and literature, especially when referring to LatinX students' academic achievement and success.

Therefore, in this final chapter, and in true CRT fashion, I explore manifestations of racial realism (Bell, 1992) in the twenty-first century as applied to the experiences of LatinX students while they navigate higher education moving forward. While not exhaustive, I identify and discuss manifestations that LatinX students, their families, and communities are facing in their higher education pathways: the aftermath of COVID-19, the repeal of race-conscious admissions, and college affordability. From there, using the characteristics of the white supremacy culture framework (Jones & Okun, 2001), I examine how the definitions of success discussed in Chapters 2 and 3 are deeply rooted in white supremacy, racism, and other forms of systematic oppression. Ultimately, I argue that re-envisioning LatinX student academic achievement and success begins within the home or wherever LatinX students find their place of community that sustains their lives and dignity (hooks, 2018). As hooks (2018) describes it, "Communities sustain life—not nuclear families, or the 'couple,' and certainly not the rugged individualist. There is no better place to learn the art of loving than in community" (p. 129). Therefore, I conclude this book by re-envisioning LatinX student academic achievement and success by incorporating a profound concept that student success definitions and measures have yet to consider—*LatinX Intergenerational Bendiciones* (blessings). I offer the *LatinX Intergenerational Bendiciones Framework for Student Success*, a powerful alternative to prevailing success metrics, focusing on the shared cultural, familial, and community bonds that sustain LatinX students throughout their educational pathways. As Stokes (2024) reminds us, "The goal is not to *belong*; the goal is to find value and beauty within the struggle itself. It is our obligation to support Latinx students and other students of color in their collective journey toward freedom, even if freedom is never realized" (p. 13). Aligned with this commitment, I argue that the *LatinX Intergenerational Bendiciones Framework for Student Success* transcends individual achievement to emphasize the importance of the collective process and the shared intergenerational milestones of LatinX students, their families, and communities. By centering the experiences, wisdom, and contributions of multiple LatinX generations, this framework recognizes the critical role of family and community in sustaining LatinX students' sense of self-worth, identity, and purpose in their educational pathways.

TWENTY-FIRST CENTURY MANIFESTATIONS OF RACIAL REALISM AND LATINX STUDENT SUCCESS

Covid-19

An application of racial realism (Bell, 1992) to the disproportionate impact of COVID-19 on LatinX students' academic achievement and success is not an anomaly but rather a reflection of the deep-seated racial violence that has long existed in the United States. The pandemic acted as a catalyst, exacerbating pre-existing disparities and shedding light on the pervasive nature of white supremacy and racism within institutions of higher education. LatinX students, who were already navigating a racialized higher education system, found their challenges compounded by the pandemic. For instance, the digital divide that LatinX students from elementary to graduate education faced during remote learning such as the lack of access to high-speed Internet and functioning devices further hindered their academic progress, stressing the racialized nature of technological access in education (Victorino et al., 2024).

Furthermore, the disproportionate impact of COVID-19 on LatinX communities, including higher infection and death rates, overrepresentation in essential jobs, varying risks of exposure, unemployment, economic loss, having an undocumented status, and insufficient access to health care, reflects the racial structural violence that these communities have historically faced (Garcia & Danek, 2023; Pedraza et al., 2022). The Centers for Disease Control and Prevention (2022) reported that LatinX individuals were twice as likely to die from COVID-19 compared with their white counterparts. The isolation, anxiety, and depression reported by LatinX students during this time can be seen as the psychological toll of enduring systemic racism, which the pandemic only intensified (Victorino et al., 2024). Racial realism would also suggest that the increased mental health challenges experienced by LatinX students during the pandemic are indicative of the cumulative impact of living in U.S. society where racial stressors are a daily reality. The concept of racial realism would frame these mental health disparities not merely as individual challenges but as symptoms of a broader, racially stratified society.

For LatinX students, the long-term effects of COVID-19 are far from over. Institutions of higher education and their actors need to address several key areas of concern for the future of LatinX student success. Institutions of higher education and their actors must also be conscious of the financial hardship caused by the pandemic, which have led many LatinX students to stop out due to inability to pay tuition and fees (UCLA Latino Policy & Politics Initiative, 2022). For instance, between Fall 2019 and Fall 2021, LatinX undergraduate enrollment declined by 7 percent, signaling a significant shift in enrollment trends. Students from economically disadvantaged backgrounds, many of whom are LatinX, have become increasingly less likely to enroll in two-year colleges, which may limit their access to higher education opportunities (Victorino et al., 2024). Additionally, the learning loss experienced by LatinX students in K-12 settings during the pandemic likely left many less prepared for the academic demands of their first year in college and beyond (Lara et al., 2021). This lack of preparedness could further impact LatinX academic achievement and success in years to come. Institutions of higher education and their actors across the nation must be proactive and provide personalized academic support, financial assistance, and mental health services to address the long-term effects of the pandemic on LatinX students.

RACE-CONSCIOUS ADMISSIONS AND AFFIRMATIVE ACTION

In June 2023, the Supreme Court voted (6–3) in favor of the *Student for Fair Admissions, Inc. v. President of Harvard College* and *Student for Fair Admissions, Inc. v. University of North Carolina*, which effectively dissolved all race-based affirmative action programs in the U.S. higher education system. Prior to this decision, 12 states had previously dissolved race-conscious admissions practices: California (banned in 1996); Louisiana, Mississippi, and Texas (1996–2003); Washington (1998); Florida (1999); Michigan (2006); Nebraska (2008); Arizona (2010), New Hampshire and Oklahoma (2012); and Idaho (2020) (Baker, 2019). Research pertaining to the effects of repealing affirmative action finds that the enrollment of BIPOC students is negatively impacted as they result in lower admission and enrollment rates across different institutional types of higher education (Baker, 2019).

The repeal of race-conscious admissions and affirmative action by the Supreme Court in June 2023 is another example of racial realism in action. The dismantling of affirmative action was not an unexpected development but rather an inevitable consequence of a system designed to maintain racial hierarchies. For LatinX students, the repeal of race-conscious admissions programs represents a significant setback in their access to institutions of higher education, particularly at selective institutions. Historically, affirmative action has played a crucial role in creating opportunities for LatinX and other BIPOC students to attend universities where they might otherwise be underrepresented. Without these programs, the structural barriers that LatinX students face—such as socioeconomic disadvantages, underfunded K-12 education, and limited access to college preparatory resources—become even more pronounced.

The experiences of California after the passage of Proposition 209, which banned affirmative action in 1996, provide a clear example of the consequences of such policies (Bleemer, 2020). The University of California (UC) system saw a significant decline in the enrollment of BIPOC students, particularly at its more selective campuses. UCLA and UC Berkeley, for example, experienced a 25 percent decrease in BIPOC enrollment, and these institutions have struggled to recover their previous levels of racial and ethnic diversity (Bleemer, 2020). Overall, the percentage of BIPOC students enrolled in 1998–2000, the period after the year Prop. 209 took effect, fell at least 12 percent across the University of California system (Bleemer, 2020). BIPOC students were less likely to apply to top-rated schools, instead applying to less selective options. This accounts for the significant disparity in change between UCLA and UC Berkeley and other UC campuses, ultimately leading to lower degree attainment. This trend has potential nationwide replication following the 2023 Supreme Court ruling.

Through a racial realism lens, the decline in LatinX enrollment at selective institutions is not merely a byproduct of changing policies but reflects the systemic functioning of white supremacy and racism within institutions of higher education and the U.S. government at large. Repeal of affirmative action can be seen as a mechanism wielded by the white dominant racial group who seeks to preserve its power and privilege to maintain control over access to educational opportunities. By removing race-conscious admissions practices, the system effectively reverts to a status quo that favors white applicants or legacy admissions, thereby reproducing inequity. Moreover, the absence of a diverse student body at selective institutions can create a campus climate where LatinX students feel isolated and unsupported. Reducing racial and ethnic diversity also deprives all students of the benefits of learning in a diverse campus environment, which is crucial for preparing graduates to navigate an increasingly diverse nation and global workforce. Institutions of higher education and their actors across the nation must continue exploring lawful and effective practices that will increase diversity in admissions and enrollment.

COLLEGE AFFORDABILITY

The relationship between college affordability and the rise of the student debt crisis is closely connected, especially for LatinX students. Goldrick-Rab and Steinbaum (2020) argue that while higher education should be a public good, access to it decreases as students struggle to afford it. Specifically, LatinX communities have the highest workforce participation rate of any racial or ethnic group in the United States. Still, they are less likely to hold high-paying jobs, which limits their abilities to pay for college and avoid accumulating significant amounts of debt (Excelencia in Education, 2019). An application of racial realism demonstrates that this does not result from individual choice but reflects a racialized capitalist system that restricts access to wealth-building opportunities for LatinX communities. This systemic limitation on earning potential directly impacts LatinX students' ability to pay for college, resulting in them taking out large amounts of debt. Measuring college affordability is complex, and institutions of higher education often place the blame for LatinX borrowing rates onto individuals rather than recognizing the impact of a broader capitalist system (Gándara & Zerquera, 2021). Employing racial realism underscores that this tendency to blame individuals for their financial struggles is part of a larger narrative that masks the role of white supremacy, racism, and capitalism in perpetuating the racial-wealth gap.

LatinX students consider various factors when approaching how they will afford college and minimize or prevent their debt (Gándara & Zerquera, 2021). Many LatinX students have additional responsibilities, such as working to support themselves through college and caregiving for family members, which leads them to consider their families when considering making financial decisions (Crisp & Nora, 2010; Gándara & Zerquera, 2021). For many LatinX families, debt is considered a family responsibility that impacts their college choices and borrowing behaviors (McDonough et al., 2015; UnidosUS, 2020; Venegas, 2007).

When choosing which institutions of higher education to attend, LatinX students often view community colleges as more accessible and affordable. As discussed in Chapter 3, community colleges typically offer lower tuition fees than public four-year institutions, and their proximity to LatinX students' homes reduces the need for relocation or extensive commuting. This proximity enhances the financial accessibility of college affordability for many LatinX students (Martinez & Fernández, 2004; Nuñez et al., 2013). However,

Gándara and Zerquera (2021) found that community colleges pose their own financial challenges as LatinX students attending these institutions are less likely to receive Pell Grants, and federal student loans may be inaccessible due to these institutions opting out of the federal loan system. Applying racial realism suggests that these institutional limitations are not accidental but are part of a system that continuously adapts to maintain racial hierarchies, even in spaces that are, at face value, supposed to be more accessible. Institutions of higher education and their actors across the nation must recognize these systemic barriers and work to implement policies that provide equitable financial support and resources for LatinX students.

THE CHARACTERISTICS OF WHITE SUPREMACY CULTURE AND LATINX STUDENT SUCCESS

Okun (1999, 2021) offers well-defined characteristics of the white supremacy culture to name how white supremacy cultural norms manifest and perform widely within any given organization. Okun (1999, 2021) argues that the characteristics of white supremacy culture are used to adopt attitudes and behaviors that are harmful to everyone. White supremacy norms are ingrained in the very fabric of our nation, often internalized unconsciously, and are subtle. The nine characteristics of white supremacy consist of the following:

- **Perfectionism:** The belief that mistakes are personal failings because there is only one "right" way to do things.
- **Sense of Urgency:** The pressure of time to achieve results quickly, often at the expense of others, especially relationships and individual well-being.
- **Defensiveness:** The inability to take responsibility or be accountable for behaviors or actions that cause harm.
- **Quantity Over Quality:** An emphasis on measurable outcomes and metrics rather than the quality of relationships. There is a disconnect between achieving an intended outcome and attending to the needs of those involved.
- **Worship of the Written Word:** The prioritization of written documentation and formal communication as the only "right" or valid form of knowledge sharing and production.
- **Only One Right Way:** The belief that there is a single "right" way to approach things, often aligning with white cultural norms.
- **Paternalism:** Decision-making is controlled by those in power without including the perspectives of those affected by the decisions.
- **Either/Or Thinking:** A binary way of thinking that frames issues regarding two opposing options without considering complexity or nuance.

- **Power Hoarding:** The unwillingness to share power, distribution of resources, knowledge, and/or decision-making processes with others, particularly marginalized groups.
- **Fear of Open Conflict:** Aversion to confrontation or disagreements, often placing the blame on the person raising issues rather than addressing the issues themselves.
- **Individualism:** The prioritization of individual achievement and autonomy, often at the expense of collaboration and collective well-being.
- **Progress Is Bigger, More:** The assumption that expansion is inherently positive, regardless of whether those experiencing the growth are being well-served.
- **Objectivity:** The belief in an objective, neutral perspective, often dismissing the importance of subjective experiences and emotions, especially those of marginalized communities.
- **Right to Comfort:** The belief that those in power are entitled to emotional and psychological comfort, often prioritizing "logic" over emotion.

An application of the characteristics of white supremacy culture can assist in contextualizing how indicators used to define LatinX student academic achievement and success often reinforce white supremacy and racism, placing the onus on the individual instead of the system. As an example, and for this analysis, I draw from three definitions of student success (Ewell & Wellman, 2007; Hearn, 2006; Nuñez et al., 2013) and nine indicators identified as specific to LatinX student success (Crisp et al., 2015). Hearn (2006) emphasizes the importance of effectively defining and measuring student success, stating that while graduating with a desired degree is the most significant indicator, focusing solely on graduation rates can distort institutions' reputations. Hearn (2006) argues that while graduation rates are simple and straightforward metrics highly regarded by policymakers, educational leaders, the public, and students, they can unfairly enhance the reputations of selective institutions while harming the perceptions of those serving a broader range of students. Hearn suggests that defining and measuring student success are a continuing challenge for scholars and institutional leaders in higher education. Ewell and Wellman (2007) argue that "student success" is a complex concept that covers many aspects, including the entire educational pipeline from high school graduation to college enrollment, retention, and degree completion. It also includes the quality of learning and skills gained through college and positive educational experiences like student engagement and satisfaction. Nuñez et al. (2013) define success broadly and multi-dimensionally, encompassing factors such as "initial enrollment characteristics, academic performance, social sense of belonging, persistence, and degree completion" (p. 2). This wide-ranging definition aligns with discussions from the NPEC symposium and commissioned papers, emphasizing the central characteristics of completing a postsecondary degree or credential in determining LatinX student success. Finally, as discussed in Chapter 3, Crisp et al. (2015) found that the leading indicators of LatinX student success are course grades or grade point average (GPA), persistence, and completing a postsecondary degree or credential. As detailed in Chapter 3, Crisp et al.'s (2015) research further identifies nine specific factors influencing LatinX student success:

1. LatinX students' sociocultural attributes such as gender influence persistence, grades, and the likelihood of postsecondary degree or credential completion.
2. LatinX students' self-confidence regarding academic tasks contributes to their persistence, grades, and postsecondary degree or credential completion.
3. LatinX students' awareness of their ethnic and racial identities, belief systems regarding justice-oriented equity, responsiveness to stereotypes, and engagement in adaptive coping might contribute to their persistence in postsecondary degree or credential completion.
4. LatinX students' precollege characteristics, such as how well they perform in high school, can dictate how well they will perform in college, especially regarding their grades and persistence to a postsecondary degree or credential completion, regardless of institutional type.
5. LatinX students' college experiences, such as college affordability, financial aid packages, student and employment status (e.g., full-time or part-time), and academic performance, influence their postsecondary degree or credential completion.
6. LatinX students' internal motivation and commitment profoundly impact their drive to succeed and academic performance.
7. LatinX students need supportive relationships from peers, parents, mentors, or others who contribute to their grades and persistence in pursuing postsecondary degrees or credentials.
8. LatinX students who have negative experiences due to hostile campus climate may deter their persistence and postsecondary degree or credential completion.
9. For LatinX students, the institutional type they attend may impact their persistence in obtaining a postsecondary degree or credential completion.

I want to clarify that applying the characteristics of white supremacy culture to these student success definitions and nine indicators is not about blaming individuals or groups. Instead, the purpose of identifying the characteristics of white supremacy culture is to demonstrate how institutions of higher education and their actors unconsciously adopt these norms and standards, which ultimately impede LatinX students' progress toward a postsecondary degree or credential completion. As a result, institutions of higher education and their actors, while claiming to be advocates of "student success," only allow LatinX students to participate if they conform to white supremacy cultural norms. Taken together, the characteristics of white supremacy applied to the nine indicators of LatinX student success are as follows:

- **Sociocultural Attributes (e.g., Gender Differences)**: The characteristic of **Paternalism** often manifests in institutions of higher education by imposing a single standard of success, usually ignoring the unique sociocultural attributes, like gender, that impact LatinX students. Institutions of higher education and their actors determine success without involving LatinX students, their families, or communities. For instance, the higher persistence rates of LatinX females might be undervalued due to gender stereotypes and false assumptions that they do not need support. This oversight can lead to inadequate support for LatinX females, reinforcing gender inequities and limiting their educational pathways.

- **Academic Self-Confidence**: **Perfectionism** and a **Sense of Urgency** create an environment where LatinX students might feel immense pressure to meet unrealistic standards, often affecting their self-confidence and cognitive abilities. Only certain types of achievement are valued and usually stem from white cultural norms that frequently reflect a sense of urgency that prioritizes speed and efficiency over the quality of educational experience. These traits ignore LatinX students' additional challenges and create pressure for them to conform to white cultural norms that do not acknowledge their culture or social identities and potentially lead to stress and feelings of inadequacy. This is especially true when LatinX students are pressured to meet timelines and benchmarks that do not account for navigating systemic oppression, balancing family responsibilities, or dealing with financial pressures.

- **Ethnic/Racial Identity and Coping Strategies**: **Either/Or Thinking** and **Objectivity** may suppress the value of LatinX students' awareness of their ethnic and racial identities. By reducing success to rigid, binary terms, institutions of higher education and their actors may occupy an "objective" stance and overlook the complex ways these students navigate their identities and cope with challenges. This lack of recognition can lead to alienation, reducing motivation and persistence.

- **Precollege Characteristics: Power Hoarding** and **Defensiveness** appear in how institutions of higher education and their actors assess LatinX students' pre-college characteristics. Traditional paths are often favored, while nontraditional paths, like gap years or community college attendance, are undervalued, leading to insufficient support for LatinX students. The lack of recognition and support for nontraditional pathways can result in higher pushout or stop-out rates among LatinX students.
- **College Experiences (e.g., College Affordability and Financial Aid): Worship of the Written Word** and **Quantity Over Quality** manifest in the rigid application of policies and metrics, often overlooking the lived experiences of LatinX students. This can limit access to financial aid and other resources essential for their success. Financial strain, accumulated debt, and limited support can lead to decreased academic performance and higher pushout or stop-out rates.
- **Internal Motivation and Commitment: Individualism** undermines recognition of LatinX students' internal motivation and commitment by overemphasizing personal responsibility while ignoring racism and white supremacy. This can obscure the importance of familial and community support. The pressure to succeed independently can lead to burnout and disengagement.
- **Supportive Relationships: Right to Comfort** and **Fear of Open Conflict** can hinder the development of supportive relationships for LatinX students. Institutions of higher education and their actors that prioritize the comfort of those in power may fail to create environments where supportive relationships can thrive. The characteristics of white supremacy might stifle critical conversations about how current definitions of success fail to serve LatinX students. Without support networks and transparency to openly discuss racism and white supremacy, LatinX students may feel isolated, alone, and misunderstood.
- **Campus Climate: Fear of Open Conflict** and **Defensiveness** can prevent institutions of higher education and their actors from addressing hostile campus climates. When institutions of higher education and their actors avoid confronting racism or dismiss LatinX students' concerns, they perpetuate environments that discourage persistence and postsecondary degree or credential completion. A hostile or unwelcoming campus climate can significantly reduce LatinX students' engagement, as they do not feel welcome, increasing their chances of being pushed out or stopped out.
- **Institutional Type: Only One Right Way** is often reflected in the devaluation of LatinX students' diverse educational paths, such as

attending community colleges or minority-serving institutions. This narrow perspective can lead to inadequate support and recognition of LatinX students in these institutions. Undervaluation of alternative educational pathways can limit resources and support for LatinX students, decreasing their chances of persistence and successful postsecondary degree or credential completion.

Application of white supremacy cultural characteristics within institutions of higher education significantly impacts LatinX student success, which perpetuates norms that marginalize and exclude these students' needs. White cultural norms reinforce a narrow, one-size-fits-all definition of success that is often misaligned with the realities of LatinX students, their families, and communities. To truly support LatinX students, institutions of higher education and their actors must identify how and when these characteristics are manifested, actively dismantle these harmful norms, embrace anti-racist practices, and offer personalized recourses that uplift these students. In the next section, I conceptualize *LatinX Intergenerational Bendiciones* to disrupt white supremacy cultural norms of LatinX students' academic achievement and success. *LatinX Intergenerational Bendiciones* embraces anti-racist practices that culturally affirm LatinX students, their families, and communities.

LATINX INTERGENERATIONAL BENDICIONES: A RE-ENVISIONING OF STUDENT SUCCESS

As a Spanish-as-a-second language learner, I have consistently struggled to speak the language fluently. My conversational skills have suffered from a lack of practice, though my writing and reading abilities have often compensated for this gap. However, I know I am not alone in grappling with losing the Spanish language within my family and community. I once asked my grandmother, "Why didn't you teach my dad Spanish, or us, your grandchildren?" She responded, "I barely knew it myself, and what I did know, I was discouraged from speaking at school." Intergenerational pressures ensured that Spanish was not passed down to me to help me navigate the U.S. educational system "successfully," which meant conforming to white cultural norms. Although I have since healed from these conflicting messages, I still encounter expectations that I should know Spanish or feel ashamed of not speaking it. Today, I no longer view the absence of the language as a point of shame but rather as a complex part of my cultural identity shaped by white supremacy, racism, and other forms of systematic oppression beyond my control.

My partner spent his early years in Bolivia with his father. When he returned to the United States, his experience diverged from mine. He could not speak English and was placed in an English as a Second Language (ESL) track—a completely different experience, yet in a way two sides of the same coin. From our conversations, this experience left him insecure, lacking confidence in his academic abilities, and, worst yet, lonely. We often discuss our household pedagogies that emerged from our childhoods, our grandparents' driving forces in how we developed, and our parents making sacrifices to provide a life better than their own. I always ask my partner about *dichos* (sayings) as I have gathered them from my experiences, chosen family, students, and peers through the years. When I told him I was writing this book on LatinX student success, he asked, "How would you define success for us?" I proceeded to explain that was the goal of my work ahead.

In the concluding weeks of writing this book, I struggled to name "success" without using the word "success" since it was never truly designed or defined with LatinX students, their families, or communities in mind. I asked him, "While growing up in Bolivia, how did you all talk about someone successful?" With a growing grin, he stated, "*Tiene mucho bendiciones*" (They have a lot of blessings) *or con muchas bendiciones* (with a lot of blessings)." It was at this moment that goosebumps arose on my skin. That was what was missing from how I have come to understand and experience blessings. While my grandmother only spoke English to me, the sense of blessings resonated with me powerfully. She often said, "Let's count our blessings" or "We are blessed." While blessings in Spanish and English frequently carry religious undertones, that is not the sense I am referring to here. Instead, I draw from Delgado Bernal's (2001) pedagogies of the home, which emphasize bilingualism, biculturalism, commitment to communities, and spiritualities as tools for cultural affirmation, resilience, and support in navigating institutions of higher education. Additionally, I incorporate Pérez Huber et al.'s (2024) focus on intergenerationality, which explores sharing stories, dreams, ideas, and reflections across generations. Taken together, these sensibilities help me conceptualize *LatinX Intergenerational Bendiciones*.

Embedded in pedagogies of the home, *bendiciones* (blessings) encompass the teachings, values, and resilience inherited from previous generations, which empower LatinX students to navigate educational spaces that disrupt white supremacy, racism, and white cultural norms engrained in metrics of success in institutions of higher education. Pérez Huber et al. (2024) emphasize centering intergenerationally, grounded in the belief and practice of sharing "stories, ideas, reflections, and dreams" (p. 1265). Sharing as a belief becomes critical for advancing *LatinX Intergenerational Bendiciones* because it shifts the focus of student success from merely an academic metric to a broader understanding that honors the shared intergenerational milestones of LatinX students, their families, and communities. LatinX student milestones are cumulative across generations, marking success as not limited to individual achievement but as a collective, sustained by the LatinX community and familial ties that nurture and uphold the dignity and identity of LatinX students. In short, *LatinX Intergenerational Bendiciones* recognize the power of community, shared history, and intergenerational exchanges in shaping and supporting the educational pathways of LatinX students.

For example, the composite counter-stories of Mari, Ariel, Yamaris, and Felix are based on the many individuals I have encountered professionally and personally. Their counter-stories illustrate how the concept of *LatinX Intergenerational Bendiciones* manifests in various ways as their experiences are culturally affirmed and deeply connected to the collective experiences of many LatinX students, their families, and communities. Therefore, *LatinX Intergenerational Bendiciones* as a framework re-envisions LatinX student academic achievement and success by shifting the focus from the individual to the collective, focusing on the intersections of intergenerational wisdom, cultural affirmation, and community resilience.

LATINX INTERGENERATIONAL BENDICIONES FRAMEWORK FOR STUDENT SUCCESS

As seen in Figure 5.1, *LatinX Intergenerational Bendiciones Framework for Student Success* revolves around two concentric circles interconnected in a cyclical, ongoing process. At the heart of this framework lies the concept of *LatinX Intergenerational Bendiciones*. These *bendiciones* (blessings) represent the legacies and strengths passed down through multiple generations within LatinX communities. The focus here is on how LatinX communities draw on shared cultural, social, and emotional strengths to overcome challenges and thrive, especially within institutions of higher education.

The outermost circle reflects re-envisioning LatinX academic achievement and student success through the interplay of Cultural Affirmations, Intergenerational Wisdom, and Community Resilience. These three components work together to challenge and disrupt the dominance of white supremacy and racism in U.S. society and educational contexts. Cultural affirmation is grounded in affirming the cultural identities and diverse social identities (e.g., race, gender, class, citizenship status) of LatinX students. Acknowledging and centering LatinX students' cultural and social identities in everyday practices within educational spaces recognize both as sources of strength and resistance to assimilating into white cultural norms. Culturally responsive curricula and programming, community engagement, and social media campaigns that validate LatinX student experiences and contributions should be created. Examples include uplifting cultural and identity markers such as *dichos* (sayings) and family traditions to reinforce the value of education in informal spaces like the home.

Intergenerational wisdom recognizes that success is a collective achievement that spans across generations. Drawing on the wisdom of ancestors, family, and communities, this component encourages intergenerational mentorship programs where LatinX students can connect with elders, alumni, and community leaders to share stories of survival and strategies as a form of shared history and healing. Storytelling is a powerful methodology for understanding personal and professional academic achievement and success, and LatinX students can share family narratives of perseverance that tie to their educational pathways. Community resilience emphasizes that LatinX academic achievement and success are inherently communal. Academic achievements and success are celebrated collectively, not individually. Building community-based networks that provide social and emotional support through peer support groups, family engagement, and community coalitions is critical. LatinX student organizations and family-inclusive academic events can emphasize the importance of community in supporting academic achievement and success in institutions of higher education.

The inner concentric circle of Figure 5.1 contains strategies for disrupting white supremacy and racism in institutions of higher education with a focus

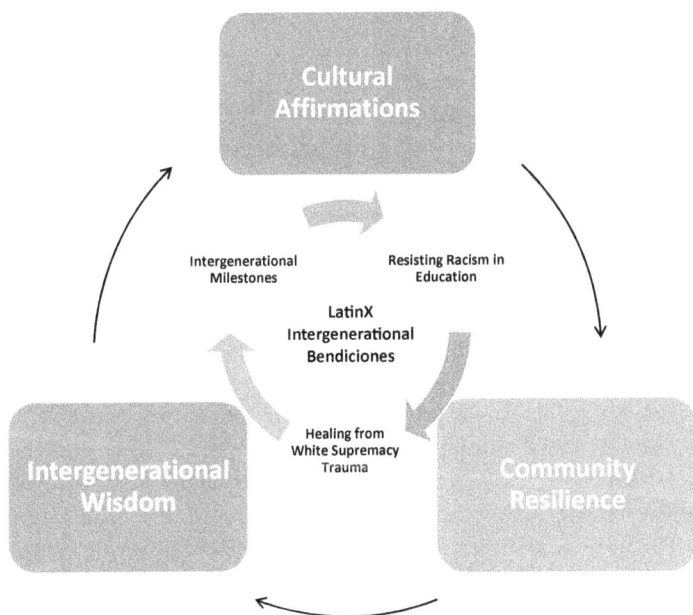

Figure 5.1 This is an example of a LatinX Student Success Model in Higher Education focusing on intergenerational milestones.

179

on Resisting Racism in Education, Intergenerational Milestones, and Healing from White Supremacy Trauma. Resisting racism in education focuses on how *bendiciones* (blessings) can disrupt racism and white supremacy embedded in academic metrics of success. Developing counter-curricular and resistance strategies, such as discussing banned topics like Critical Race Theory, allows for critical assessment of academic achievement and success based on white racial norms and metrics like GPA and standardized tests. Workshops and seminars led by faculty and activists can address anti-racist practices and offer strategies to resist oppressive educational policies. Intergenerational milestones confront the narrow academic definition of student success. For LatinX students, success includes cultural, spiritual, and familial milestones that are cumulative across generations. Institutions of higher education and their actors should recognize these holistic markers, namely well-being, community involvement, and family connections, as critical aspects of academic achievement and success. For example, institutions of higher education and their actors can honor family and community contributions during graduation ceremonies by offering familial degrees that acknowledge critical cumulative milestones and collective accomplishments. Healing from white supremacy trauma addresses the distinct barriers faced by LatinX students due to racism and white supremacy. *Bendiciones* (blessings) provide tools for healing and resilience based on collective love, joy, compassion, and support. Institutions of higher education and their actors must offer mental health resources that are culturally responsive to these challenges, including the effects of anti-DEI legislation. Healing circles, culturally relevant counseling services, and space for communal reflection can help LatinX students navigate and heal from systemic trauma.

In conclusion, the *LatinX Intergenerational Bendiciones Framework for Student Success* offers a culturally responsive approach to examining and cultivating academic achievement and success for LatinX students in higher education. Instead of LatinX students conforming to a system prioritizing assimilation and individualism, the *LatinX Intergenerational Bendiciones Framework for Student Success* seeks to affirm the intersections of cultural affirmation, intergenerational wisdom, and community resilience. In honoring *bendiciones*—material and immaterial—that are passed down from one generation to the next, blessings act as a source of strength that LatinX students draw upon despite ongoing experiences with racism and white supremacy. Finally, this framework offers a pathway for institutions of higher education and their actors to uplift the collective strength of LatinX students, their families, and communities.

CONCLUSION

The struggle for freedom is far from over (Bell, 1992). We are currently in a presidential election year, with Kamala Harris as the Democratic candidate and Donald Trump as the Republican candidate. By the time this book is published, we will be under a new presidential administration that could significantly influence the future of DEI initiatives and the broader landscape of racial equity in higher education. The outcome of this election will likely determine whether the setbacks discussed in this chapter—such as anti-DEI legislation, the repeal of race-conscious admissions, and the long-term effects of COVID-19—will continue or if there will be renewed efforts to advance DEI initiatives across the U.S. institutions of higher education. While this chapter focused on three critical areas: the aftermath of COVID-19, the repeal of race-conscious admissions, and college affordability, future research should expand to examine other factors such as LatinX students in rural areas, Science, Technology, Engineering, and Math (STEM), LatinX students' basic needs, graduate students, undocumented students, and adult learners. Manifestations of racial realism can be met with intentional resistance strategies that disrupt the dominance of white supremacy and racism in academic metrics and institutional policies. Employing the *LatinX Intergenerational Bendiciones Framework for Student Success* would provide opportunities for institutions of higher education and their actors to uplift LatinX students, their families and communities. Such necessary work would aim to ensure that the limitations of a racialized system do not define them, and that they are instead recognized for the strength and value they bring with them into institutions of higher education.

DISCUSSION QUESTIONS

Using the content within this chapter, consider the following questions for reflection and discussion:

- How can institutions of higher education and their actors develop holistic metrics that better capture the diverse and intangible aspects of success for LatinX students beyond white cultural norms?
- What strategies can institutions of higher education and their actors adopt to better support and engage with the families and communities of LatinX students, acknowledging their significant influence on their educational pathways?

NOTES

1. U.S. Census Bureau. (2021). *Hispanic or Latino origin by race: 2020 Census Redistricting Data (PL 94–171)*. Retrieved from https://www.census.gov https://www.insidehighered.com/news/diversity/2024/03/18/va-officials-scrutinize-2-universities-dei-course-syllabi. Senate Bill 377 (2022) in Georgia restricts teaching certain "divisive concepts," including elements often associated with DEI initiatives. It aims to ensure that no individual is compelled to affirm, adopt, or adhere to beliefs related to race or gender as part of their educational experience.
2. LatinX students comprise 46 percent of the undocumented student population in U.S. higher education (American Immigration Council, 2023).
3. Anti-DEI laws propose to eliminate DEI offices and positions, DEI training, curriculum content in courses and books (e.g., Critical Race Theory), DEI criteria in hiring and admissions, and related funding.
4. Translation (*with many blessings*).
5. Please refer to Georgia's House Bill 1084 https://www.legis.ga.gov/api/legislation/document/20212022/212225
6. I was inspired by the collective work of My Undocumented Life: Up-to-date Information and Resources for Undocumented Students, Families, and Allies. Please refer to: https://mydocumentedlife.org
7. My Undocumented Life: Up-to-date Information and Resources for Undocumented Students, Families, and Allies. Please refer to: https://mydocumentedlife.org
8. My Undocumented Life: Up-to-date Information and Resources for Undocumented Students, Families, and Allies. Please refer to: https://mydocumentedlife.org

REFERENCES

American Immigration Council. (2023). *Undocumented students in U.S. higher education*. Retrieved from https://www.americanimmigrationcouncil.org/research/undocumented-college-students-2023

Baker, D. J. (2019). Pathways to racial equity in higher education: Modeling the antecedents of state affirmative action bans. *American Educational Research Journal, 56*(5), 1861–1895. https://doi.org/10.3102/0002831219833918

Bell, D. A. (1992). *Faces at the bottom of the well: The permanence of racism*. Basic Books.

Bleemer, Z. (2020). The impact of Proposition 209 and access-oriented UC admissions policies on underrepresented UC applications, enrollment, and long-run student outcomes. UC Office of the President. Oakland, CA. Retrieved January 28, 2022, from https://www.ucop.edu

Centers for Disease Control and Prevention. (2022). COVID-19 racial and ethnic health disparities. https://www.cdc.gov/coronavirus/2019-ncov/community/health-equity/racial-ethnic-disparities/index.html

Chronicle Staff. (2024, June 28). DEI legislation tracker: Explore where college diversity, equity, and inclusion efforts are under attack. *The Chronicle of Higher Education*. https://www.chronicle.com/article/dei-legislation-tracker

Crisp, G., & Nora, A. (2010). Hispanic student success: Factors influencing the persistence and transfer decisions of Latino community college students enrolled in developmental education. *Research in Higher Education, 51*(2), 175–194. https://doi.org/10.1007/s11162-009-9151-x

Crisp, G., Taggart, A., & Nora, A. (2015). Undergraduate Latina/o students: A systematic review of research identifying factors contributing to academic success outcomes. *Review of Educational Research, 85*(2), 249–274. https://doi.org/10.3102/0034654314551064

Delgado Bernal, D. D. (2001). Learning and living pedagogies of the home: The mestiza consciousness of Chicana students. *International Journal of Qualitative Studies in Education, 14*(5), 623–639.

Ewell, P., & Wellman, J. (2007). Enhancing student success in education: Summary report of the NPEC initiative and national symposium on postsecondary student success. National Postsecondary Education Cooperative [NPEC].

Excelencia in Education. (2019). *How Latinos pay for college: Fact sheet.* Retrieved from https://www.edexcelencia.org/research/fact-sheets/how-latinos-pay-college-fact-sheet

Gándara, D., & Zerquera, D. (2021). Moving beyond the "debt aversion" truism. In W. Taliaferro, T. Taylor, & K. Wheatle (Eds.), *Changing the narrative on student borrowers of color* (pp. 18–27). Lumina Foundation. https://www.luminafoundation.org/wp-content/uploads/2021/02/borrowers-of-color-2.pdf

Garcia, N. M., & Danek, V. (2023). Shelter from the storm: Disaster capitalism and Puerto Rican undergraduates in post-hurricane María stateside higher education. *Teachers College Record, 125*(4), 182–211.

Goldrick-Rab, S., & Steinbaum, M. (2020). What is the problem with student debt. *Journal of Policy Analysis and Management, 39*(2), 534–540.

Hearn, J. C. (2006). Theories of student success: Reflections and future directions. *National Postsecondary Education Cooperative.*

hooks, b. (2018). *All about love: New visions.* HarperCollins Publishers.

Jones, K., & Okun, T. (2001). *Dismantling racism: A workbook for social change groups.* Change Work.

Lara, G. D., López, L. M., Barajas-Gonzalez, R. G., & Coll, C. G. (2021). COVID-19's impact on Latine students. *The Learning Professional, 42*(6), 60–64.

Martinez, M., & Fernández, E. (2004). Latinos at community colleges. *New Directions for Student Services, 105*, 51–62. https://doi.org/10.1002/ss.116

McDonough, P., Calderone, S., & Venegas, K. (2015). The role of social trust in low-income Latino college financing decisions. *Journal of Latino/Latin American Studies, 7*(2), 133–148.

Nuñez, A.-M., Crisp, G., & Elizondo, D. (2013). Hispanic-serving institutions: Advancing research and transformative practice. *Journal of Latinos and Education, 12*(3), 150–165.

Okun, T. (1999, 2021). *White supremacy culture characteristics*. Dismantling Racism Works. Retrieved from https://www.dismantlingracism.org/uploads/4/3/5/7/4357 9015/okun_-_white_sup_culture.pdf

Okun, T. (2021). *White supremacy culture: Characteristics—Showing up for racial justice*. https://www.showingupforracialjustice.org/white-supremacy-culture-cha racteristics.html

Pedraza, L., Villela, R., Kamatgi, V., Cocuzzo, K., Correa, R., & Zylberglait Lisigurski, M. (2022). The impact of COVID-19 in the Latinx community. *HCA Healthcare Journal of Medicine*, 3(3), 97–104. https://doi.org/10.36518/2689-0216.1387

Pérez Huber, L., Vélez, V. N., & Malagón, M. C. (2024). Charting methodological imaginaries: Critical Race Feminista Methodologies in educational research. *International Journal of Qualitative Studies in Education*, 37(5), 1263–1271.

Stokes, S. (2024). A sense of belonging within the imaginative constraints of racial realism: A critical race analysis of Latinx students' racialized experiences during the Trump presidency. In M. Ledesma, V. Ojeda, S. Coon, and L. Parker (Eds.), *Critical race theory and qualitative methods* (pp. 26–41). Routledge.

UCLA Latino Policy & Politics Initiative. (2022). *A change of plans: The impact of COVID-19 on Latinx students' higher education journeys*. https://latino.ucla. edu/wp-content/uploads/2022/03/Final_A-Change-of-Plans.pdf

UnidosUS. (2020). *Following their dreams in an inequitable system: Latino students share their college experience*. UnidosUS. https://www.unidosus.org/ publications/2010-following-their-dreams-in-an-inequitable-system-latino-students-share-their-college-experience/

Venegas, K. (2007). Low-income, urban Latinas' student aid decisions: The effect of family ties (ASHE/Lumina Fellows Series Policy Brief, Issue 1). Association for the Study of Higher Education.

Victorino, C. A., Ing, M., Claassen Thrush, E., Heil, S., Harris, H., Cano Matute, A., & Colchete, N. (2024). Latin* student success after the COVID-19 pandemic. *Journal of Hispanic Higher Education*. https://doi.org/10.1177/15381927241276437

Index

Page numbers in **bold** denote tables, those in *italics* denote figures. The letter n following a page number indicates a reference in the notes.

academic achievement 24–25, 61; definition of 24, 44; and ethnic and racial socialization 54–55, 56–58; and parenting practices 53–54
academic capital 77
academic performance 75, 77, 78, 79, 80
access, college 120, 123
accountability, institutional 61, 77, 82, 88
acculturation 115
Acevedo, Elizabeth 74, 97n12
acompañamiento 128
Adachi, F. 14
adaptative coping 78
administrators 75, 77, 83, 89
admissions 19, 79, 123, 165; race-conscious 168–170, 181
adult learners 16–17, 85
Adult Training and Education Survey (ATES) 23
advocates 89
affirmative action 21, 122, 166, 168–170
affordability issues 21, 22, 83, 87, 170–171, 175
African Americans 10, 15, 43, 46, 47, 48, 55, 56, 57; *see also headings under* Black
Afro-Latin@, as a term 11
Afro-LatinX identities 7, 10, 93
Aguilar, C. 128

Alaska Native and Native Hawaiian-Serving Institutions 84
Alcantar, C. M. 83
Alcoff, L. M. 9, 11, 12–13
Alemán, E. 138
Americanization programs 49
Anderson, M. L. 12
anti-Blackness 10, 11, 13, 93
anti-Critical Race Theory (CRT) 164
anti-Diversity, Equity, and Inclusion (DEI) 29, 164–166, 180, 181, 182n3
anti-immigrant sentiment 127–128
anti-Indigeneity 13
Anzaldúa, G. E. 130–132, 134, 136
apprenticeships 21, 23
Asian American and Native American Pacific Islander-Serving Institutions 84
AsianCrit 121
Asians 15, 17, 43, 55
ASPIRA program 73, 97n10
aspirational capital 124
aspirations, parental 53
assessment: effective 61; standardized 24, 25, 44
asset-based approaches 18, 29, 77, 120; *see also* Chicana/Latina feminisms; Critical Race Theory (CRT)
assimilation 49, 50–52, 118, 180; resistance to 178; structural 51
associate degrees 21, 22–23, 31n2, 80
Association for the Study of Higher Education (ASHE) 120

attainment *see* higher education attainment
authoritarian parenting style 53
authoritative parenting style 53
Ayón, C. 57

bachelor's (baccalaureate) degrees 19, 20, 21, 22, 31n2, 80
Batt, M. C. 44, 52
Baumrind, D. 53
Beginning Postsecondary Students Longitudinal Study 16
Bell, D. A. 113, 121, 166
belonging, sense of 77, 79, 83, 172
bendiciones (blessings) 29, 177; *see also LatinX Intergenerational Bendiciones Framework for Student Success*
Bensimon, E. M. 120
bias, institutional 25
Bicultural Orientation Model (Torres) 115
biculturalism 134, 177
bien educada/o (being well educated) 91
big systems four-years HSIs 86
Bilingual Education Act 65n1
bilingualism 134, 177
Black Feminist Thought 113
Black, Indigenous, and People of Color (BIPOC) communities 11, 17, 31n8, 45, 51, 121–123, 129; college enrollment of, and repeal of affirmative action 168–169; community cultural wealth 123–125; conflict amongst 46; family ethnic and racial socialization practices 54, 55–56; *see also* Black people; Indigenous peoples
Black people 10, 17; *see also* African Americans; Black, Indigenous, and People of Color (BIPOC) communities
Black/white-race binary 125
BlackCrit 121
Blackness, anti- 10, 11, 13, 93
Blackwell, M. 93–94
body/bodies: body—mind separation 136; bodymindspirit 132, 137; brown, epistemology of 135–136; *see also* embodied knowledge
borderlands 130–131

Bourdieu, P. 114, 116–117, 123
Braxton, J. M. 60–61
bridging agents 89
Brooklyn College 73, 96n2
brown bodies, epistemology of 135–136
"Brown Monolith" phenomenon 7
Brown/Browness label 7, 10
Burton, L. M. 55–56
Busey, C. L. 7, 10

California 47; Hispanic-Serving Institutions (HSIs) 22, 23; LatinX population 8; race-conscious admissions 168, 169; Title 1 programs 65n2
campus climate 87, 116, 122, 175
capital, forms of 76, 77, 89, 114, 116–118, 123–125
capitalism 132, 170
Carales, V. D. 83
cariño (care) 91
Carnegie Classifications of Institutions of Higher Education 86
cartography, Chicana feminist 137
Castillo-Montoya, M. 134
Caughy, M. O. 57
Ceballo, R. 58
Ceja, M. 122
Centers for Disease Control and Prevention 167
Central Americans 8, 9, 19, 20, 44, 94
Centro (Center for Puerto Rican Studies) 73, 97n11, 97n9
certificates 21, 23, 24, 77, 79
certification 21, 23
Chicana Feminist Epistemology (CFE) 114, 133, 137
Chicana/Latina feminisms 29, 113, 114, 138, 141, 144; emergence and impact of 129; foundational theoretical tools 130–132; methodologies 137; queer 136; tools in education 133–137
Chicanismo 7
ChicanX 9, 16, 27, 43, 92, 94, 122; *see also* Mexican Americans
ChicanX Studies 92, 94, 136
Child Development 52, 55, 56
choice, college 117, 127, 170
Chronicle of Higher Education 165
cisgender dominance 91, 92

citizenship status 7, 47, 76; Mexican Americans 46, 47; Puerto Ricans 47
Civil Rights Movement 129
class 27, 51, 125, 130, 132, 134
class paradigm of race 51
classism 122, 130, 133
climate change, and migration 8
college access 120, 123
college achievement 62
college admissions *see* admissions
college affordability 21, 22, 83, 87, 170–171, 175
college choice 117, 127, 170
college enrollment *see* enrollment
college preparation 79
college readiness 24, 44, 62, 63
Collins, P. H. 12
Colombian population 8, 9
colonial logic 7, 10, 13, 28, 132, 142
colonial rule, Puerto Rico 46–47
colonialism 125, 130, 132, 136; settler 46, 94
color-evasiveness 122
colorism 55, 56
comfort, right to (white supremacy culture) 172, 175
commitment: student 78, 175; to communities 134, 177
community colleges *see* public two-year institutions
Community Cultural Wealth 114, 118, 123–125
community standards dimension of HSIs 88
community/communities 30, 57, 166, 167, 177, 178, 179; commitment to 134, 177; engagement/involvement 178, 180; resilience 29, 111, 112, 140, 142, 178, 179, 180, 143.178
completion/completion rates 16, 19, 20, 26, 62, 63, 75, 77, 78–79, 118; community colleges 80
conformist resistance 126
congruence assumption (person-environment fit theory) 62
conocimiento (knowledge/consciousness) 131
consejitos 135
consejos 135
continuing generation college students 15–16

convivir/convivencia (co-existing) 137, 138, 142
coping strategies 78, 174
Coronado, H. M. 94
counselors 83
counter-storytelling 27–28, 30, 122, 125, 129, 141, 143
COVID-19 pandemic 6, 20, 21, 167–168, 181
credentials, non-degree 20–21, 21–22, 23–24, 31n2, 77, 78, 79
Crenshaw, K. 113, 121
Crisp, G. 44, 75, 76, 77–78, 79, 80, 81, 96, 112
critical consciousness 138
Critical LatinX Indigeneities 93–94
critical legal studies 121
Critical Race Feminisms 121
Critical Race Feminista Methodologies (CRFM) 29, 114, 137, 138–139, 144
Critical Race Feminista Quantitative Ethnography Praxis (CRF+QE) 114, 137, 139–143, 144
Critical Race Theory (CRT) 27, 28, 29, 31n3, 55, 56, 58, 76–77, 82, 113, 114, 126, 128, 138, 141, 144; anti-Critical Race Theory 164; in education 121–123, 128–129; emerging methodologies 129; and qualitative methods 129; and quantitative methods 129
critical race-gendered epistemologies 126–127
Critical Whiteness Studies 121
CRitT Walking 129
CRT *see* Critical Race Theory
Cruz, C. 135–136
Cuba 46
Cubans 9, 20, 44, 76, 119
cultural affirmation 134, 177, 178, 180
cultural capital 77, 117–118, 123
cultural deficit model 48, 49–50
cultural deprivation theory 48, 49
cultural differences 48
cultural explanations (1960s–1970s) 48–50
cultural intuition 133–134, 137
cultural knowledge 134–135
cultural nationalism 129–130
cultural pluralism 50, 51
cultural socialization 54, 55, 57, 58

culturally responsive approaches 29, 76, 77, 94, 95, 116, 178, 180
culture 89, 92, 116, 125; *see also* organizational culture; white supremacy, culture

Darling, N. 53
debt 21, 170, 175
decolonial imaginary 132
defensiveness (white supremacy culture) 171, 175
deficit perspectives 25, 28, 42–43, 44, 48, 49–50, 64, 92, 118, 119, 139
degree attainment 19, 20–21, 63, 75, 77, 78–79, 172; associate degrees 21, 22–23, 31n2, 80; bachelor's (baccalaureate) 19, 20, 21, 22, 31n2, 80; as collective accomplishment 26
Delgado Bernal, D. 113, 121, 122, 125–126, 126–127, 130, 133–135, 138, 177
Delgado, R. 113, 121, 125
Delgado-Gaitan, C. 135
demographic factors 20; *see also* LatinX demographics
deportations 8
Developing HSI Grants (Title V-Part A) funding 85
Deyhle, D. 58
dichos (sayings) 177, 178
differential racialization 125
digital divide 167
discrimination 10, 19, 54, 55, 56, 58, 165
DisCrit 121
Diversity, Equity, and Inclusion (DEI) 29, 164–166, 180, 181, 182n3
Dolan, C. V. 91–92
dominant ideology 122
Dominican population 9, 145n5; college enrollment 19; degree attainment 20; *see also Epistemic Network Analysis of Dominican Undergraduate Disaster Preparedness Model 0*
Doran, E. 83–84
dual credit transfer students 81
Dumka, L. E. 58

earnings 22–23, 170
economic capital 117, 118
economic conditions, and migration 8

economic outcomes 20, 22–23
economically disadvantaged students 17–18, 19, 50, 80, 81, 85, 168
educational opportunity gap 20, 21
educational pathways 63, 64, 77, 143, 167, 174, 175–176, 178, 179
educational pipelines 31n3
educational psychology 91, 112
either/or thinking (white supremacy culture) 171, 174
el movimento 129
El Salvadoran population 8
Elementary and Secondary Education Act (ESEA) (1965) 65n1
Elenas, C. A. 133
Else-Quest, N. M. 57
embodied knowledge 132, 137
employment opportunities 6, 20–21
employment status 78, 87
empowerment 11, 28, 30, 65, 73, 89, 114, 118, 130, 139, 177
enrollment in higher education 19–20, 25, 62, 63, 77, 79, 87, 168–169
Epistemic Network Analysis of Dominican Undergraduate Disaster Preparedness Model 0 111–112, *111*, 139–141, *140*, 142–143
Epistemic Network Analysis (ENA) 110–112, 139–143
epistemology: of the brown body 135–136; *see also* knowledge
equity 29, 121, 122
Espino, M. M. 127, 135
ethnic categorization 6–7, 13
ethnic consciousness 124
ethnic empowerment capital 118
ethnic enclaves 50, 51
ethnic identity 6–7, 13, 57, 78, 113, 114, 115, 116, 121, 174, *see also* ethnoracial identity
ethnic socialization 54–55, 56–58
ethnicity 9–10, 11, 12–13, 51, 52, 92, 93, 95, 116, 121, 125; definition of 12
ethnicity paradigm 51
ethnography: Chicana feminist 137; quantitative 29, 114, 137, 139–143; urban 129
ethnoracial identity 11, 12–13, 92, 95, 115–116
"ethnoracial pentagon" 12
ethnoraciality 11, 12–13
Eugenics 45, 51, 139

Eurocentric ideologies 27
Eurocentric research paradigms 129, 137
Every Student Succeeds Act (ESSA) (2015) 65n1
Ewell, P. 25–26, 59, 63–64, 172
Excelencia in Education 15, 31n9, 81–82, 84–85, 86
experiential knowledge 122, 143
external boundary management dimension of HSIs 88

faculty 61, 75, 76, 77, 83, 88, 89
familial capital 124
Family Studies 52, 55–56
family/families 26, 30, 48, 49, 76, 167, 177, 180; familism 57; *familismo* 91; traditions 178; *see also headings under* parent; parental; parenting
female students 90; adult learners 17; college enrollment 20; dependent children 17; low-income 17–18
femininity (*marianismo*) 91
feminism(s): Black 113; Chicana/Latina *see* Chicana/Latina feminisms; Critical Race Feminisms 121; radical 121; white 130, 136
feminist cartography 137
feminist ethnography 137
Ferdman, B. M. 113, 114, 115–116
financial aid 19, 50, 78, 79, 81, 83, 85, 94–95, 175
financial capital 77
first-generation college students 14–15, 16, 19, 81, 85, 86
Flores, J. 11
Florida: Hispanic-Serving Institutions (HSIs) 23; LatinX population 8–9
Foraker Act (Organic Act of 1900) 46–47
four-year institutions 20, 63, 77, 84, 87–88
Frey, W. H. 9
funding, Hispanic-Serving Institutions (HSIs) 85–86
funds of knowledge 114, 119–121

Gallegos, P. V. 113, 114, 115–116
ganas (determination) 124
Gándara, D. 171
Garcia, G. A. 87–88, 89, 90
Garcia, N. M. 135, 137, 138, 139

García-Louis, C. 93
Garvey, J. C. 91–92, 113
gender 7, 20, 27, 78, 90–92, 115, 116, 130, 134, 141, 174; consciousness 126; expression 91, 92, 95; identity 91, 92, 95, 125, 132; roles 91, 95; socialization 91; *see also* critical race-gendered epistemologies
geographic proximity 87; public two-year institutions (community colleges) 81, 170
goals, parental 53
Godinez, F. E. 133
Goldberg, D. T. 12
Goldrick-Rab, S. 170
Gómez, L. E. 9–10, 46, 47, 48
Gonzalez, G. G. 49
González, N. 114, 119
Gordon, M. M. 50–51
governance, Hispanic-Serving Institutions (HSIs) 88, 90
grade point average (GPA) 24, 25, 44, 77, 78, 79
grades 77, 78
graduate school enrollment 87
graduation rates 25, 59, 87, 172
Greenberg, J. B. 119–120
grounded theory 129
Guadalupe Hildago, treaty of (1848) 46
Guam 46
Guatemalan population 8
Guimond, A. B. 116

Haney López, I. 9, 45–46, 125
Harper, S. R. 123
Hauser-Cram, P. 54
healing 114, 130, 138, 142, 179; from white supremacy trauma 179, 180
health: benefits of college attendance 20; *see also* mental health
health science schools 86
Hearn, J. C. 59, 60, 63, 172
Hernández, E. 113, 114, 115, 135
Hernandez, I. 83
Hernández, T. K. 10
heteronormativity 91, 92
Higher Education Act (HEA) (1965) 84
higher education attainment 19–24; *see also* degree attainment
Higher Education Opportunity Act (2008) 85
Hill, N. E. 58

Hispanic Association of Colleges and Universities (HACU) 86
Hispanic-Serving Institutions (HSIs) 22, 23–24, 28, 75, 76, 77, 83–90, 96; critical dimensions for servingness and student success 88; funding 85–86; governance 88, 90; institutional actors' student support 88–90; investment in x; LatinX servingness 87–88; and Latinx student success 84–90; leadership 90; organizational culture 86, 87–90; Seal of Excelencia 22, 23, 31n9; typology of 86–87
Historically Black Colleges and Universities (HBCUs) 84
Hitlin, S. 12
Hofstadter, R. 45
Holland, J. L. 62
Hollinger, D. A. 12
homophobia 132
Honduran population 8, 9
hooks, b. 166
HSI STEM (Title III) funding 85
HSIs see Hispanic–Serving Institutions (HSIs)
Hughes, D. 55, 56, 58
human capital 76
Hurtado, A. 130
hypodescent 45, 47

identity: cultural 178; see also social identity/identities
ideology: dominant 122; Eurocentric 27
immigration 125, 127–128
immigration experiences 76
immigration policies 95
immigration status 7, 115, 125, 128; see also undocumented students
imperialism 125
In-state Resident Tuition (ISRT) 94–95
incentive structure dimension of HSIs 88
inclusion 29, 122
Indigeneity 93–94; anti- 13
Indigenous peoples 6–7, 10, 93–94; see also Black, Indigenous, and People of Color (BIPOC) communities; Native American(s)
individualism 172, 175, 180
institutional accountability 61, 77, 82, 88
institutional actors 75, 76, 77;

administrators 75, 77, 83, 89; counselors 83; faculty 61, 75, 76, 77, 83, 88, 89; funds of knowledge 120; leaders/leadership 61, 90; use of social capital to empower students 89; student affairs professionals 75, 76; and student success 61, 75, 76, 77, 83–84, 88–90
institutional bias 25
institutional brokers 89
institutional types 25, 75, 78, 80; see also four-year institutions; Hispanic–Serving Institutions (HSIs); Minority Serving Institutions (MSIs); public two-year institutions (community colleges)
integrative agents 89
intercultural capital 118
intergenerational milestones 177–178, 180
intergenerational wisdom 178, 179, 180
intergenerationality 138, 177; see also LatinX Intergenerational Bendiciones Framework for Student Success
intersectionality 7, 13, 14, 19, 27, 30, 92, 95, 113, 116, 133; quantitative 129

Jain, D. 81, 82
Jiménez Román, M. 11
Jones Act (1917) 47
Jones, S. R. 113
jotería (queerness) 136–137
Jotería Studies 92, 136
justice: justice and accountability dimension of HSIs 88; social justice 121, 122, 126, 139, 143

Kiyama, J. M. 120
knowledge 131; cultural 134–135; embodied 132, 137; experiential 122, 143; funds of 114, 119–121; see also epistemology
Kuh, G. D. 24, 44, 61

Ladson-Billings, G. 121
language factors 49, 50, 76, 125, 176–177; see also bilingualism; linguistic capital
Lara, I. 132

LatCrit *see* Latino Critical Race Theory
lateral transfer students 18, 81, 82
Latin*, as a term 14
Latin@s 11
Latinidad 7, 10, 93
Latino Critical Race Theory (LatCrit) 76–77, 121, 123, 125–129; definition 125
LatinX, as a term 5, 14, 30
LatinX demographics 7–9, 76; average age 9, 19; distribution of population 6, 8–9; migration patterns 6, 7, 8; population growth 6, 7, 8; racial and ethnic categorization 6–7; size of population 7–8
LatinX Intergenerational Bendiciones Framework for Student Success 29, 167, 176–180, 181
LatinX servingness 87–89
LatinX student identity development 114–116
Latinx student success 75–80; characteristics of white supremacy culture and 171–176; and institutional types and actors 75, 76, 77, 78, 80–90; prevalent theoretical frameworks on 114–121; and social identities 90–95
Latinx-enhancing institutions 87
Latinx-enrolling institutions 87
Latinx-producing institutions 87
law/legal systems: and construction of race 45–46, 121; and white supremacy 9, 121, 126
leaders/leadership 61; Hispanic-Serving Institutions (HSIs) 90
learning disabilities 42–43
learning loss 168
legal studies 121, 125
Lewis, O. 48
licensures 21, 23
Lifespan Model of Latinx Ethnic Identity Development 115
linguistic capital 124
lived experiences 87, 122, 123, 132, 143, 175
lobbyists 89
Lohfink, M. M. 15–16
Lorde, A. 11
low-income students 17–18; *see also* economically disadvantaged students

lucha (the struggle or fight) 134
Lugones, M. 136
Lumina Foundation 21

machismo (masculinity) 91
McNair Program 145n8
majoritarian narratives 27
Maldonado Dominguez, K. J. 94
male students 90; adult learners 17; college enrollment 20; community cultural wealth 124
manifest destiny 46
Marable, M. 11
marianismo (femininity) 91
Marshall, S. 56
masculinity (*machismo*) 91
maternal influences 124–125
media literacies 129
membership dimension of HSIs 88
Mendez v. Westminster (1946) 47
mental health 95, 168, 180
mentoring 58, 78, 89, 126, 128, 173; intergenerational 179
meritocracy 122
mestiza consciousness 131, 134
mestizaje 10, 131
methodological nepantla 138, 139
Mexican Americans 8, 9, 43, 44, 45, 76, 92, 94, 124, 129; Americanization programs for 49; citizenship status 46, 47; college enrollment 19; *consejos* for women PhDs 135; and "culture of poverty" 48; degree attainment 20; ethnic socialization 58; funds of knowledge 119–120; white racial positionality 47; *see also* ChicanX
Mexican—American War (1846–1848) 46
microaggressions 19, 122, 128
micro-credentials 21
migration patterns 6, 7, 8
Milian, C. 5, 30
Minority Serving Institutions (MSIs) 25, 84, 176; *see also* Hispanic–Serving Institutions (HSIs)
mission dimension of HSIs 88
mixed methods research 129, 137
Model of Latina and Latino Ethnoracial Orientations (Gallegos and Ferdman) 115–116

Model of Latino Identity Development (Ferdman and Gallegos) 115
Moll, L. C. 119, 120
Montero-Sieburth, M. 44, 52
Moraga, C. 130, 132, 136
motivation 78, 134, 174, 175
MultiCrit 121
"multiple capitals" approach 77

nation-based paradigm 51
National Center for Education Statistics 19, 23
national policy, and student success 63
National Postsecondary Cooperative (NPEC) symposium (2006) 45, 59, 64, 77; commissioned papers 45, 59, 60, 64, 77
National Skills Coalition 22, 23
National Student Clearinghouse Research Center (NSCRC) 20, 24
nationalism, cultural 129–130
Native American-Serving Nontribal Institutions 84
Native Americans 46, 55
navigational capital 124
nepantla (in-between space) 131, 138, 139
networking coaches 89
New York State, LatinX population 8, 9
Nieto, S. 46, 47
non-degree credentials 20–21, 21–22, 23–24, 31n2, 77, 78
nontraditional college students 16–17
Nora, A. 81
nos/ortas (us/others) 131–132
Nuñez, C. 7, 75, 76–77, 78, 79, 80, 86, 89, 96, 172

Obama administration 8
objectivity 114, 122, 132, 133, 172, 174
Office of Postsecondary Education (OPE) 85
Oliver, M. 123
Omi, M. 12, 51
one-drop rule 45, 47
only one right way (white supremacy culture) 171, 175–176
open conflict, fear of (white supremacy culture) 172, 175
open-access policies, community colleges 80–81

oppression, systematic 5, 9, 11, 29, 52, 92, 113, 116, 121, 122, 144
oral histories 129, 132
organizational culture, Hispanic-Serving Institutions (HSIs) 86, 87–90
Ortiz, V. 51–52

Paredes, A. D. 94
parent—child socialization 52–53, 92; and academic achievement 53–54; see also cultural socialization; ethnic socialization; racial socialization
parental goals, values, and aspirations 53
parental involvement 53, 58
parental level of education 14–15, 16, 53, 54, 78
parental monitoring 53
parenting practices 53–54
parenting styles 53, 54
Paris, treaty of (1898) 46
part-time students 82
participatory research 129, 137
paternalism 171, 174
patriarchy 90, 91, 130, 132, 142
Patton, L. F. 123
Paulsen, M. B. 15–16
pedagogies of the home 134–135, 177
Pérez, E. 130, 132
Pérez Huber, L. 26, 127–128, 138, 177
Pérez, M. S. 137
perfectionism 171, 174
permissive parenting style 53
Perna, L. W. 61–62
persistence in higher education 16, 44, 61, 62, 63, 75, 77, 78, 79, 118, 172, 174
person-environment fit theory 62
personality types 62
Pew Hispanic Research Center 8
Pew Research center 22
phenotype 125
Pietri, Pedro 73, 74, 97n5, 97n7
pláticas 137
pluriversal cultural wealth 124
Plyler v. Doe (1982) 19
policy, state and national, and student success 63
political advocates 89
population factors see demographic factors; LatinX demographics
post-college attainment 62

poststructuralist perspectives 113
poverty 17, 18; culture of 48
power 9, 11, 12, 117, 121, 130, 133;
  see also empowerment
power hoarding (white supremacy
  culture) 172, 175
Predominantly Black Institutions 84
Predominantly White Institutions
  (PWIs) 25, 77
privilege 9, 11, 52, 121
progress is bigger, more
  (white supremacy culture) 172
Promoting Postbaccalaureate
  Opportunities for Hispanic
  Americans (PPOHA) (Title V-Part B)
  funding 85
psychology 62, 112, 113; educational
  91, 112
public two-year institutions
  (community colleges) 18, 20, 28, 63,
  75, 77, 80–84, 84, 96, 170–171, 176;
  affordability 170–171; completion
  rates 80; institutional actors'
  student support 83–84; and Latinx
  student success 80–84; open-access
  policies 80–81; programs offered
  80; proximity to students's homes
  81, 170; rural dispersed community
  colleges 86; scheduling options 81;
  transfer pathways 81–83; urban
  enclave community colleges 86
Puerto Rican institutions 86
Puerto Ricans 8, 9, 16, 27, 44,
  76; citizenship status 47; college
  enrollment 19; degree attainment 20;
  funds of knowledge 119
Puerto Rico 85; colonial rule
  46–47
purpose dimension of HSIs 88
Pusser, B. 63
PWIs see Predominantly White
  Institutions (PWIs)

qualitative approaches 25, 122, 133,
  142; boundaries of 129; Chicana
  feminist 137, 138; and Critical Race
  Theory (CRT) 129
QuantCrit 129
quantitative approaches 25, 114, 133,
  142; Chicana feminist 137; and
  Critical Race Theory (CRT) 129;
  eugenic origins of 139

Quantitative Ethnography (QE) 29,
  114, 137, 139–143
quantitative intersectionality 129
quantity over quality (white supremacy
  culture) 171, 175
queer Chicana/Latina feminists 136
Queer LatinX students 91, 92, 124,
  136–137
Queer pláticas 137
Queer Theory 113
QueerCrit 121
Quintana, S. M. 55

R1 four-year institutions 86–87
race 9–11, 12–13, 27, 28, 51, 52,
  92, 93, 95, 116, 122, 126, 130,
  134, 141; law/legal systems and
  construction of 45–46, 121;
  see also Critical Race Theory (CRT)
race-conscious admissions
  168–170, 181
racial and/or ethnic empowerment
  capital 118
racial categorization 6–7, 9–11, 13, 45
racial discrimination 10, 19, 54, 55,
  56, 58, 165
racial identity 6–7, 13, 78, 113,
  114, 115, 116, 121, 174;
  see also ethnoracial identity
racial microaffirmations 125
racial paradigms 51
racial realism 166, 167–168, 169,
  170, 181
racial socialization 54–55, 56–58
racial-wealth gap 170
racialization 7, 13, 45–46;
  differential 125
racism 5, 10, 11, 27, 28, 29, 44,
  48, 113, 118, 122, 123, 130,
  132, 133, 142, 166; and conflict
  amongst BIPOC communities 46;
  definition of 11; legal systems
  and perpetuation of 121; primary
  functions 11; resisting racism in
  education 180; systemic 11, 126
racist nativism 127–128
radical feminism 121
Ramirez, J. J. 89
reactionary behavior 126
readiness for postsecondary education
  24, 44, 62, 63
religious values 76

remote learning 167
Rendón, L. I. 124
research institutions 86–87
resilience 26, 28, 64, 134, 165, 177, 180; community 29, 111, 112, 140, 142, 143, 178, 179, 180
resistance 130, 134, 178, 181; conformist 126; reactionary behavior 126; resisting racism in education 180; self-defeating 126; transformational 125–126
resistance capital 124
resource agents 89
respeto (respect) 91
retention/retention rates 25, 26, 63, 117
reverse transfer students 18, 81
Revilla, A. T. 136
Rios-Aguilar, C. 120
Rivas-Drake, D. 116
Rivera, Gabby 74, 97n12
Rosa, J. 13
rural dispersed community colleges 86

Saavedra, C. M. 137
Salas-SantaCruz, O. 136
Salinas, C. 14
Sánchez, G. K. 94
Sánchez, N. C. 135
Sandoval, C. 130
Sandoval Girón, A. B. 6
Santiago, D. 18, 22, 23, 81
Seal of Excelencia 22, 23, 31n9
segregation 49
segregationist educational explanations (1800s–1950s) 45–48
self-confidence 78, 174
self-defeating resistance 126
self-identitification 6–7, 12, 91, 131
"servingness" 87–88
settler colonialism 46, 94
sexism 122, 130, 132, 133
sexual orientation 7, 91, 92, 95
sexuality 27, 130, 132, 134
Shapiro, T. 123
Silva, C. 7, 10
sitios y lenguas (spaces and discourses) 132
small communities four-years HSIs 86
Smart, J. C. 62
Smith, P. J. 57
social capital 77, 89, 117–118, 124

social class *see* class
social constructions of race/ethnicity/ethnoraciality 9–13
Social Darwinism 45, 51
social identity/identities 13, 14, 121, 125, 132; affirmation of 178; ethnic 6–7, 13, 57, 78, 113, 114, 115, 116, 121, 174; ethnoracial 11, 12–13, 92, 95, 115–116; gender identity 91, 92, 95, 125, 132; intersectional 7, 13, 14, 19, 27, 30, 92, 95, 116, 133; and LatinX student success 90–95; racial 6–7, 13, 78, 113, 114, 115, 116, 121, 174; self-identity 6–7, 12, 91
social justice 121, 122, 126, 139, 143
social reproduction 117
socialization: gender 91; parent–child 52–54, 92; *see also* cultural socialization; ethnic socialization; racial socialization
socialization assumption (person-environment fit theory) 62
socioeconomic status 20, 54, 86, 115, 118
sociological explanations (1970s–present) 50–52
Solórzano, D. G. 11, 27, 121, 122, 123, 125–126, 129
"some college, no credential" (SCNC) students 24
Soto, L. D. 48, 49
Spanish language 176; elimination of use of 49
Spanish-Cuban-American War (1898) 46
spatial analysis 129
Spera, C. 52–53, 53–54
spiritual capital 118, 124
spirituality/spiritualities 91, 131, 134, 177
standardized assessment 24, 25, 44
state policy, and student success 63
Stefancic, J. 125
Steinbaum, M. 170
Steinberg, L. 53
STEM fields 77, 85, 181
stereotypes 25, 48, 54, 78
Stewart, D.-L. 113
Stokes, S. 167
stop-out 24, 31n10, 168, 175
storytelling 27, 179; *see also* counter-storytelling

structural assimilation 51
student affairs professionals 75, 76
student development theories
112–113, 123
student engagement/satisfaction 24,
44, 61, 63, 123, 172
student success 24–26, 44, 45, 64–65;
defining and measuring 59–64,
172; person-environment fit theory
and 62; transitions for the success
process 62; *see also* Latinx student
success
Students for Fair Admissions, Inc.
cases 166, 168
subjectivity 133, 137
symbolic capital 117
systematic oppression 5, 9, 11, 29, 52,
92, 113, 116, 121, 122, 144
systemic racism 11, 126

Tate, W. F. 121
Tatum, B. D. 11
Taylor, M. 17–18
technical education/training 23, 80
technology dimension of HSIs 88
Telles, E. 51–52
testimonios 129
Texas: Hispanic-Serving Institutions
(HSIs) 22, 23; LatinX population 8,
9; race-conscious admissions 168;
undocumented students 19
theories in the flesh 132
Third World Feminisms of Color 130
Thomas, S. L. 61–62
Tinto, V. 63
Title 1 programs 65n1, 65n2
Torres, V. 113, 114, 115
Torres-Guzmán, M. 134
Tovar, E. 83
Trans-LatinX students 91, 92
transfer students 18, 77, 79, 81–83, 85
transfer-receptive culture 82–83
transformational resistance 125–126
Tribal Colleges and Universities
(TCUs) 84
TribalCrit 121, 128
Tribally Controlled Colleges and
Universities Assistance Act (1978) 84
Tribally Controlled Community
College Assistance Act (1978) 84
Trinidad Galván, R. 138
Turk, J. M. 17–18

two-year institutions *see* public two-year
institutions

U.S. Bureau of Labor Statistics 22
U.S. Census Bureau 6, 7, 8, 9, 19, 20
U.S. Department of Education 22, 85
U.S. Department of Labor 21
UCLA Latino Policy & Politics
Institute 93
Umaña-Taylor, A. J. 58, 116
UndocuCrit 121, 128
undocumented students 18–19, 81,
94–95, 121, 124, 125, 128, 134,
164–165
unemployment rate 22
University of California (UC) system
169
upward transfer students 18
urban enclave community colleges 86
urban ethnography 129
urgency, sense of (white supremacy
culture) 171, 174

Valencia, R. R. 47
validation theory 83
values 177; parental 53; religious 76
Valverde, L. A. 75, 76, 79–80, 96
Vazquez–Hernandez, R. 47
Vélez-Ibañez, C. G. 119–120
Venezuelan population 8
"ventajas" 124
vertical transfer students 18, 81, 82
Villalpando, O. 122, 123
Villenas, S. 49, 58, 133
vocational education 23

walking *pláticas* 137
Wellman, J. 25–26, 59, 63–64, 172
Western research paradigms 129, 137
Whalen, C. T. 47
White Anglo-Saxon Protestant (WASP)
society 51
white feminism 130, 136
white supremacy 5, 10, 13, 28, 29,
48, 64, 116, 118, 122, 123, 130,
132, 142, 166; and conflict amongst
BIPOC communities 46; culture, and
LatinX student success 171–176;
ethnicity paradigm and 51; healing
from trauma of 179, 180; legal
systems and perpetuation of 9,
121, 126

whiteness 9, 13, 47, 87, 115, 118, 121
whites 9, 15, 17, 56
Winant, H. 12, 51
wisdom, intergenerational 178, 179, 180
women: as carriers of American culture 49; *see also* female students; feminism(s); *marianismo* (femininity); maternal influences
Workforce Innovation and Opportunity Act (WIOA) (2014) 21

written word, worship of (white supremacy culture) 171, 175

xenophobia 6, 127

Yosso, T. J. 27, 121, 122, 123–124, 129, 142
Young Lords 73, 97n6

Zerquera, D. 171

For Product Safety Concerns and Information please contact our EU
representative GPSR@taylorandfrancis.com
Taylor & Francis Verlag GmbH, Kaufingerstraße 24, 80331 München, Germany